Does it really need to be this hard?

Abbie Broad

Now Watch Me Fly

Copyright © 2020 by Abbie Broad

All rights reserved. No part of this publication may be reproduced, distributed, or transmitted in any form or by any means, including photocopying, recording, or other electronic or mechanical methods, without the prior written permission of the publisher, except in the case of brief quotations embodied in critical reviews and certain other noncommercial uses permitted by copyright law. For permission requests, write to the publisher at the address below.

Now Watch Me Fly
43 Southdown Road
Cosham
Portsmouth
PO6 2ED
United Kingdom

www.nowwatchmefly.co.uk

ISBN: 978-1-5272-7104-3

Book design: The Art of Communication www.book-design.co.uk

To My Boy 'Jack'
thank you for keeping me grounded.

Rest in Peace 02.10.07 – 01.06.20

Contents

A letter to the reader 1

Introduction
Lisa, me, and mindset 9
Lisa 11
The beginning 12
They'll believe it, when you do 15
Who is this book written for? 17
Why mindset is important 20
Getting the most from this book 22

Chapter 1
The Science of Mindset 25
What is Mindset? 27
Behaviours and Habits 28
The 4 Stages of Competence 29
Core Drivers, Values, and Beliefs 30
Mindset Motorway 31
Why is mindset a struggle for women in business? 34
Why are you really doing this? 40
The Process 42
Working with a coach 43

Chapter 2
Big 7 No. 1 – Self-Doubt to Self-Confidence 47
Self-doubt: A lack of confidence in oneself and one's abilities. 49
Self-confidence: A feeling of trust in one's abilities, qualities, and judgement 50
My struggle with self-doubt 56

How I found self-confidence 63
Where self-doubt shows up in business 71
Top tips – Self-doubt to self-confidence 73
Book recommendation 75

Chapter 3
Big 7 No. 2 – Isolation to Connection **77**
Isolation: The process or fact of isolating or being isolated 79
Connection: A relationship in which a person or thing
is linked or associated with something else 81
My struggle with isolation 83
When you find connection 92
Where isolation shows up in business 100
Top tips summary – Isolation to connection 102
Book recommendation 104

Chapter 4
Big 7 No. 3 – Confusion to Clarity **107**
Confusion 109
Clarity 110
My Struggle with Confusion 112
How I found clarity 118
Where confusion shows up in business 128
Top tips summary – Confusion to clarity 131
Book Recommendation 135

Chapter 5
Big 7 No. 4 – Fear to Courage **137**
Fear 139
Courage 140
My struggle with fear 141
Where I found courage 154

Where fear shows up in business 165
Top tips summary – Fear to courage 166
Book recommendations 169

Chapter 6
Big 7 No. 5 – Guilt to Forgiveness **171**
Guilt 173
Forgiveness 174
My struggle with guilt 176
How I embraced forgiveness 186
Top Tips Summary – Guilt to Forgiveness 195
Book recommendation 197

Chapter 7
Big 7 No. 6 – Time Fatigue to Time Management **199**
Time Fatigue 201
Time Management 202
My struggle with time fatigue 204
Learning to manage time like a boss 215
Where time fatigue shows up in business 227
Top tips summary – Time fatigue to time management 228
Book Recommendation 231

Chapter 8
Big 7 No. 7 – Overwhelm to Resilience **233**
Overwhelm 235
Resilience 236
My struggle with overwhelm 237
How I built resilience 246
Where overwhelm shows up in business 260
Top tips summary – Overwhelm to resilience 2625
Book recommendation 264

Chapter 9
Inspirational Stories **267**
Emma Hannay – Stamped with Love. 269
Jennie Smith – Sole to Soul.. 273
Jess Walton – Fresh Air Learning 277
Kari Ann Roberts – Emotional Strength Coach........................ 280
Tracey Blake – Aloe Energetix Health and Wellness 288
Vicki Hudson – Vicki Hudson Reflexology................................... 290
Sami Turner – Sparkle with Sami 293

Conclusion – Does it really need to be this hard?........... **297**
Postscript 303
Support for the onward journey.. 303
Work with me 305
Acknowledgements and thanks... 307

A *letter* to the reader

Hello friend, how are you?

If you're holding this book in your hand thinking, Jeezz they will publish anything these days. If you're flicking through the pages to see how large the print is, because if it's too big she must be dumb, if it's too small she's probably boring. If you're filled with excitement and anticipation ready for the challenge. If you're exhausted and in need of a lifeline, or confused and overwhelmed by the road ahead. If you're looking and hoping that magic sentence is going to pop out and cure you of your struggles, or you're trying to decide if you have time to read it. If you're wondering what could there possibly be in this book, that you haven't already read, seen, or listened to. If you're praying that this is not just another Look at Me Now – rags to riches story, that is only going to make you resentful. If you're wondering when is all this anaphora going to end, and when is she going to get to the point? Then welcome to the tribe. You and I are going to get on like a house on fire.

This is not a book about money or success. At least not the typical success you read about. This is a story about struggle. About joy. It is my story. Of my why, my goals, and my pursuit of happiness. To honour the memory of a dear friend and how I use the skills she taught me to pay it forward. How I am inspired every day through surrounding myself with passionate individuals who all have their own stories to tell. This is an insight into my journey and the mindset tools I use to navigate my journey, but the journey is far from over.

Growing up, it was never my plan to own a business, never a dream or even a goal. I love being around people, and I love to feel useful, and, honestly, my own limiting beliefs never really allowed me to even consider it. I didn't do very well at school, academically that is; I had a lot of fun and a lot of friends, so in that respect I was nailing it. I didn't go to college because I was too focused on meeting my immediate needs. I had no concept of how to look at the big picture or how to play the long game. For me, I wanted money, clothes, and a car; a holiday with my boyfriend; and to have fun with my friends. So, I went to work, lived an average life, and bounced from shitty relationship to shitty marriage until finally, in 2002, everything changed. I met Lisa, and by 2010, at the age of 39, I finally went to college and I haven't stopped learning since. In 2015, I discovered coaching. Having chosen to embark upon this very definite path of self-discovery, when coaching popped up on my radar, it just felt right. It was like the mothership calling me home. I loved coaching and coaching loved me back – finally, at the age of 45, I found my purpose. Even then, I still hadn't considered myself capable of running a business. But soon after gaining my diploma, a chance opportunity came along, and before I knew it, I had a business bank account, 1000 business cards, a website, and no job!

    I can honestly say it has been a rollercoaster of emotions. I am an expert in reframing and whilst I almost welcome failure as a tool for further self-discovery, I look back now and wonder if it really needed to be quite so hard.

    I was inspired by the 1988 film *Working Girl* and Melanie Griffiths' epic performance. From the age of 17, all I ever wanted to be was her. A working woman. Turning up to the office every day. Saying hi to people, doing my bit and being a part of something. I admired her determination to break away from the hand she'd been dealt. Her constant pursuit of passion and fulfilment. Always thinking there must be more to life than this. I was so inspired, and this was my dream. An office. A desk. Serving others, both below me and above me. In the middle, never at the top. I never once dreamed of being my own boss. I convinced myself at an early age that it was ok, even honourable, to serve. To help other people realise their dreams and make their pathway to financial success, better, quicker, and easier. Unlike other entrepreneurs – I couldn't see past my own limitations. I never imagined that I could be the one to lead. To be my own boss. To take my ideas and my passion and turn it into a profitable business. Even once I began my entrepreneurial journey, I was still labouring under this assumption – and very quickly I began to experience the struggle. 7 big struggles to be precise: Fear, Isolation, Confusion, Guilt, Time fatigue, Overwhelm, and Self-doubt. My fixed and limited mindset meant that instead of finding a way to reduce the struggle, I simply powered on. Believing that I had no time or money to invest in finding a solution.

Overcoming mindset struggles is a constant process of focusing attention, building confidence, and shaping new and effective behaviours. The challenges don't disappear, they just change. We learn to embrace the struggle. Make it our friend. Without struggle there is no success. We must struggle, and we must fail in order to succeed. I know because I walk that path every day. The difference is today I choose my struggles, I welcome failure as a tool, and I trust that I will learn and grow with every step I take. Instead of battling our behaviours, values, and beliefs, we can start to know them and understand them. We can decide which are helpful and which hold us back.

Like best friends. We tap into and connect with the one that we know will be the most helpful. One is great when you want diet advice. Another is fab for offloading and moaning about your husband, job, or kids. Another is a great listener who will allow you to work through your shit and come out the other side inspired and refreshed.

Struggle happens when we listen to the wrong friend. Allowing their fears and beliefs to leak out onto our own. Injecting their views and opinions onto us. For example – I would not ask my friend Donna to come help me sort my loft out. She is terrible at tidying up, and she loves to hoard stuff. She would not want to help me, because for her that would be a nightmare. I would ask Sandra. Sandra sorts like a boss. She would go through that loft like a Tasmanian Devil, and before you could blink, that shit would be done.

If I am in a panic or need help with my kids or the dog, if I needed someone to knock up a quick meal at the last minute, or if I were drowning in overwhelm and needed help, I would call my sister. When I'm doubting, confused, or procrastinating about work, a client, or a new online programme or workshop, or if I have to do a presentation in front of an audience and I feel nervous or full of self-doubt, I call on my tribe.

You see, we are all part of a team. Your core behaviours, core values, and core beliefs work just like your friends, and mindset is about finding the right friend that can help and benching the ones that don't. Maintaining connection and friendships is vital, and we wouldn't leave out or ignore a friend. If we do, we feel it; our values, behaviours, and beliefs work in much the same way. Meeting and using these friends is essential, and when we don't, it feels shitty. We start to question ourselves and become confused and in effective. When this happens in our business, it can be exhausting. If you value creativity – as I do – yet you ignore or neglect it, then before long, your passion and joy will start to decline. So being able to stay present with all the friends (behaviours, values, and beliefs) that are helpful, useful, and kind is how we stay happy, healthy, and productive.

Now there are of course 'friends' who are simply not helpful. Ever. They are negative, miserable, and downright bad for us.

But we keep them around because their misery and negativity are somehow comforting. We have gotten so used to them; we can't seem to let them go.

Ok – so sometimes we need to let 'actual' people go, or at least let go of the impact they have on us. Imagine that some of your behaviours, values, and beliefs were the 'not so helpful friends'. They exist within you, and if those 'negative friends' are all in your head, having a party, and tearing the place up, you need to get them out quickly. Mindset practices are how we kick them out, or at least how we get them to shut up and behave. Limiting beliefs, negative self-talk, and unresourceful behaviours such as self-doubt, guilt, procrastination, avoidance, and overwhelm are the friends you need to let go of.

This book will – I hope – offer you a way to begin that process of choosing the behaviours, values, and beliefs that help reduce the struggle and increase your joy and productivity. The negative beliefs and behaviours don't completely disappear, and honestly, we need them. Change is not about losing parts of ourselves; rather, it is about learning new things about ourselves and using those new and resourceful thoughts and behaviours to take action.

Ok, so if you're not exhausted by my use of metaphor, hopefully you are now starting to see and feel that this mindset malarkey might actually not be quite the bore-fest you thought it would be, that this book is not just a collection of tips that you can't action because you are too busy thinking that you're not good enough, or you don't have time to stop and learn something else. I hope that you are starting to see that this is a journey, and my book and my story are like a friend. A useful, helpful friend. One that will absolutely clean out your loft, listen to you off load, and help you to find a better and easier way to be present in your business and in your life. I hope this book inspires you, brings you joy, and makes you laugh. I hope it helps you learn more about who you are and who your real 'friends' are. This book will introduce you to a mindset that will enable you to consistently meet challenges head on. To avoid overwhelm, procrastination, self-doubt, and fear to make your business journey fun, exciting, and successful.

What I wish I had known from the start: if you are going to be your business and you are your product, then you had better make damn sure you understand every inch of how you work. I hope that I have written the book that I needed back at the start.

I am not a marketing expert. I am not an expert in starting a business. I know nothing about sales tactics, profits, ROI, and KPI's and I know very little about advertising or social media.

So, what do I know? What I do know is people. *And I see you*. What I trust is the power of coaching. What I have learnt is that through a coaching process, you can find the answers that you need to build confidence, focus attention, and shape behaviours that will allow you to succeed. Being a start-up or business when you are your product is always going to be an emotional journey, and that's ok. Emotion is where all the good stuff happens. We are nothing without our emotions. We just need to master them. We cannot operate on emotions alone. Mark Mason states in his book *The Subtle Art of Not Giving a Fuck*:

Decision making based on emotional intuition, without the aid of reason to keep it in line, pretty much always sucks. You know who bases their entire lives on their emotions? Three-year-old kids. And dogs. You know what else three-year-olds and dogs do? Shit on the carpet. (2016, p. 35)

The world needs emotionally intelligent people. The world needs more entrepreneurs. The world needs those willing to use their own skills and passion to benefit others, and if I can help you benefit the world by sharing your skills and passion, then I am absolutely going to do that. I can help you to recognise your value, build your self-belief, overcome stuck behaviours, gain clarity, and seek information that will reduce noise and focus your attention. I can also help you create behaviours that will ensure your success. All you must do is be willing to put in the work.

Now, if you are easily offended and hate the F word, then a word of warning. I keep the F bombs to a minimum. Although anyone who knows me well will tell you when I get going, I can give Mark Manson and Dan Meredith a run for their money. Seriously I honestly think I would crush either of them in an "F bomb face off". I am, however, not actually all that proud of this particular skill. I kind of hate it. So in person – yep it's going to happen; it is a weakness I embrace, but when I write, I try to save it for when it really matters, rather than using it as a full stop, or question mark as I am known to do from time to time in conversation.

If you hate metaphor and you bought this book in the hopes you could flick straight to a list of *How to's* you could follow that would offer the golden ticket to success, you might be disappointed. I love metaphor. I am a visual and creative thinker, and for me the answers to all the problems in the world lie somewhere in a metaphor. It's how I process information; I need it to fit. For learning to make sense, I have to make it relatable to me, and I hope that works for you too.

If you're irritated by conversational-style writing and a constant need to verbalise pretty much every thought that has gone through my head or you're thinking 'this woman sounds nuts', and you are frantically searching for your receipt, then ok. Just stay with me for a few more lines and then I will let you go. Am I a bit nuts? Probably. Passion is energising and obsession is motivating and combining my passion for coaching and my obsession for self-actualisation does mean that I can come across as a bit crazy at times. But if you're looking for help to get you to where you want to be, isn't a passionate, obsessed, and slightly crazy person exactly who you need?

If you're still worried that having your own business is too much of a leap, know that though my life looks very different to what it was before, I still have imaginative, practical answers and solutions for everyday problems and needs. I still get to serve others. I still get to support help and inspire others to reach their dreams. The difference is, I don't watch from the side-line. I don't hold back and sacrifice my own dreams. I am there with you every step of the way, while we take this journey together.

My entire business model is based around friendship, fun, familiarity, connection, coaching, helping, and supporting. It has worked for me, and I am certain it can work for you too.

Does it really need to be this hard? Fuck NO! It doesn't. Because together we are a team, we are a tribe, we are friends. Your success is my success. So, are you ready? Then let's do this.

Much Love
Your friend *Abbie* x

INTRODUCTION

Lisa, me, and **mindset**

*"A good friend will let you into their life.
A good coach will let you into your own."*

Lisa

Curiosity is where my journey began. This was the first thing I learned from Lisa. She opened a Pandora's box when she uttered the words: "Who are you blaming for all of this Abbie?" WTAF! My face went pale, so I was later told; and yes, its corny but it's true. My whole life suddenly flashed in front of my eyes. Every shit decision, every nasty relationship, every mistake, struggle, and moment of self-pity, all speeding past me like a freight train. That was the moment that my whole inner narrative started to make sense. The "why me", the "what did I do to deserve this", and the "if I just do more …" When the freight train finally passed, the weirdest thing happened. Instead of feeling judged or broken or upset, I felt energised. I felt taller suddenly. I stood up, as I had in fact slumped onto the floor and turned my head towards the window. The sunlight was warm and bright, and I had to close my eyes. "Is this what the light at the end of the tunnel feels like?", I asked myself.

Curiosity explains why I am who I am now. My willingness to get down and dirty with curiosity is what drew me to coaching and is what fuels my very being. I am a positive person. Annoyingly positive sometimes. And you won't ever catch me turning up to a pity party. Not unless I can come dressed as a unicorn waving a confetti cannon. I won't sit with you in pity. If you just want to wallow in self-pity, then I am annoying to be around.

I am not naive in my relentless pursuit of personal joy. Curiosity is painful and has been present during my lowest and highest moments. We can't just ask ourselves questions and hope that we will come up with an answer. We must be curious and allow ourselves to be vulnerable too.

Lisa taught me to be curious. How to lean into the uncomfortable process of becoming self-aware. And it is bloody uncomfortable sometimes. But ever since the moment I met Lisa, with everything that I have been through and let's face it, put myself through, none of that discomfort compares to the feeling of utter despair that I was experiencing before that moment. Avoidance, shame, guilt, and a lot of self-medicating is a shit place to be, and so I remain curious. Even when it pinches, I trust that the door will always open to what is on the other side.

Curiosity plays a fundamental part in coaching and in growth. If you are challenging yourself to do something new, like starting a business, then you need to get down and dirty with curiosity too. Coaching helps to facilitate that process, and I could not have done this without Lisa's help and expertise. I look back now at how patient she was and how no matter how hard I resisted, she always remained calm, kind, and empathetic.

Curiosity and vulnerability remain my constant companions, and with Lisa gone, not a day goes by when I don't ask myself, "What would Lisa be asking me now?"

The beginning

I met Lisa in 2002, just weeks after I got married and was already pregnant with my second child. We were, I suppose, forced together through circumstance; our husbands were best friends, and so we met regularly and soon became good friends.

Although much younger than me, Lisa was an old soul, balanced, humble, and wise. And it wasn't long before I started to experience some rather unusual thought processes after spending time with her. She was, to be fair, training as a person-centred counsellor at the time, and as I discovered for myself later in my own training, you need to practice as you learn – so I guess I became her very willing guinea pig.

Each time we met, despite being surrounded by children, friends, family, conversations, and the occasional "drama", I always felt completely listened to. My life back then was a shit storm. I make no secret of how unhappy I was, and to be clear, there were huge reasons why this was true. Some of them yes, were on the outside of me. People and situations that made me doubt my worth and my very existence. People and situations that caused me to feel helpless, sad, anxious, and depressed. People and situations that confused and upset me. However, these people and situations were not the focus of our conversations.

I had suffered the consequences of wearing my low self-esteem and self-doubt like a printed t-shirt for the last 30 years. Self-doubt had gotten me to a very uncomfortable place. Thankfully, after meeting Lisa that all began to change. It all changed with these four words: "Just say thank you".

Do you ever feel uncomfortable when someone pays you a compliment? Even though you know it's well deserved, do you ever just want to walk away? Every time I would go to visit Lisa, she would comment: "I like your top" or "nice earrings" or "you look beautiful today". And every time, I had a self-deprecating or sarcastic comeback. Sarcasm is our family's superpower and one I used tirelessly to defend myself from any kind of vulnerability or curiosity: "Oh, this is old", "Oh yeah they were cheap", or "well I have had a bath and brushed my hair so that's probably it".

And every time without fail, Lisa would pause, look me right in the eye, smile, and say, "just say thank you". It was so painful. I would laugh. Not a good laugh, but an uncomfortable laugh like when you don't quite hear what someone said, but instead of asking them to repeat it you laugh weirdly and then walk away. 18 months we did that dance. 18 months of birthday parties, BBQ's, nights out, weddings, and piss ups. Every time the same dance. I dreaded it. It was like some sort of initiation ceremony.

You can't come in until you have felt the pain of your own self-awareness. I didn't get it. Why was she doing this? It didn't make me dislike her, quite the opposite I was drawn to this initiation like a puzzle trying to be solved. Knowing I would walk away beaten and frustrated, still I needed to try.

Then, one day, it happened. I don't remember what day exactly; I do remember it was sunny and I had lost a bit of weight and for once I was feeling good. Back then those days were few and far between, so I was going to make the most of it. All the way to Lisa and Andy's house I was planning my response. *Today I'm going to win. I'm going to show her. I am going to say thank you. This will make her think. I bet she won't ask me today. I bet she only says it when she thinks I look rubbish to try to make me feel better. I bet she won't say it.* I know now, of course, Lisa would never have done that.

We arrived and I got out of the car, off loaded all the food I had made, because I know that if I bring food that will make people like me and think I'm a happy housewife. Because that's what normal housewives with no job and loads of time on their hands do, isn't it? They bake and sew and decorate and go to PTA meetings and help their kids with homework, right? Anyway. I got out of the car and stood smiling and waiting for it. And sure enough. After a big long hug. Lisa was a pro at hugging, she stood back and said, "you look lovely and that perfume is delicious". "Thank you", I said, "I love it too".

She smiled, kindly and with so much love in her eyes. "There you go", she said.

I thought I was going to be smug, and we would laugh and joke about it. Instead what happened next was a feeling I will never forget. It was as though a surge of energy rose inside of me, from my feet to my head. I could not move. I was fixed to the spot. I literally was paralysed for what was probably seconds but felt like minutes. The world stopped spinning; I swear. Yes, I know, another dramatic life changing moment, but I swear the world slowed down for just a split second. It was as though it was waiting for me to catch up.

When I finally regained the movement in my feet and the ability to talk, I started to follow Lisa up the driveway to her house (while carrying a big bowl of chocolate covered strawberries – which to this day I don't know how I didn't drop) and I said, very quietly almost in a whisper: "Fuck. I get it now. Is it always going to be this painful?"

"If it's uncomfortable, then its working", said Lisa.

They'll believe it, when *you do*

When you're given a second chance at life, it's hard not to find yourself utterly consumed by it. I owe my new life to Lisa and her unwavering determination to help me to see that I had choices. She would take no credit for what I have achieved, and every time I went to thank her, she would simply reply, "This isn't about me Abbie, you are doing the work, not me, make it about you".

Lisa did not have all the answers – she never once told me what to do. Even when I begged her to. She knew that for me to make the changes on the outside of my life, I needed to experience the realisations on the inside. Take responsibility for the part I was playing, and, through curiosity, start to make better choices. I used a little poetic licence with the quote at the start. Honestly, it is my wholehearted belief that with the right help and support we are each capable of anything. All any of us need to do in life is to know ourselves so we can be ourselves.

Who knew that learning to take a compliment would be

such a life changing moment? My inability to accept or take compliments and tendency to belittle or dismiss any kind of praise with sarcasm or deflection was at the centre of everything that was wrong in my life. "Abbie, you are awesome", Lisa would say. "But no one else is going to see it, until you do". This rather eloquent and slightly painful statement was repeated to me quite recently when I asked a fellow coach, "why am I struggling so hard to convince people to pay me for coaching?" "Abbie, they will believe in you when you do". Urgghhhhhhh, shit. Yes. Feel like I should have known that. That was the point in my business journey when I realised, I would have to go back to the beginning and redo the steps of mental resilience. Learn how to love myself again – in the business sense. Learn how to be the best version of me. Learn how to be confident and fearless again and, yes, learn to take a compliment.

There is nothing worse than being excited about someone's product, only to hear them apologising for it, holding back from promoting it, or hesitating to place value in it. I had my second chance at doing life, and the lessons I learnt are still what guide me today. I owe my life to an angel. She saved me. This time I needed to save myself. It took a bit of time to work it out, but the moment I realised I have choices and began to choose curiosity over control, and the moment I chose vulnerability over perception was when it really started to get better. I couldn't have written this book without sharing with you where it all began for me. Not everyone will have to have experienced these personal ups and downs – although I offer many of you will have. I needed to share with you what got me to this point, what makes me tick, and what brings me joy. In this book, I hope to share with you my skills and my short comings, my vulnerability and my purpose. I do this with hope. Hope that after reading this book you not only get to know me a little better, but more importantly I hope that you get to know yourself a lot better. Because when we know, like, and trust ourselves, we are invincible.

Who is this book written for?

We will all struggle from time to time, with life and in business, when we choose to work for ourselves. When we do something we feel passionately about, money is often not our top priority. My clients tend to be women, and more often than not they are over 40. They have chosen to use their creative skills to earn an income, but their priority is working around their other commitments. Or they wish to reduce their workload to avoid the stress and overwhelm they felt while working in a corporate business. Whatever their reason, the goal of earning money is always present; however, the pressure they feel to maintain the peace and the balance that led to that choice in the first place can sometimes become distracting.

My clients do not come to me for expert business advice. They come to me for support, for a safe space. They're looking for a place to share their thoughts and feelings and for a way to make it work. The inspiration for the title, *Does It Really Need to Be This Hard?*, came directly after a session I had with a client who was struggling to build enough confidence to be more visible online. It was the question I had been asking myself for years. The struggle comes when things don't quite go to plan and the "choice" we made starts to feel "burdensome" and "up for debate". A woman's place in society and the workplace has changed enormously over the last few decades, and yet we still struggle to be our own first priority. We would rather disappoint ourselves than disappoint others. We have stories and narratives playing in our heads that jump up and grab us every time we try to be brave or do something new, exciting, or challenging. Something for us.

I had no idea that the issues I had battled and overcome in my private life would be the exact same shit that would force me to get in my own way again in my business. Mindset is what saved me – remembering that I have choices about how I think, feel, and act, and all I needed to do was step back and work that process.

Because of the shift in mindset and the work that I have put in, I am now a raging success. That is, if we were to be measuring success by joy, fulfilment, and inspiration. Financially, my business still has a way to go. I am not done. My business is still growing, and this is, I believe, where my empathy for those struggling and just starting out is so valuable. I not only remember what it feels like to struggle, but I still work my process every day to stay focused, confident, and motivated. Only now, it is a practice that I enjoy, rather than a search and rescue mission. I am sharing my story here as a representation of where I have been and how far I have come – to inspire others to keep going and to share some tips along the way that I believe can make all the difference.

This book is for women in business or those working from home. For those who have chosen to follow their passion and who require support to navigate the demands of work and home. For those who have just started out and for those who are experiencing a change of circumstance or dip in motivation. For those who lost their jobs recently after Covid19 and those whose businesses where cruelly put on hold because of lockdown and social distancing, and who are now struggling to regain confidence and momentum to get back in the game.

It's also for women in business suffering with menopause and struggling with issues of fatigue, anxiety, and brain fog that they have not had to deal with in the past. For every woman out there, working and trying to support her family and quietly doing her best, while silently struggling to be present for everyone else other than herself. I see you.

You already have everything you need to be a success. You already know everything you need to know. It is all right there inside of you; it has been there the whole time. I hope I can help you to reach inside and start to use that strength. I want to support you through vulnerability and help you to be not only brave but courageous too.

I see you, I hear you, I know you because you are what the world looks like.

For those who are their product, coaches, therapists, and creatives, this book will provide insight into who you are and where your strengths lie. And for those already on the roller coaster, who may have hit a low point, it will teach you the tools to overcome and rise again.

If you are at the start of your journey, in the honeymoon phase or the "I'm gonna quit my job – screw the boss, I'm off to start a business" phase, then you may not yet have come up against some of the issues I address. Or at least you have not yet suffered the consequences of emotional struggles, and this may indeed mean you will not have to experience just how hard it can be. That is great. I would suggest you stick with it if you can, read it through and then pop the book up on a shelf, not too far away, and be sure to grab it as soon as you start to feel the struggle. As your business grows, you will face new obstacles and your values and resilience will be challenged. So the first time you cry "I want to give up", you have no money left for Christmas, you look and feel like Waynetta Slob, your inner critic is calling you a fat failure, or you can't remember what your husband and kids look like or why you started this all in the first place – you can jump right back into the exercises and use them to navigate all these new situations.

Why *mindset* is important

My mission since starting Now Watch Me Fly is to provide accessible and affordable coaching to business owners with the same kindness and friendship as it was offered to me many years ago. We all deserve to play the leading role in our own life, and coaching makes this happen. Developing your business is about building the belief that you can do it! If you have been struggling, then the good news is you are not alone. In fact, very few people are born with that mystical "Entrepreneurial Mindset". Most of us are hardwired with an "Employee Mindset". We are told to work hard, be grateful, ask permission, and limit ourselves and our aspirations.

Networking meetings and marketing strategy will not unpick that mindset. We need to first admit that it exists and then work to change it. Women, especially but not of course exclusively, will be distracted by their inner narrative. And when deciding to start a business alone, fear and uncertainty will undoubtably play a part, triggering your brain to set off warning sirens and shut down borders just to keep you safe – avoiding the things that feel difficult and sending you in circles just to avoid the discomfort of disappointing your beliefs. The all too familiar stories play through our minds: "You can't do that. What will people say? You are going to fail so don't bother trying". Instead, we opt to disappoint ourselves and live with the struggle.

Mindset is how we choose to view the world, the information that is on the outside, and how we choose to process it on the inside. I will explain more about this in the coming pages; for now, I'll assume you agree that the mind is a powerful tool. Have you ever experienced jealousy and allowed it to consume and distract you? Have you experienced guilt, when realistically you know you have not actually done anything wrong? It is a choice, right? Stuck behaviours are caused by limiting beliefs. Procrastination manifests through fear. Confusion is triggered by low self-esteem. We have all felt these emotions and subsequently displayed these behaviours. So, would it surprise you to learn that all of this is bullshit? Low self-esteem is bullshit. Limiting beliefs are bullshit and fear ... don't get me started on that one. Ok so fear is real, but the limitations we place on ourselves because of it are bullshit. These are all choices. And I say this with kindness, and empathy: if you are not changing it, you are choosing it. When we apply the right mindset to the right set of circumstances, we begin to see the bullshit, sift it out, and make better choices. We start to focus attention, build confidence, and shape behaviours that will reduce stress, anxiety, hesitation, and confusion; we move forward.

This is not new information. I am willing to bet that every person reading this book will have already read seen or watched something about mindfulness, meditation, CBT (Cognitive Behavioural Therapy), self-improvement, mindset, or emotional intelligence. I bet every one of you has read a quote on Facebook or Instagram and thought, "Hmm, I totally get that". I am a quote junkie.

All of it boils down to this: YOU are not your stories or your thoughts. You are not your emotions or your beliefs. You are your actions, and with the help of this book I hope you get a step closer to being able to reduce your struggles and begin to take consistent action in your business – to thrive in it and to enjoy it.

You do have to put some work in. I am not a magic fairy. And this is normally where people start to curl their nose and say to themselves, that sounds hard, or that sounds too good to be true, or they question the evidence: *What? I just think myself to success, do I? Surely there is a catch? Actually, I think I will stick to the struggle because honestly, I don't know who I am without it.* Many of us are in fact afraid of success and it is the winning that stops us from competing. Now, if you opt to settle for a mediocre life, one that is okay and just a bit better than most, then enjoy; we are not all designed for greatness. But if you start a business, invest money, and want to earn a living, then you need to get out of your own way because winning is all there is.

Getting the *most* from this book

The book begins with an insight into my definition of what mindset is and why we need to use it well – my rather unscientific, scientific explanation. Having an understanding of your core values, drivers, and beliefs will offer insight into where they can pop up and either help or hinder your process. I have provided you with a link in the Summary Section of the book where you can go to download exercises to help you identify your core drivers, values, and beliefs. You may want to complete these exercises before reading further into the book; however, this is not essential. I do recommend completing them prior to using the additional exercises that are also available online.

The book has been divided into chapters that cover the big 7 struggles for women in business: Fear, Confusion, Guilt, Self-doubt, Isolation, Overwhelm, and Time fatigue. I share with you the stories of my struggles with each of these and how I eventually overcame them. I have included exercises in the workbook download for each of the struggles that you can then apply in your business to regain control of your thoughts, reduce the noise, and build mental resilience.

I have also included examples of the core mindset coaching conversations I use to help them my clients transform their mindset from limitation to growth. These can be applied in almost any situation in which confidence, communication, motivation, or action are required. If you are experiencing a struggle right now, then you might want to jump ahead to a particular chapter or exercise. By all means go ahead. And be sure to circle back to the start when you can. When working through the exercises, be open to what they mean for you. I give a lot of my own examples – I encourage you to think purposefully as you read and ask yourself "what is my version of this", "what am I feeling when I work through this", or "how will I implement this in my journey"?

Each time you embark on something new, up your game, grow your reach, become more visible, the same process is repeated. While coaching is about teaching you the strategies to do this for yourself, it is my heartfelt belief that we will always need support. There is no need to go it alone. The most successful entrepreneurs and businesspeople DON'T DO ANY OF THIS STUFF ON THEIR OWN. They all have help and pride themselves on having gurus, coaches, mentors, and trainers and a network of people that have all the skills and talents that they know they do not have. Working alone does not mean you have to be alone and although you may not yet be ready to employ staff and consultants to aid you in your business journey, you absolutely can reach out for help. I offer a variety of ways to connect and work with me online, and I would welcome each one of you to join me. I have shared links and information about how to do this in the summary at the end.

CHAPTER 1

The Science of *Mindset*

"Having the right mindset is paramount for success."

CHRISTINE EVANGELOU

What *is* Mindset?

The established set of attitudes held by someone.

So that is the definition but what does it really mean, you might ask? What is it? Why is it important to me? And how do I get one?

Mindset is not just one thing. It is a combination of practices that enable a person to think purposefully and consciously – to take in information and process it in our conscious mind rather than allowing the information to sink deep into our emotions where pretty much anything can happen.

There are many books on the subject that offer a more scientific explanation. I like to keep things simple, and I am a sucker for figurative language, so, sit tight; this is how I explain what mindset means to me.

Mindset is like a window: if the one you are looking through is dirty or broken, the world will look dirty and broken. Step to the side and look through a different window, one that is clean and free from cracks. The world will immediately look quite different. The world did not change – you just decided to step to into a better place from which to see it.

Our world is experienced through our senses: sight, sound, smell, touch, and taste. Millions of bits of information come at us every second. How we interpret that information is determined by our unique values, drivers, and beliefs. How we filter that information before it hits our values, drivers, and beliefs is through our mindset.

There are several mindset tools designed with a particular outcome in mind that we can use. I have given examples of these in the workbook download that accompany each chapter. When practiced over time, these tools begin to merge to form our default mindset. At first the practice is purposeful and conscious but over time it becomes easier and requires less input from us. In the process of coaching, this is the moment when things begin to change – when a person can start to see and feel the difference. Life does not change, how you are experiencing it does. When we think differently, we feel differently, and if we feel differently, we act and behave differently. This is how Mindset helps you to create the core behaviours that will propel you forward and release you from the struggle.

Behaviours and Habits

A lot has been written about the science of behaviours and habits. It is in fact one of my favourite pastimes to immerse myself in a good audio book on this very subject. Interestingly, behaviours and habits are not the same thing; they form in separate parts of the brain. Pippa Lally is a health psychology researcher at University College London. In a study published in the *European Journal of Social Psychology*, Lally and her research team decided to figure out just how long it actually takes to form a habit.

Their study of 97 participants concluded that the average time to create a cue-dependant or subconscious habit was around 66 days (Lally *et al.* quoted in Ranpura and Fraser). The much publicised 21-day timeframe is in fact a myth, and her research produced a spectrum of results from 18 up to as much as 254 days, allowing for a multitude of variables. Shifting our mindset to respond quickly to new ways of thinking begins with behaviours. Practice the behaviour over time, insert the relevant cues to trigger our brain, and, eventually, we have our default mindset. Ok so it's a little more complex from a scientific point of view, but in reality, it's not that complicated.

The *4 Stages* of Competence

Creating new behaviours can be tough. It takes conscious effort and it is important to recognise that learning will take time and, at least to begin with, our behaviours will be a conscious choice.

Noticing our own learning is great practice. Pay attention to where you begin and notice when a shift occurs. Over time these new behaviours become our normal behaviours, like recycling our rubbish, using a bag for life, or switching off lights when we leave a room. These practiced behaviours become less conscious over time and eventually result in the formation of a habit. Habits sit in the basal ganglia part of the brain where automatic responses sit.

Getting things done in our business, overcoming hesitation and procrastination, and building confidence through behaviours is how we keep moving forward. The 4 stages of competence provides a great model of how, with practice, we can learn new ways of thinking and doing that will eventually become automatic. As we commit to learning anything, our mind will take us through this 4-stage process.

1. **Unconscious Incompetence** – *I don't know what I don't know.*
2. **Conscious Incompetence** - *I am now aware of what I don't know or can't do.*
3. **Conscious competence** – *I am now doing something different and it takes awareness and conscious thought to make it happen.*
4. **Unconscious Competence** – *I now have this new skill /*

knowledge / behaviour that I can implement without thinking, it's automatic.

Whether we are learning a new procedure at work, setting up our new phone, or learning to walk, our conscious and unconscious mind will be tirelessly guiding us through each of these steps. Mindset coaching follows this same method through focusing attention, building confidence, and shaping new behaviours. Each time we want to do something new the cycle repeats.

Core Drivers, Values, and Beliefs

We each have core drivers that exist in our head. These drivers push us forward and will often dictate our actions. Core behaviours develop over time to help us to satisfy these drivers; these include being organised, reliable, tidy, or efficient. They are our default and we defy them at our peril. For example, if a tidy person decides to marry or live with an untidy person, eventually there is going to be a problem.

Core values belong in our heart: passion, creativity, love of learning, and connection. For me one of my core values is growth, so if there is an opportunity to learn something "I'm in"; I seek growth every day, and it makes me feel great. If our values are challenged or ignored, it can be very distracting. Values are powerful and we will defend them at all costs.

Core beliefs are tricky. Beliefs exist in our head for sure, but we feel them in our stomach. When a belief we hold is saying, "Who do you think you are? You don't belong here", we feel fearful and sick to our stomach. Beliefs can, of course, be positive and motivating too; the trick is to always have the good ones to hand to dispute or dismiss the bad ones.

Each of our drivers, values, and beliefs will play a part in how we perceive and process the information we take in. They are what makes our map of the world unique. Mindset practices help us to notice when they pop up and to decipher their meaning. For example, if we are struggling with self-doubt, then it could be that a core belief has been triggered and by applying mindset practices we can work past this doubt and build confidence. Sounds simple right? It is. We just need to put the work in to create a strong infrastructure.

When we deal with information coming at us, our emotions and feelings are triggered. Once they join in, without infrastructure, all hell breaks loose. The resulting internal dialogue, conflicts, and confusion are exhausting.

In simple terms if you fail to meet your values, use your behaviours well, and reframe your limited beliefs, you will, without doubt, fall prey to the BIG 7 struggles.

I have included an exercise for each of these in the downloadable resources. I would invite you to take a look and complete these for yourself.

Mindset Motorway

Imagine all these emotions, drivers, feelings, behaviours, values, and beliefs are cars travelling around your body, smashing into the information being absorbed through your senses. Without structure and guidance, they are permanently "off roading" – basically, your vehicles have all been carjacked and they are off on a joy ride.

Our mindset acts like a road, with traffic lights, sat navs, stop signs, and traffic police keeping order, directing you to the best route, slowing you down, or speeding you up. It is a perfectly slick system that keeps everything moving in the right direction, guiding you to your destination via the easiest and best route. It is not always the fastest route; it is the route that offers us the best chance of finding our destination again and again, relying less and less on the sat nav.

Most of us will have a variety of mindset roads that we can access; the magic is knowing which one is going to be the most useful at any given time and being able to access it quickly without falling prey to detours, pot holes, and dead ends.

Familiar or default mindsets develop over time through repeated behaviours and circumstances. An employee, fixed, or limited mindset comes as a result of imposed beliefs and restricted imagination. A business or entrepreneurial mindset begins when we challenge ourselves to succeed, and gratitude or growth mindsets develop as a result of a committed process of self-awareness.

Through daily practice, you get to choose your default. We can choose the default mindset we want to access, like selecting your preferred debit card when buying online – the question that pops up each time we click BUY NOW, do you wish to make this your default card? My default will always be growth. When I need to, I can switch to entrepreneurial, business, or gratitude, and with my training and dedicated practice, my mind trips easily from one to the other without much effort. I almost always have the right mindset to fit the situation. Almost. I am not perfect and certain people and situations will of course trigger my fear mindset, miserable whining moaning mindset, or my inner bitchy mindset, and when that happens take cover! Thankfully, they are way down the default list, and the second they appear, I work hard to shut them down quickly.

So, the same traffic goes up and down the Mindset Motorway, we just get to choose which road is the best one to use that day. This book will offer you an insight into how you can tap into your growth and entrepreneurial mindset quickly and more easily and notice when the emotions start creeping in. Daily practice will help you to create this filter to manage and overcome many of the struggles you are experiencing.

Ok, great Abbie; so how do I build my traffic system? I hear you cry. Like this.

Mindset coaching begins by focusing attention on where the traffic is going and where it needs to be. Questions and exercises help you to create signs that pop up and direct you so you can relax, build confidence, and trust you are going in the right direction. Practice helps create the behaviours that teach you to drive the traffic more purposefully. Eventually, everything is running like clockwork. By learning and practicing mindset tools and techniques we can thrive. Struggle is exhausting and mindset tools give us energy. We all know how it feels to be off roading. It's bumpy, it's muddy, it's exciting for a while, and then we just want to puke. Mindset coaching brings structure and allows us to navigate the emotional journey, with calm, with purpose, and ultimately to reach our destination, ready for action.

In this book I share with you how I built the entrepreneurial roadway, added the signs, and plugged in the sat nav so I could remember the good routes. I will also share with you many of my bumpy off roading experiences and how I eventually made it through and back to solid ground.

Why is mindset *a struggle* for women in business?

Truth is, it is a struggle in life not just in business. Only difference is, when we operate inside our own lives, it is easy to hide. And it is not until we are challenged, that we even notice there is a problem. There is a lot to lose in life for sure: missed opportunities, relationships, grief, loss, good luck, bad luck, nice people, nasty people, money worries, and our health. Stuff happens to each of us at some time in our life, and it is often our mindset that determines what we do, how we feel, how we respond, and how we recover.

Once we reach a certain age, most of us will be carrying a fair amount of baggage. Not a great way to describe it, but it fits the purpose. We are weighed down by the life we have led. If we are lucky, we have worked through and learnt from those experiences.

But the baggage can leave its mark. Even when we think, "well I'm over that", the scar can still be seen, felt, and experienced. Hiding somewhere in the back of our mind is a trigger, and sooner or later something or someone is going to pull it! In business, we are challenged on a daily / hourly basis. And it is not the big stuff. Its stupid crappy stuff like, *should I post this or not? How do I find out how to do this? What if people don't want what I do? Did I remember to get the stuff for tea?*

Coping with success is an even bigger battle: *Oh no what if people think I'm greedy or resent me or judge me? What about my friends who are struggling? Do I deserve to be happy, rich, successful? What's so special about me? If I am successful, then there must be a price to pay. No one can really be successful and happy ... can they?* So, we start to avoid, apologise, and hide. Did you know that fear of money is an actual thing? We can actually be afraid of having money, and this will cause us to self-sabotage any efforts to bring income into our business. There are 7 main sources of struggle in business. All our anxiety, stuck behaviours, and doubt stem from experiencing these emotions. Some will pop up before we even get started.

The Big 7
- Fear
- Confusion
- Isolation
- Overwhelm
- Guilt
- Self-Doubt
- Time

The "Big 7" as I like to call them are at the root of many of our struggles. They cause all sorts of problems. Anxiety, procrastination, stuck behaviours, overthinking, hesitation, and some can even make us sick. Like actually – go to the doctor's type sick! Isolation is a killer. That is no exaggeration. Connection is a fundamental core human need. As stated in Abraham Maslow's hierarchy of needs, first published in his 1943 paper 'A theory of human motivation', after our basic needs of air, water, food, shelter, and safety comes love and companionship. If we deny ourselves connection with others, we will fail. We will struggle. We will become anxious, and eventually, depression and other illnesses will take over.

For me – finding myself in a pit of depression that no amount of positive self-talk or "Ted Talks" could get me out of was the point I decided enough was enough. Luckily, taking action to reach out to other small business owners is what saved me. I thought it was going to be their expertise that helped. What I found was something far simpler: connection. I needed to be with people, physical actual people. People who could see me. See my pain. And who wanted to help.

I have a super family. I am blessed beyond my wildest dreams to have children and a husband who have wholeheartedly, often to their own detriment, supported me, my dream and my why. By detriment – I mean to support me has meant a lot of missing out, a lot of "when we can afford it", and a lot of Aldi's ketchup. But in business, that is not enough. When attending networking events, and when I finally started to get out into the world again, I realised that the only real struggle was limited mindset. Trouble is, we pride ourselves on the struggle. Women especially. We are not particularly good at asking for help – at least not the right help, and herein lies the problem.

Women in business will often hold back from asking for help because.

1. They don't know they need it: *If I'm working hard then no one will notice how terrified I am.*

2. They are used to the struggle and cannot let it go: *If I am working hard then my family won't resent me for not being there.*

3. They don't want to admit defeat: *If I struggle, then that means I'm getting somewhere ... right?* (wrong)

We ask for help and advice in networking groups and from friends and partners. But we are asking the wrong questions and often to the wrong people. Let's be clear, there are many awesome networking groups out there that will offer invaluable support and advice. Connecting and interacting in these groups is an essential part of being in business. But what I learnt early on was that you must know what it is you need from these groups for it to be truly effective.

Creating an entrepreneurial mindset will help you to know what you "actually need" and help you to ask the right questions. The big issue I see is that we ask for the wrong kind of help because we are avoiding or trying to outrun our own values, drivers, and beliefs. We avoid asking the question because we fear what the response might be. Fear of success, of letting go of our self-assigned labels (more about this later), is a common reason why we avoid asking for help. For fear that it might in fact work.

"If I'm working hard then no one will notice how terrified I am."

A woman struggling to stay on top of the orders she has for clients will work herself to the point of exhaustion. She will then go home. There, she will start on all the other stuff, like bathing the kids, making tea, cleaning the house, engaging with her husband *etc*. Then at 10.30pm, she sits down, picks up her phone and messages a friend or posts on her FB profile about what a failure she is as a mother because her kids had to have pizza again. Or they have a project at school, and she forgot to get the stuff. Or she will offload how she will have to give up her business because it is not making any money, even though she is working basically 18-hour days. She is failing. She asks:

"What should I do"?

"How can I keep going"?

"Does anyone else feel the same or is it just me"?

I appreciate this is quite a stereotypical example of a woman's role in the home and for sure you will have your own version of this. Sharing the parenting and household duties is of course far more common these days, the point I am offering here is the connection between what is expected and what is in fact achievable. As women, we find ourselves in constant need to beat ourselves up for what we don't achieve and rarely congratulate ourselves for what we do get done.

What follows is usually a lot of advice: *You should do this. You should do that. Have you tried this app?* or *I know someone that does blah blah blah*, followed by sympathy. *Oh, you poor thing. I know how you feel. Life is hard.* Then the positivity parade. *Keep going you can do this. You are the strongest person I know. It will be worth it.*

But ... she doesn't want the advice because she hasn't got time to action it. The positivity parade has the complete opposite effect and just gives her more ammunition to beat herself up with. She is exhausted so she takes the sympathy, maybe feels better for a day or two and then goes right back to the struggle. Nothing changes.

> **"If I am working hard then my family won't resent me for not being there."**

Now, pain and struggle are a part of life. Without pain there is no point to life. The good news is, we can choose the pain (most of the time) that we want to carry. We can choose our struggles. But what is happening here is she is experiencing pain and struggle and reaching out for support to off load and numb that pain. But she is not asking the right people or the right questions; she is in fact avoiding, because time, money, and her mindset are getting in the way. When you are experiencing 1, 2, or all 7 of the Big Struggles, you will inevitably be getting in your own way. Knowing what you need to do and yet sabotaging or limiting your efforts to actually engage in the solution.

Time is telling her that she cannot stop. There is no time to sit and focus on herself or her mindset. She doesn't have time for that hippy wanky shit. She has actual stuff she needs to get done. Money worries are shouting – "there is always a price to pay". Guilt says, "that money could be better spent on your kids". She is convinced she cannot afford expert help because she has supplies to buy or marketing to pay for. She will spend ££££'s on printing leaflets but not ££'s on addressing the issues that could help.

"If I struggle, then that means I'm getting somewhere … right?"
(wrong)

Mindset is telling her she does not have time to sit and create an action plan or chat about what is really going on because she must work hard. She does not want to be fixed because that means admitting defeat. She does not want to know what is going on because that could open a whole can of worms. Guilt, fear, and confusion mean that she will avoid addressing the real problem: *If I look inside – I might not like what I see. Working on me sounds hard. I think I'll just keep battling on.*

Fear stops her from asking the right questions because she is terrified of appearing vulnerable. It is easier to deal with the pain of exhaustion than it is to experience the pain of what is really going on and spend time unpicking that shit.

I know because this was me.

Why are you *really* doing this?

Women who decide to go into business, certainly those later in life, do so because of someone or something that has happened to them. Something they have experienced. Overcoming illness, grief, depression, and struggle are great motivators. Also, seeing a need and wanting to help people, or sharing a life changing or positive experience with others can be just as motivating.

We always have a why that is bigger than whatever it is we are working on. Understanding that why and what it truly means is at the heart of our motivation. And I bet your why is not what you tell people it is. There is always a deeper meaning. We must be honest with ourselves (we do not have to share it) to understand it so we can use it properly.

> **"When you have been given a second chance at life, you feel compelled to pay it forward."**

I tell people that my why is to help other women succeed in business. That I love and believe in coaching so much so that I want to share what I know to help others. That is true. But. It is not "MY WHY". I do what I do because it makes ME feel good. I do it because my best friend died and in order to honour her memory, I pledged to make the most of every second of my life. I do it because I feel guilty for being alive when she is gone.

She would kill me with her bare hands if she heard me say that! So, I use that why in the most positive way that I can. I use it to reach out to others and help them the way she helped me, to do something that brings me joy, to indeed make the best of every day, and to love and cherish myself, my family, and my friends.

But when my body is saying "take a break you are exhausted", my WHY is saying "don't you fucking dare. You keep moving. All the time there is life in your body you keep moving". I think it's why I talk so fast.

Struggle does not have to mean unsuccessful. You would be amazed at the number of women out there running incredibly successful and profitable businesses, who are struggling. They're working too hard; trying to outrun themselves; avoiding guilt, shame, and vulnerability; and trying to prove they can.

At what cost? Your kids don't recognise you. You look and feel like shit. Financial success is something you now feel like you need to apologise for. You are failing as a mum and wife and daughter and sister because YOU decided it would be a good idea to follow your dreams. The baggage. The struggle is all in your head. You cannot outrun your own mind. 'Everywhere you go, there you will be'. Guilt is rife. *Daddy who's that strange woman in the kitchen drinking wine through a straw and crying? Oh, that's just Mummy. She is the person you should look up to, out in the world being a success. She's the one that pays for holidays and you know, Christmas.* So, you see our mindset is the key to all of this and, therefore, I have chosen to do what I do.

Does it really need to be this hard? No! Seriously. No, it does not! you just need to focus attention on what your actual struggle is. Build your confidence by asking the right questions and create effective behaviours that give you the time to work on all the rest.

Now you might be thinking, *Jeeeeez Abbie that all sounds a bit negative and pessimistic.* Hold on, OK? So there is work to be done; however, it is not all bad news. This is not a cautionary tale. Overcoming struggles or mindset obstacles does not have to be an uphill journey.

The world needs you, your product, and your service. We need passion and kindness in the world more than ever before.

So, I am here to tell you...

You are already amazing. You are already successful. You are already everything you need to be. You already know everything you need to know. And I am going to help you to remember that every single day.

The *Process*

This is coaching. It is positive and future focused. Applying even just a few simple techniques into your process can make a big difference. It is not rocket science, and it does not involve digging deep into your past and unpicking stuff you would rather forget.

Mindset is simply about choosing how you want to experience the world. Recognising where you may be looking through a dirty or broken window and learning how to step to the side, more quickly and easily. My hope is that by reading this book and sharing in some of my trials and tribulations that you will begin to see how powerful a shift of mindset can be. There is so much amazing advice and support out there to help you set up, grow, and scale a business, but without the right mindset, most of it will be obscured by the cracks in the glass and hidden by the dirt. I am going to help you to step to the side and see it all through a clean and crack-free window. Examples of the process of developing our mindset through Socratic questioning can be found in the workbook download: coaching conversations to build motivation, clarity, inspiration, and take action.

Working with a *coach*

Coaching has been a life changing therapy for me. First as a process of personal growth, and now as a tool that I share with others. It is delivered in a multitude of ways, and there is pretty much a coach for everything these days. Sports coach of course; weight loss, emotional strength, holistic, and wellbeing coaches; mindset coaches; mentor coaches; transformational coaches; business coaches; life and relationships coaches; birthing coaches; and even a writing coach. I can't tell you how relieved I was to find out that writing coaches existed, and in truth this book would never have made it off of my computer without the unwavering support of Dr Jennifer Jones. Coaching is, however, still a tough sell, at least in the UK. Countries such as Australia and the US have been leaning into this incredible therapy for decades, as it has become an accepted partnership and way of life for individuals and businesses. As a start-up coach I certainly struggled to demonstrate to my potential clients why they should engage with my services, separating coaching from other techniques such as counselling, training, and mentoring. Clients often come with mixed ideas of what and how coaching works, so I use this simple metaphor to demonstrate the difference and to help meet their expectations.

Imagine you have tripped over on the pavement and you are on the ground in a heap. People are watching, you feel vulnerable and exposed.

> **A Counsellor** would stop, bend down, and ask, "is it ok if I sit here with you, till you are ready to get back up?"

A **Teacher or trainer** might stop and say, "I can help you to get up. Put your hands flat on the ground and push. Bring your feet up to your chest and bring yourself up to your feet."

A **Mentor** could ask, "Can I help? I have been on the ground many times; this is how I got up."

A **Friend** would stop, reach down, pick you up off the floor, and carry you back home.

A **Coach** will most likely stop and ask, "What happened? How did you get here? What do you need to do to get back up? What can you do next time to stop yourself from falling?"

Now most of us when faced with fear, pain, and vulnerability will immediately opt for one of the of the first four options because they keep us in our comfort zone. At least to begin with. They feel like an immediate solution to our problem, something to take away the pain. Coaching requires us to be almost entirely in our stretch zone, and when we are already overwhelmed, struggling, and afraid, the last thing many of us will do is volunteer for more discomfort.

There are many thousands of self-help books, business scaling courses, networking, coaching, and empowerment materials found in shops and online, but not one of them can offer the transformation you desire without your commitment to taking action.

This book is no exception. There is no magical formula to follow. My promise to help reduce your struggle, as with all such books, comes with a caveat: *you* must take action. *You* must commit to a journey of curiosity and growth in order to have the life and the business you desire.

And this takes time. In my role as a coach, I walk beside my clients through the stretch zone, not in front of them. I walk beside them, facilitating their process, supporting them to gain clarity on their inner strength and use it to set achievable specific and measurable goals that move them forward. It can be uncomfortable, as we have discovered, but if you are willing to trust the process, lean into the discomfort, and embrace the change, it can be the most incredible ride.

So, are you ready? Are you up for the challenge? Fantastic, let's begin.

CHAPTER 2

Big 7 No. 1
Self-Doubt to *Self-Confidence*

> "I am just one of millions of people who have been told that in order to fulfil my dreams, in order to contribute my talents to the world, I have to resist the truth of who I am. I for one am ready to stop resisting and start existing as my full and authentic self ... My identity is not my obstacle. My identity is my superpower. Because the truth is, I am what the world looks like."
>
> AMERICA FERRERA

Self Doubt

A lack of confidence in oneself and one's abilities.

For me, self-doubt comes from a belief. The stories that I tell myself each time a trigger goes off and I start to feel uncertain or afraid. It can look and feel a lot like fear, confusion, or overwhelm, so it is important for me to first be clear about what it is I am experiencing. It can feel like being inside of a big box. Being in the box means we experience things differently and our thought processes are limited. We cannot see out.

When we take a closer look at the definition of self-doubt, we see that to experience self-doubt means we are in fact doubting our abilities. What we are saying is, "I am not particularly good at this" or "I don't have the ability to do it" or "I don't know how".

But instead, what happens is a loop of limiting beliefs begins and logical thought goes out of the window. You begin a cycle of doubt, fear, and confusion, rather than saying to yourself, "I don't know how to do this – who can I ask?"

Is what you are being asked or expected to do beyond your capabilities, or is your brain putting up safety barriers to prevent you from even trying?

Doubt has its place, for sure. For example, at my current level of fitness, I doubt I could climb Mount Everest, and I doubt Elon Musk will pick me to go with him to outer space. This is based on logic and a realistic approach. It is not limiting me; it's just, well, reality.

Doubt does not always work like this, particularly when we are already into our stretch zone, like when we're running a business. Instead of solution focused thinking, doubt starts a story. A story that says: *You are not good enough yet. What if people don't like you? You need to know more before you can do* this. You are not an expert, so you have no right to charge for your services. Read more, learn more, then maybe you will be ready. Perfectionism, hesitation, and procrastination are just a few of the ways in which self-doubt can push us into overwhelm and exhaustion. Self-doubt is no longer something that I battle every day; however, it does still come up for me. It's triggered by people, events, criticism, and challenge. When I feel my values are in question, self-doubt can still come up. I manage it much better these days, thanks to the mindset tools I use. What used to be days of overwhelm, fear, and procrastination is now a more structured and curious process.

Noticing the triggers as they happen is the first step to knowing when self-doubt has forced me to jump inside the box.

Mindset tools enable you to question this trigger and notice the effects. Are we playing out a story from our childhood? Are we responding with our inner child? Once we have clarity on the trigger, we can then start to look at how this is affecting our thoughts. Putting a hold on old patterns of behaviour means we can then question what happens next, rather than automatically defaulting to old responses.

Self-confidence

A feeling of trust in one's abilities, qualities, and judgement

The opposite of self-doubt is confidence. Self-confidence. Composure. Poise. Presence. Trust. To get from self-doubt to self-confidence, we must understand the belief or the 'story' behind it. The struggle comes when we allow a belief to drown out our logical and more positive narrative. Even when we have done the work and learnt the lessons, new situations can and will trigger our stories. If you're holding back from something because you feel you lack confidence, and you're planning on waiting until you're feeling confident before acting, then that can be an exceptionally long wait. Have you ever stood at the end of a high diving board waiting for courage to wrap its arms around you and lift you high up into the air and then guide you down smoothly into the water? Trust me you could be there for a week; you are still going to be terrified. When we notice the narrative, the story that is happening inside our head, we can then choose a new response. Confidence comes as a result of taking that new action; therefore, choice is where our confidence lies. Mindset tools allow us the opportunity to make a choice. With practice, it becomes less prescribed. However, in the beginning we need to consciously practice these techniques. Like exercising our bodies, we must exercise our minds too. Standing on the edge and looking over, you have a choice. Either choose the mindset that enables you to jump even though you are afraid, or the one that makes you walk the walk of shame back down those slippery steps. We know from past experiences that sometimes you just need to jump, smash into that water, and hope that your tits don't flop out of your swimsuit on the way back up. Confidence comes as a result of action. And sometimes your tits flop out; sometimes they don't. If they do, we learn that next time we might need to strap those puppies down.

Celebrating is a marvellous tool for noticing when we have chosen this new mindset. The ability to shift from one mindset to another is the game. We will always be triggered. There will always be self-doubt, the trick is being able to step to the side and begin to see the situation in front of you differently. Choose the mindset that offers the best opportunity to gain the result that you want. Allow for confidence to build, act, and overcome your feelings of self-doubt.

My *struggle* with self-doubt

BLENDING IN

I learnt at an incredibly early age that if I was afraid, I should just blend in. As a small child, when I felt afraid or nervous, I would stand very still and imagine myself as invisible, just so as not to be noticed. Having an identical twin certainly helped. There was always someone else beside me to take the heat. I would simply disappear into this weird dual identity where I could hide who I really was. However, this meant that I never really learnt how to show the real me. This was often a behaviour that was reinforced by those around me. My nan called us 'the twins' till we were almost 15 years old. We were always treated like a package deal. We were bought the same gifts at birthdays – friends always feeling like they had to include the "other one". All reinforcing my story of *"you don't matter"*.

My mum and dad did everything they could at the time to encourage us to be individual. Kate became a tomboy because that was the easiest way to separate our identities. She wore blue and I wore red (pink wasn't really an option in the 70's). It also meant we got a variety of toys. We had an Action Man and a Sindy so that made for a far more interesting game. We were put in separate classes at school, and we had different friends. Once we were old enough to walk to school alone, Kate immediately refused to let me walk with her and her friends. At the time, I thought it was mean and unkind, but all she wanted was to be herself for a few minutes each day, without the constant shadow. None of this worked. None of this was able to quiet the voice in my head. The story I was telling myself was "*stay hidden, stay safe*".

I grew up the youngest of 3: my older sister Rebecca, the "brainy well-behaved one" and me and my twin sister Katherine (Kate). Kate was born 6 minutes before me and boy did everyone love to remind me of that. Not Kate, she couldn't care less. Although there was always an unspoken feeling that she was the older sister and, therefore, her role was to protect me. And she did – so many times! Kate was the first to do everything. She is taller than me and, like Rebecca, she was a hell of a lot brainier than I was. Academia was not my safe space, at least not back then.

My dad was a submariner, and he would go away for months on end. Sadly, I have very few memories of him much before the age of 10 or 11. My mum was basically a single parent on a low-income, coping with 3 kids under 5. My mum loves to tell the story of how she would spend every day going backwards and forwards to the shops, climbing the stairs to our little maisonette. How every day we were immaculately dressed, and the house was always spotless. Looking after 3 kids had forced her to make sacrifices and hold back from things she wanted to do. And she had to rely heavily on my grandparents for support. My favourite story is about how my dad was offered an opportunity to go to Australia with the Royal Navy. My mum refused to go, as she couldn't face the thought of the journey with 3 small children. She deeply regrets this, and if I were offered that opportunity now, she would move heaven and earth to make sure I took advantage of it. What the actual fuck … I could have been Kylie frickin Minogue if my mum had been braver. Stories like this just reinforced my story, *"you're the reason they struggled"*.

Having experienced many years of obsessive-compulsive behaviours, following bouts of postnatal depression, I can now, looking back, truly empathise with how hard it must have been for my mum. My mum did not know she was having twins until around 6 weeks before we were due. I'm nearly 50, and back in those days scans and ultrasounds were not readily available. When her blood pressure reached boiling point and she was the size of a house, the doctor finally sent her for an X-ray. She was told, "Mrs Edwards it's twins – identical twins and they are both feet first. We are putting you on bed rest for the next 6 weeks, until we can induce you". Now for anyone who has experienced complications due to pregnancy, you will understand me when I say – I can see now why my mum had postnatal depression and where my feelings of self-doubt started to emerge. I love my parents and they love me. That is not in doubt. But growing up feeling like the kid that was not planned, hearing stories of how hard it was for my mum, and feeling like it was my fault that life was hard, some of that rubs off. All my life I have tried not to bother people. Trying to fit in. Making myself small. Not having my say and apologising, basically for everything.

The story I was telling myself: *They didn't want you; you were extra. Unplanned. You are the reason they struggle. Kate was the one who was meant to be here. You are just the backup.*

Now I had a fantastic childhood, and I was, of course, blissfully unaware of all of this at the time, and yet these messages do get through. I am very aware of how unwittingly we can impose our own beliefs onto our children. My own daughters often remind me of how they experienced my early parenting skills with stories of incidents that I have no memory of now. How my own obsessive behaviours impacted them and how my low self-esteem meant their childhood was not all it could have been. I waste no time in regret. I simply choose to do better now. To impart the lessons I have learnt to help them to be the amazing mums I know that they will one day be.

To be clear, my parents are the best: loving, supportive, reliable, and involved. They're resilient, loving, amazing parents, leaning into their role as grandparents with calm, devotion, and unwavering kindness.

I have done the work to understand how as children we absorb messages and create stories that become our version of the world. Importing our map of the world unconsciously onto our children and handing down the family script is just part of life. My parent's upbringing affected them, just as mine affected me. My only awareness of this came to light through my self-development and learning later in life. As a parent myself now, I can say hand on heart I too have handed over a fair amount of baggage to my kids. We are all just learning, and I have taken the responsibility to do the work on myself to make sense of what it means to me and how I can now move forward with my life and make peace with my past. Not delete it, not resent it, not blame it, just accept it as part of who I am.

My self-doubt led to crappy relationships, a whole lot of missed opportunity, and heartache – until I began to do the work. Through coaching, I built my mental resilience. I learned how to grow my mindset to allow for a more constructive approach to my situation. Thankfully in my personal life, these limiting beliefs are no more. I made my peace with them many years ago, and I can honestly say life is so much easier because of this.

When it came to developing my business, there were many times when these old beliefs would come back to the surface. Fear made me hide, self-doubt told me to blend in. See, if you don't pursue new clients, you can't be disappointed when nobody wants you. If you hesitate and limit yourself, then you cannot fail. I hid for a long time at the start, and although I felt safe, I also felt sad and unfulfilled, not to mention unsuccessful.

So I chose to go back to the drawing board, so to speak, and redo the steps to mental resilience. I adopted a more resourceful and confident mindset and again was able to overcome the limits that I had placed on myself. I no longer hide or try to blend in or make myself small, and this process is down to one thing: being me. I honestly believe that if we want to experience true and meaningful relationships and connections in our lives, we must show up as ourselves. I now show up as the real me every day in my life, warts and all.

INTO THE STRETCH ZONE

When taking the leap to start my own business, feelings of self-doubt that I thought were gone came back like a wave, crashing over my head, grabbing my shoulders, and pushing me down. It took a while to realise what was happening, and by the time I came up for air, I was lost, exhausted, and inches from drowning. Dramatic? – a bit. Real? - absolutely.

Later in life, we get to choose the learning we want to take part in, and when we embark upon a learning experience, it can be terrifying. If we are lucky, we have chosen to follow our passion; thus it stands to reason it will be an emotional ride. When embarking upon the next stage of my journey, I had not prepared myself for all the stuff I thought I had dealt with to come crashing back over my head.

The first time I noticed this wave of doubt, was when I began my training as a counsellor. Back in a classroom – not my comfort zone (at least that was what I thought) – with people I believed to be smarter and far more deserving of their place in the room than me.

The story I was telling myself was *OMFG Abbie you do not belong here; they are going to figure out you are a fraud; you are going to look stupid; you best get your game face on don't let them see how scared you are.*

Surrounded by people and feeling vulnerable, exposed, and

no Kate to hide behind. Ok, I thought. *You have one choice, Abbie: man up or leave now.* Thankfully, I manned up. I manned up so hard I thought my head would explode. I rose to the challenge and I excelled. I answered the questions. I read all the books. I did all the homework. I competed against my fellow classmates – not to outdo them – but simply because I had to survive, to keep my head above the water. I went from academic failure to teacher's pet overnight. Perfectionism, overachieving, and desperation were my new best friends.

All driven by my passion for self-actualisation and my low self-esteem when it came to academics. I believed that I wasn't as clever as everyone else, and therefore, I had to overcompensate. I kept telling myself, "If I do everything that is asked of me, maybe no one will notice the gaps".

Ok, so this did not turn out too badly for me. I did do very well, and I gained a lot of confidence from the process. I was even able to give myself a little pat on the back (a small one mind you, but still it was progress).

When a few years later the opportunity to train as a coach came up, I jumped at it. This time I knew what to expect. I understood my learning style, and although I was almost crippled with anxiety and overwhelm (due mostly to the fact it was being taught on webinar) and I had no feckin clue what a webinar even was, it was cool. I would just apply the same behaviours that got me through last time. Be the most organised, be the one with your hand up. Help everyone else to do well too, because now my core need for co-dependency had kicked in: *"Big up everyone else that way they will like you more. If you can't be clever be kind"*.

Now I was taught by the best in the business, and the learning process I undertook was far more challenging than I ever imagined it would be. I was expecting to be told what to do; instead the learning was more of an "offering of knowledge and self-reflection". Jeez, it was so uncomfortable. They knew what was going on: they could see the circles I was running in, the processing I was doing, and the pressure I was putting myself under. I hit my stretch zone hard. Questioning and doubting my every move. This sent me in circles and every day was a merry-go-round of pain, discomfort, curiosity, reflection, and realisations. It was awesome, and for the first time since completing my counselling training, I truly felt alive and energised to be back in this learning environment. It was also exhausting. By the time I had qualified and taken the subsequent Train the Coach programme too, I had my learning process nailed. I had experienced several moments during my training where my overpreparing and perfectionism had tripped me up. These lessons came hard. Like a punch in the gut type of hard. I thought I was done. But no. These lessons kept coming. We cannot go back from a place of self-awareness. Once we have opened that box, it is impossible to go back to a place of un-knowing. With self-awareness comes vulnerability, and so as the lessons kept coming, so did the pain and discomfort.

Then came starting a business. Oh, my days this has been the toughest test of my self-doubt to date (except maybe writing this book!). When I took the leap to quit my job and go it alone as a coach, I experienced yet another wave of self-doubt. This time the wave really did take me under. I was way past the Isle of Wight and halfway to France, before I was plucked out of the water by a passing lifeboat (metaphorically that is). I had found myself in yet another room, surrounded by people I thought were better than me. Except this time the room was the entire internet. Adverts, posts, videos. Everywhere I turned people were succeeding, looking like they knew exactly what they were doing. Everyone except for me. Where did they learn all this stuff? How do they know what to say? I don't know how to sell. I don't want to sell. That all looks icky. I can't do that. I really did not know what to do this time. I just wanted to blend in and hide, but this was not an option. Blending in was exactly what I could not do.

We want to sell our stuff, but we do it in a way so as not to bother anyone. We apologise for intruding onto their newsfeed with "our little offer". We try to hide who we are. We don't do videos or FB lives because that is what confident people do, and that's just annoying. It's fine if someone scrolls past our post; it's only words after all. But if we put on a video and no one likes it, OMFG! Devastation. They are rejecting me. The real actual me this time, and I cannot have that, so I am not doing a video. I will just keep posting other people's quotes in the hope that I inspire someone.

SELF-DOUBT CYCLE

Self-doubt hides what is really going on. Because I was so used to doubting myself in the past, it was almost like an old friend had retuned. We got on like a house on fire and before long we were best buddies again. I took her everywhere. She carried me through my counselling training and my coaching diploma and then followed me into my business. She would show up most days, spouting on about how she didn't think that someone like me deserved to be offering help to others. "Who was I to call myself an expert? and really charging other people, ummm nah. Nope." During my training, the self-doubt brought fear, confusion, and overwhelm. The fear of failing, the fear of someone finding out I did not belong. The confusion of where this was all leading and the overwhelm, did I mention overwhelm? Trying to balance life's demands, while selfishly pursuing my dream. But what for? Why? I just kept thinking, I don't know enough, so I worked 10 times harder than I needed to. In my learning I overachieved and pushed myself to ridiculous lengths, trying to outrun self-doubt. So how was I going to do that in business? What do I need to learn now? But instead of opting for a book on building a business or maybe finding someone in business to ask, I chose to hide and question my abilities as a coach. The story I was telling myself was this: *You are failing because you are a crap coach, because there are other coaches out there that know more than you. No one is going to take a fat housewife with a hobby in coaching seriously – what do you even know anyway?* The added noise of having no money, isolation, and now deep depression was too much. By some miracle I did get a few clients to start with and that was great. Scary and exciting all at once. But instead of just going out and being myself and trusting that this was of course going to be a learning curve, I reverted straight back to procrastination and all the avoidance behaviours and coping strategies that I had adopted during my training.

Now to be clear. Wanting to learn more and grow your skills is not something to avoid. Continuing professional development (CPD) is literally essential – as a coach, therapist, and honestly in any business. However, the danger comes when growth becomes an obsession. Because of my self-doubt, I kept thinking that I needed to know more and that at some point I would wake up and say to myself, "that's it Abbie you've read all the books, watched all the webinars, you're golden – go out and charge a fortune because now you know everything. You are as good as all those other 'proper coaches". Instead of using my time and resources to get more clients, practice my skills, learn, and fail, and fail some more, I hid. I got so engrossed with doubting my abilities and thinking I needed to know more that all my energy was going into chasing this unrealistic destination of "Done". I did this to the point at which when a client did cancel, I was relieved.

I would get myself into such a state before every session: *Have I got all the tools and exercises? Have I written out all my questions? What if I go blank and forget what to say? OMG what if I say the wrong thing? What if they think I'm shit? I cannot let them down.*

Now any good coach will tell you that we can only be so prepared for a session, and the best we can offer our client is to be present, listen, and facilitate. You do not need notes for that. And that is how I was trained. I was trained by the best and yet my beliefs (the ones I thought I had left on the driveway at Lisa's house 10 years before) were telling me otherwise. Overpreparing defines my procrastination behaviours. When I describe struggle I am, in reality, describing procrastination. At first, I couldn't identify with this, as for me procrastination meant faffing and being disorganised. I was far from that. What I have since learnt is that procrastination is a combination of behaviours, any of which postpone, prevent, or distract you from achieving your goal. I distracted myself with perfectionism and overpreparing based on fear and self-doubt. Low self-esteem popped up a fair few times too, as my childhood stories of 'you are not talented', 'you are not the brainy one in the family', 'you are average' started to play out in my mind. My core drivers to be prepared and not let anyone down often joined in, and hiding in the shadows, waiting to pounce was the ever present assassin, self-sabotage: "You will never really be good enough so fail now, fail quick, and then no one will know you even tried".

> Covid19 caused many micro businesses to be put on hold. Many never recovered. With so much uncertainty, self-doubt once again came flooding back. Just when life and my business were balancing nicely, and I had started to find consistency, lockdown was announced, and it was

snatched away in a matter of hours. The world seemed to just stop spinning. Like so many of my coaching and networking colleagues, I was pivoting, doubting, and reacting at such a rate that within days I was exhausted. My core values to serve and support went into overdrive, and with no clear guidance or information as to what was needed, every step felt like I was treading on rotten floorboards. Am I doing the right thing? What do people want? What do I need? Every decision felt riddled with doubt and the uncertainty grew. Doubting whether I could meet the challenges that lay ahead, I began to retreat, thinking that this situation was best left to the experts. The story I was telling myself: *I have nothing to offer here.*

This was a time of unimaginable fear and confusion, and one I hope we never have to see again. I was struggling. I wanted to get on and help and give my clients at least the support they needed, but I had no clue where to begin. After a rather long day of Zoom calls and phone calls, my voice began to fade. My face was flush, and my chest was tight. "Oh god this is it I have it!" Luckily, my good friend Nicky is a nurse, and she came round the next morning and took my temperature. She gave me a tentative all clear and suggested I stay put and rest. Thinking I might be ill, thinking I might not be able to work gave me the shock I needed to stop. I took stock and made some choices. I stepped away from social media and emails for a day, and while writing a list of all my passwords and the songs I wanted played at my funeral, I started to think back to the last time I had felt this panicked. Self-doubt is a merry-go-round, and the

> more you fight it the faster it goes. You must stop and do the work. My slight brush with death, or at least the thought of it, gave me all the motivation I needed to step back and think. When was the last time I felt like this? What was the trigger? How did I get past it that time? What was the self-talk then? What is the self-talk now? If I can dig deep now and remember how I got out of this last time, maybe I can do the same again this time. And that is exactly what I did.

How I found *self-confidence*

SEEK ABUNDANCE

Last time I felt panicked was right at the start of my business journey, the day I discovered networking. Going from self-doubt to self-confidence is a process of steps. Recognising the belief and rewriting the story. It was not until in March 2018 when I started networking that I realised it was not just me. What a realisation that was. It was almost as powerful as the "just say thank you" moment ... almost. I walked into a networking group and found, to my amazement, a room full of people all struggling with the same things as me: fear, isolation, confusion, overwhelm, guilt, exhaustion, and self-doubt. Now to be clear, at this point I was still blissfully unaware of the fact my only actual problem was me. I just thought I was shit at being in business. Once I began to talk with them, it became clear to me that they too were doubting their talents and holding back. In fact, their talents were solid, only their confidence needed work. Now from the outside looking in, I was thinking, "all these people are amazing; their products and businesses are so cool; they are so talented." And they dutifully would reciprocate with, "Abbie you really know your stuff, you are awesome", but I was back to deflection and doubt.

Why was this happening? Why was everyone struggling to stand up and talk about their business for 1 minute. Why were they holding back? Fear, confusion, and overwhelm, all wrapped up in a box of self-doubt. Not one of them had taken the decision to set up their business lightly. They had all trained and qualified and invested. They were all fantastic at what they did. They just needed to see it too. That is when the penny dropped, and I decided to switch my focus from constantly doubting my coaching skills to developing a growth mindset around my business. To learn how to navigate all the traffic that was tearing around my head. To begin to make sense of what was driving me to behave in this way and to, most of all, accept who I am, recognise my worth and learn to just say "Thank you".

Before long, I realised that my decision to focus on my own mindset as part of being an entrepreneur was something that others in my network could benefit from too. Through conversations with my new friends, it was evident that we were all suffering from the same debilitating condition: procrastination. Clients began to approach me for support, and while still navigating this path for myself, I willingly sat beside them and supported their growth.

When we start to look at what feels right, we begin to notice not only where our passion lies but where our energy and motivation are too. Life coaching had been an amazing journey for me, and yet not one that had brought huge reward. Being around these amazing entrepreneurs triggered a fire inside of me that I could not ignore. I began to look at the parts of my business that really energised me, where I found my flow. For a brief time, I was lucky enough to have been involved in training and instructing new coaches. I loved this. So, what was it that I loved so much? Teaching, training, mentoring, instructing, creating learning materials, and imparting coaching to others. How could I use these drivers and apply them to my business? I wondered.

In time and with help I shifted my business to mindset coaching for women in business. By appreciating the skills I valued most and using them as the platform, this shift came quickly, and I pushed forward with confidence. I have been where these ladies are. I know the struggle. I can adapt my skills as a coach to help them to navigate this journey and use my passion for writing and creativity to produce materials, workshops, and lessons to help them overcome these mindset blocks. There is often a temptation when we shift or pivot in our business to think we need to learn something new or buy into something that will help us get to where we want to be. A simple exercise in seeking abundance can show we already have exactly what we need. Combining what we have with what else we might need greases the wheels and makes goal setting much more effective. I did, of course, have a lot of work to do to make this happen; however, had I focused only on what I lacked (a website, a business plan, a marketing strategy, any clients, *etc.*), I probably would not have got very far. By choosing to lead with what I have, my core drivers, my passion, my skills, and my experience, it became a far more manageable task.

> At the start of the Covid19 crisis, I could feel self-doubt creeping in. I already had my 5-year, 3-year, 1-year and 90-day goals planned out and suddenly everything was called into question. I found myself struggling to commit to what I needed to get done, doubting that

anything would be enough. Wondering what my clients would need. Is this a time to be raising my profile? Reaching out to help all those in need? I soon realised that everyone was in need and so I had to do something. Where can I be most useful and stay confident of making a difference, I asked myself, having realised that my struggle was again a result of my chosen mindset. My tribe. My paying clients and my community, that is where I feel safe, useful, and confident. *Look at what you already have Abbie*, I said to myself, *you don't need anything more*. My confidence began to return. To be clear, this really was an incredibly difficult and unpredictable time, and even those with the strongest business mindsets were shaken by the enormity of the tasks ahead. However, stepping back meant taking back control of my energy and my power, and accepting that I needed to do what was right for me was how I changed the game. I decided very quickly that 'big fish little pond' was the way to go. I cannot heal the world, so I need to focus on me, my family, my clients, and my tribe. I put all my energy and focus into serving them. Where my tribe are concerned, I have no issues with doubt. They are like an open book to me, and I know every page like the back of my hand. Choosing to focus on where I knew I could not fail was how I removed self-doubt and rebuilt my confidence. This gave me a solid foundation from which to work, so when the time was right to reach out to a wider audience and offer my services, doubt was no longer as issue. Using what I already knew and sandwiching it between the bits I was less sure of helped to get it done. Recognising your abundance is a great way to grease the wheels. Choosing

> to notice what you already know, rather than only on what is uncertain, helps your inner voice of doubt to stay just quiet enough to start making progress. I took all the uncertainty and buried it amongst everything that I already knew: my tribe, my skills, and my why.

OWN YOUR STORY

The first time I realised I had a story to tell was when I signed onto the counselling course. It was an experience unlike any I had ever encountered, and the whole thing excited and terrified me all at the same time. Looking back, I probably pushed through because of Lisa – I didn't want to let her down.

I arrived at the centre for the first day of college feeling sicker and more excited than I had ever been before in my life. I had decided to go with the "you have nothing to lose" mindset, and I have to say it was working. I had attended a 12-week introduction course a few months earlier and nailed it, so after my initial rumble with self-doubt, I quickly picked myself back up and thankfully did not make a complete fool of myself. The yearlong course was challenging at times, and I loved every single second of it. I became utterly addicted to the activity of growth and how it energised me. One of our final assignments was to give a presentation. A story about us, our life our interests our passion, and our why. Why we were there on the course, and what brought us to this point. I went balls deep on the project as I had done on all the assignments – something that was to turn out to be a bit of a pattern for me in the future. As I sat facing my classmates and read my story, flicking through the album I had created, the photos I had painstakingly selected and the words I had so carefully chosen, the tears poured down my face and I struggled to speak. Was this really my life? Was this really my story? I had never pieced together the parts of my life before to see the full extent of what made me who I am. The person that I was right there in that moment. Riddled with doubt, I had questioned so much of what I was going to say, for fear of judgement, for fear of appearing weak. But as I began to speak, all the doubt drifted away. What did I have to lose? "It begins with you", Lisa said to me one day when we were sat in her garden. "It begins with you". I get it now, I thought as I sat in front of the teary-eyed faces of my classmates. Some scrabbling for tissues others just staring as I spoke. Now my story has a few sad bits, but overall, it is not a tragic tale. It was my unabridged honesty that resonated that day. I felt the transformation. That was the moment I realised my story matters.

The next time I told my story was during a presentation on my coaching training. I had come a long way since the photo album, and I was now rocking the power point presentation. My core driver for perfection was in overdrive: "I must get this right", I kept saying to myself. Instead of choosing the more relaxed chat to the audience approach that many of my classmates had chosen, I went in hard. I chose to remain off camera and read from a script, while my painstakingly perfect power point slides played out across the screen. The presentation was great, and it set the bar high for those that came next. However, I could not help feeling a sense of deflation. Why did I have a script? Why did every word matter so much? Why did I choose perfection over authenticity and engaging with the audience? Because I chose to be off camera, so my script could be perfect, I was disconnected from the audience, and I had panicked several times during the presentation that no one could hear me. Allowing self-doubt to dictate my choices was a behaviour I would repeat many times throughout my coaching journey, and to this day I still battle with perfectionism. Perfectionism born out of fear and self-doubt.

The next time I told my story was when I met Rico, and we were designing my website. Rico worked painstakingly hard to ensure "my story" was visible for all to see. Working with Rico helped me to feel confident throughout that process and when challenged to be visible, he helped me to overcome my discomfort and to be ok with vulnerability.

Self-doubt is an easy fix; you just need to know what has triggered it. If you own your story, warts and all, you then have the power to fix it. If you are blaming something or someone else, then they hold the power. Self-doubt is just the box we use to hold all the other crap in. I still have bumps in the road. Each time a new opportunity comes up, I can literally feel myself being drawn to those old behaviours. Overprepare, cover all bases, do not let the fear show. Rehearse, rehearse, rehearse. Trouble is, not only does this not work, particularly on a Facebook live or in a conversation, it masks the authenticity. It causes hesitation and it is basically a waste of time and energy. As your business grows, so will you. You need to get better at managing your energy, and wading through self-doubt, procrastination, and stuck behaviours are a waste of your resources. It makes things take longer, and it's exhausting. When you own your story and embrace your past experiences, you have the capacity to draw confidence from your past struggles to meet new challenges in the future.

TRUST YOUR UNIQUENESS

For me, using my unique selling points (USP) – which is a marketing term for just be yourself and show us what makes you different from the rest – is about knowing who I am. If you are the product, then you need to understand yourself inside out: how you work and how you play. Your USP is your motivation, your purpose. It is where you find flow, and where you will always find your why.

When we are creating a brand or marketing our product, we want our USP to shine. For me, this was a process of understanding where my specific skills were of value to my clients. What was it about me that attracted clients, and also what was it in me that helped build confidence in my offer? We need to operate at the truest version of who we are. When we say it's ok to just be me, we can let go of doubt because there really is no one to compare ourselves to. And therefore, nothing to doubt. Yep – so that is a little easier said than done, although there is a lot of confidence to be gained by simply knowing and understanding who we are on the inside so we can be the best we can be on the outside. USP is not just a marketing strategy it really does underpin your whole business.

For me, this began with understanding my core drivers and behaviours, core values, and core beliefs. There are exercises to download that will help you to identify your core behaviours, values, and beliefs. I would encourage you to check these out once you have read the book.

Navigating a journey through doubt to confidence is about using the behaviours, values, and beliefs that work for you. Understanding when they are helpful and when they are not. For example, my core value for connection means that being in a room full of people fills me with joy. My core driver for consistency means that when I begin a task, I must finish it. Great for the ironing – not so great when you have 32 things to do that day. This core behaviour pops up regularly, and I have gotten particularly good at noticing when it starts to impact my productivity. While on the surface it appears I'm getting lots done, the reality is that I am powering through to complete and ignoring other work and my health. It starts to become beneficial again when I take on a new client, for example, as I work tirelessly to ensure I onboard them efficiently and give them all the support they need as they begin their coaching relationship with me. Beliefs can be tricky, however; not all beliefs are negative. They are not all shitty narratives from our past. Beliefs can be powerful too. My belief in the life altering transformation brought about through coaching is unshakeable. It motivates me at every step and encourages me to keep going. We do not ignore any of our values, behaviours, or beliefs, we just find a way to make them work for us. More about this in the coming chapters.

> Throughout my life, when faced with challenges I dig deep – especially when I feel self-doubt creeping in. I am an expert in reflection and tend to overdo it when doubt becomes too big to manage. This was the case when Covid19 entered our lives, triggering not just doubt, but fear, confusion, and overwhelm. Thanks to my mindset coaching tools, I was able to stop and step back before things got too difficult, and as with all situations, there were lessons to be learnt.

WHERE SELF-DOUBT SHOWS UP IN BUSINESS

Self-doubt shows up in all sorts of ways in our businesses. From a daily hesitation about posting on social media to questioning our very existence and the value of our business. Self-doubt surrounds us throughout our lives, and it enjoys nothing more than getting together with its best friends, fear, confusion, procrastination, and overwhelm. We imagine that those around us who appear confident and decisive are that way because they are immune to self-doubt. I can assure you this is not the case. Over time those that choose to practice a growth mindset will indeed develop their confidence to act and be less distracted by their inner pessimist or judge. They are not, however, immune. As a coach, I judged myself in the beginning for not knowing it all. For not always having the answers when it came to growing my business, and this caused me to experience huge amounts of self-doubt. I wasted time and money trying to "feel" confident because I was listening to the voice of self-doubt telling me *you don't know enough; you are not good enough*. Being a coach does not make you immune to self-doubt, or any of the other Big 7 struggles for that matter, it just makes you more aware of what needs to be done.

As you will learn throughout this book, I do, to this day, still experience the struggle. I am just far better at noticing it, being curious about what it means to me, and finding strategies to work through it. So, the trick here is to notice self-doubt and shine a light on it before the rest join in. Work the process to be curious and avoid judging yourself for having doubt in the first place. This will help you to avoid falling into a pity cycle. I call it this because self-doubt can lead to self-pity and when the others join in – fear, confusion, and procrastination – it quickly becomes a pity party, and you do not have time for that. Self-doubt is almost always triggered by a limiting belief. Understanding the stories that we are telling ourselves is probably a good place to start. Notice the trigger, listen out for the story you are telling yourself. Think, what is important to me here? What is the story telling me? Is it telling me I can or is it telling me I can't? What are my options?

Top tips – Self-doubt to self-confidence

Understanding and being who you are, honestly and authentically, is a perfect starting point for self-confidence. We just need to trust ourselves to do it. For me, the moment I leaned into my personality and decided that it was ok to be who I am in my business as well as in my life was a game changer. For so long I had tried to hide the fact that I was terrified.

That I felt more comfortable treating my clients like friends than customers. That I am still a work in progress, and that I wake up every day just wanting to be useful. These are now the biggest assets of my business. They are what enable me to work with the people I want to work with. They mean I get up every day feeling excited and inspired because today I get to see my friends. They are what makes business fun for me. So, I am not as terrified now as I used to be; however, I am not ashamed to admit that I was or that I still have days when self-doubt washes over me.

Where Self-doubt shows up	Top Tips to Beat Self-doubt
You hesitate way too long before deciding or taking action.	A quick pros and cons list can help when hesitating about deciding or taking action. Stick to the facts and set yourself a time limit to act.
You find yourself on a loop of procrastination – doing lots and getting nowhere.	When procrastination kicks in stop and step back. Take time to reassess your goals and re-prioritise your tasks.

You make poor judgements about your abilities and question support from others.	When you begin to doubt your ability to complete a task or take on a new challenge, take a few minutes to check in on your credibility skills. When have you done this before? What or who helped then? Can you do this again?
You get caught up in perfectionism.	Perfectionism tends to be more about avoidance and doubt than it is about standards. Decide before you start what 'done' looks like. Set a time limit to get it done and learn to be ok with 'ok'.
You avoid stepping out of your comfort zone.	Avoiding stepping out of our comfort zone means that we miss out on great opportunities to grow our business. The smallest step in the right direction can make all the difference. Commit to one action at a time and celebrate your progress.
You apologise for and under-price your offers.	Lack of confidence around your offer can mean inconsistencies in promotion and pricing. Identify your Ideal Paying Client, and create an offer that meets their needs.

You seek out co-dependency instead of collaboration.	When opportunities arise to collaborate with others take a few minutes to ask yourself what this opportunity means for you and your business. Does it meet your values? Will it be good for you and your ideal paying clients? Are you sharing the fun or shifting the burden?
You feel out of control because your inner critic is running the show and she is making some BAD choices.	Negative self-talk can be extremely destructive to our productivity and our self-esteem. First notice who or what triggers the negative self-talk. Then think about how you want to act.

BOOK RECOMMENDATION

The Book of Gutsy Women by Hillary Rodham Clinton and Chelsea Clinton.

A great book for motivation, perspective, and confidence is the brilliant The *Book of Gutsy Women* by Hillary Rodham Clinton and Chelsea Clinton. I am an audio book junkie, and listening to these amazing inspirational stories of bravery and absolute determination was like having confidence pumped directly into my brain. Stories of so many women you may or may not have heard of throughout history.

Women taking a stand, sticking up for what they believe in, and making a difference, often to their own detriment. A powerful insight into their incredible journeys. If you are ever sat thinking *I can't do this, what if I fail, It's too hard, I don't know how,* ... a few chapters of this book will put that negative self-doubt right in its place.

The book tells the story of 100 gutsy women throughout

history, and honestly gutsy does not even come close to describing the courage, bravery, and determination these women showed in often the most oppressive and horrific of circumstances. These are stories of women living their values and beliefs every single day to overcome insurmountable odds and accomplish their goals. All have one thing in common: they faced challenges, negativity, interference, and difficulties from outside of themselves. Endless triggers that could easily have prevented them from pushing through. Had these women given into the voices of self-doubt, fear, and uncertainty, the world would be a vastly different place. Civil rights, racism, oppression, medicine, politics, sports, and entertainment all would be quite different right now, if it were not for the determination of these magnificent women and the 1000's more whose stories may never be told. Do not ever doubt yourself. Do not ever let anyone tell you, you can't achieve greatness. Especially not if that voice is coming from inside of you. Be a cheerleader. Be a warrior. Be gutsy. Be you.

CHAPTER 3

Big 7 No. 2
Isolation to *Connection*

*"Motivation comes from working on things we care about;
it also comes from working with people we care about"*

SHERYL SANDBERG

Isolation

The process or fact of isolating or being isolated

Isolation, confinement, remoteness, segregation, solitude, aloneness, detachment, and withdrawal. Wow those are not words that we really want to use to describe how we are experiencing our businesses, are they? Feeling isolated can be devastating. We crave connection and gain energy from having people around us. The right people, that is. However, we can be operating very effectively within our lives and our families and still be experiencing isolation when it comes to our business.

I am blessed with an amazing support network of family and friends, yet when I left work to start a business, the feelings of isolation were catastrophic. Our passion, energy, purpose, and motivation are directly linked to the people and situations we chose to engage with. And connection sits very securely within our core values. Without it our heart will literally break. So, for me, defining the feeling of isolation in my business is a combination of physical geography and emotional connection. Isolation causes a multitude of struggles, fear, confusion, self-doubt, and overwhelm. Because without connection, we struggle to process our thoughts and emotions. We self-medicate and become addicted to things that are not good for us, because our body and soul are literally crying out for the happy hormones we get when we meet with friends or when we feel wanted and useful.

In 2015 during his phenomenally successful Ted Talk, Johann Hari describes a study performed on rats that were isolated and given a choice of drugged water or clean water to drink. The isolated rats chose the drugged water and inevitably became addicted and subsequently died. They gave the same choice to rats who had all their mates around them, balls to play with, and lots of stimulation. Those rats barely touched the drugged water, and they all thrived. It's a great Ted Talk, and it made me cry. Coming from a long line of diabetics and self-medicators, the message hit home.

My family's drug of choice is food. Alcohol yes, but mostly food. Numbing pain with food is something my family have done for generations. Upset ... eat. Happy ... eat. Bored ... eat, drink. Stressed .... drink, drink, eat. Busy ... snack. Celebrating ... eat, drink, eat, eat. Giving up your job and sitting at home alone, cut off from the world, is painful, and eventually you will become so consumed with numbing the pain, your business will die, no matter how hard you work or how much you love it. Connection is vital for a business to survive. And if you are the business, then you need to GET OUT!

> The Covid19 lockdown was surreal, and many businesses closed or ceased to trade during the pandemic. Many moved online, and thankfully my business transferred instantly and my audience and reach in fact grew during this time. Many people forced to self-isolate or restricted from their normal daily routines – walks to the shops, coffee with friends, and going to work – were starting to suffer. Of all the horrors that Covid19 brought, isolation and disconnection were second only to the virus itself.

Connection

A relationship in which a person or thing is linked or associated with something else

> Finding ways to stay connected during Covid19 became the new national pastime. Celebrities showing up on Facebook and Twitter, super stars sending messages to the nation, and of course sports stars and fitness coaches showing up every day to help keep kids entertained and active – all in the hopes of staying connected. The elderly and the vulnerable undoubtedly suffered; however, the younger generation felt the weight of this enforced isolation more, I believe, than most. Being unable to go to school or work, to socialise and have time with friends, really took its toll. Not to mention being with their parents 24/7!

Connection can be experienced on so many levels: physically, spiritually, mentally, and verbally. When we connect with a person, there is a profound feeling of comfort and belonging. It gives us energy and feeds our soul. If we are lucky, we get to experience connection throughout our lives from our parents, siblings, and family, to making our first friends at school to our partners and spouses and when we meet our babies for the first time. Even our pets. We only need to look on social media to see how much we love our animals. In our lives, we seek out connection on a subconscious level and in an instinctual way. Children and animals connect without hesitation and lean beautifully into the feelings that it brings. As we get older, it starts to become a more prescribed process. Going on dates, job interviews, and meeting the in-laws. Connection starts to feel a lot more like something we do rather than something we are. When we are connected, we experience joy and it is most often because our values are being met. We can connect with TV shows or a great audio book. We go to the gym rather than working out alone. We find jobs and hobbies that make us feel good, energised, and alive. When work takes us away from the natural hustle and bustle of an office, team or workplace connection immediately begins to be lost, and so when we consciously make the choice to isolate ourselves physically, we need to be purposeful in our behaviours to seek out other ways to connect.

Social media and the internet can be a double-edged sword. We have all these people wanting to inject themselves into our lives and wanting us to reciprocate. However, if we are not meeting our core values through these connections and getting at least a small amount of physical interaction, then social media can start to feel like an empty void. It triggers self-doubt, procrastination, fear, and judgement. So, we want to connect with the right people, those who share our values, and combine that with consistent actions to engage with actual human beings. Our family and friends can, of course, offer deep connection; however, when it comes to our business values and goals, we will need to look further outside of our immediate circle. Our family support us, but they may not appreciate our why. This is your dream, not theirs; so they probably won't "get it" – for that, we need business buddies and fast.

My struggle with isolation

MANAGING ANXIETY

I had no idea that isolation would become the defining point of my early journey as a start-up. Nor did I imagine that it would also define the biggest shift in my business growth a few years later during the Covid19 pandemic.

At the start of my business, I found myself isolated and full of anxiety. I had no idea how damaging isolation could be to a new business. I had just left a job that was practically destroying me emotionally, and I thought that the worst was behind me. "I'm a coach now", I said to myself. "I have done the work; I have developed the skills and resilience to overcome whatever comes my way. I just need to get out there and coach and everything will be fine". Little did I know that whatever anxiety and stress my previous job was causing me, nothing would compare to the mental anguish I was about to endure – when I meet with new clients or chat to other business owners, going through the same things I did, a little shiver goes down my spine.

This, this right here is why I wrote this book. All the other struggles that I have endured have been a walk in the park compared to the devastating feeling of isolation. If you do nothing else, if you take only one thing from this book, let it be this: connection is vital. Find it wherever you can. Get out of your house whenever possible, and if that is not possible, get out of your own head. Build relationships with others who inspire and support you. Spend time talking with and asking questions of those who understand your struggles. Be sure to engage with positivity and expertise and avoid injecting yourself into situations that are ineffective. Connection is vital; it does, however, need to be the right kind of connection. So, go where you will be supported and where you will be challenged to grow. And remember – no one else will do this for you. So whatever connections you make or advice you take, be sure to take action. You cannot talk your way into growing a business. Watching Monty Don on BBC2 will not get your veggie patch sorted. You need to listen to what he says, be inspired by the size of his marrows, and then you need to get up and go plant your own seeds. Water them, nurture them, and reap the rewards. You must take action!

My energy comes from being in a room with others, and for a while I let that hold me back from introducing new offers into my business. "I don't want to be a faceless coach at the end of an online course", I would say to my mentors when they were encouraging me to expand my offers and take them online. "It's not who I am; I like to be with people when I coach". Years later, I am coaching almost entirely online. I realised that connection is about having your needs met. When we can meet our core values through connection – how and where we do it matters a lot less than actually doing it. I still top up my face to face time with clients, only now this is achieved through events, workshops, networking, and the occasional afternoon of tea and cake.

By January 2018 I had been a "fulltime coach" for 4 months. I had left my job, and since then I had been desperately trying to get my head around social media and trying to get clients. I had signed on with the Life Coach Directory – which proved handy and I did get a few clients. I even had a couple of referrals. But nothing consistent and nothing that was going to come close to paying my bills or looking like an actual income. I was barely covering the cost of all the crap I was buying on Amazon and the frantic spending, like agreeing to advertise on websites and in publications that I thought would give me clients, but instead just took my money and I never heard from them again. WTF! Anyway, I had some lovely clients and they have continued to support me to this day. I will forever be grateful to those who stuck with me in the early days, when I honestly had no clue what I was doing except trying to survive.

Christmas 2017 was horrendous. We had so little money at this point that the noise in my head was almost deafening: *this is your fault; you have put us in this horrible position; you are the reason that we can't afford to pay for our weekly shopping, let alone fucking Christmas!* I am not a fan of Christmas, but December 2017 was the worst ever. I had flu too. The horrible bone aching, head crushing, lung stinging, kill me now kind, and it went on for weeks. January came and I was by then in a deep depression. Isolation, procrastination, fear, and confusion had taken me to a place I thought I would never come out of. *Should I get a job? People won't take me seriously. What if I get a job and then coaching work comes in?* Between that and trying to navigate the feeding, peeing, and pooping schedule of a then senior Labrador, I wondered where I'd find the time for a job; I was working way too hard at being in business, there was no time to earn money. Oh my god, looking back on it now, I shudder at how much time I wasted dicking about trying to make sense of it all.

So, January, anxiety, depression confusion, and poverty. Well not poverty, but seriously struggling to make ends meet and all the time blaming myself. Then, just after my birthday in mid-February, when flu and desperation had moulded me into what can only be described as a fat 'Gollum' – Dave finally broke his supportive silence and said, "Babe this was supposed to be your dream, it looks more like a nightmare".

I cried so hard that day I thought my eyes would melt. Not nice movie crying; it was more like howling and snorting and groaning. Tears and snot all down my face and onto my sleeve as a laid on my bed curled up in a ball wondering what the hell I was doing wrong. I had never felt more alone in my entire life.

DESPERATION POINT

> When years later we were forced into self-isolation and ultimately lockdown, I feared the worst. The anxiety I had felt at the start of my journey through isolation was a memory and an experience I did not wish to repeat. I feared for myself but more so for the rest of the world. Pictures on the news of deserted cities and families talking through windows and loved ones lying alone in hospitals, sick, and often dying. "The world is already so sick", I said to Dave while we watched Boris delivering the news. "Mentally sick, we will never recover. What about of all those people clinging to the few moments of connection they have each day? What about all those that are working hard to maintain their mental health and now they can't do any of the things they want to do? I don't care about me; I'm used to being at home. I don't have a life that I need to escape. But the kids, not seeing their friends; you Dave, you think you want a few weeks off, trust me you will be climbing the walls after a week". All I could think about were the friends I have whose relationships are not like mine. Those with kids who need entertaining or relationships already on thin ice. Clients and colleagues unable to work, their business is their income, but it is also their passion and their joy. What will become of them? I was terrified, and for a few days I joined the wave of overwhelm that poured onto social media, trying to make sense of what

> was happening. I started to feel the anxiety welling up inside. Not for myself this time but for the entire world and everyone I loved, and I began to remember how isolation had almost ended my business before it even got started.

That day lying on my bed curled up in a snotty ball. The voices in my head were deafening. One of those voices, thankfully became a little louder: *What the fuck Ab; you are a coach, if you were a client what would you be saying? What questions would you be asking? What solutions would you be exploring?* The penny dropped. Abbie, coach thyself! Seriously how did it take me this long to work it out.

I was so used to puking all my procrastination and processing onto the people at work and onto other coaches, that once that opportunity had been removed, I had no way to process all this shit. That and the fact that I had no clue how to run a business! I thought all I had to do was be willing to work hard. We hear all the stories of rugged determination and how it pays off. I just thought that is what you did. Once the penny had dropped, my brain started to reboot. I had been at a point of mental exhaustion way before I had even left my job, and so it was no surprise that all of this had become overwhelming. Lying on that bed, clarity began to appear as little tiny bursts of positivity, popping like bubbles in my imagination.

Then a few days later, during a regular social media displacement/distraction moment, I spotted a video on Facebook. I forget the exact title, but it was something like, 'running a business is hard, coping with isolation is tough, come and join us for our next monthly meeting and connect with others'. Oh, my days, what? Hang on a minute? Stop the merry-go-round, are you telling me that I am not the only person laid on their bed crying every night because all they want to do is have a business? WTF WTF WTF! I watched the video with tears streaming down my face hanging on every word, talking back to the screen, "yes, I know; yes, that is me; yes, I feel that too". It was both painful and heart-warming at the same time. And there it was, the moment I realised isolation was the problem. Not me. Not my skills as a coach. Not my selfish need for joy and fulfilment in a job that I love. I was simply the rat in the cage without any friends, drinking from the drugged-up bottle, stoned, and slowly dying. So, I was not dying or drugged up, unless you count sugar by way of biscuits, cake, and chocolate as a narcotic. I was not dying, but my joy and my passion were. Finally, I could see a way forward and out of this living hell.

I booked a place at the next meet up, and the rest, as they say, is history. I had become so desperate at this point that I went in feeling like I had nothing to lose. My confidence was enabled by the shear fact I was finally doing something. Physically getting up and out and purposefully deciding to act was more powerful than the struggle at that point. Nothing changed that day except how I was choosing to respond to my struggle: *Get up, get out, you love people Abbie. Go find some.* I used the desperation to motivate me rather than letting it hold me captive. I left that meeting with new friends, new purpose, new motivation, and feeling like I had everything to fight for. It was a game changer, and to this day I will be forever grateful to the people in that room. Every single one of them. Networking became my lifeline. I began to interact on social media, reaching out and having conversations. Building relationships, asking questions, and attending meetings like they were my own personal team briefings. It suddenly felt like I had gone from 'party of one' to a huge corporation. A business full of experts in every field and a constant source of expertise and reassurance. I grew so much during that time. I began to also realise that I was not the only person struggling with what appeared to me to be ridiculous obstacles. I found myself surrounded by other people all trying to overcome their own struggle. It was alarming to think that so many others could be suffering. If it's so hard to start a business, then why is everyone doing it? I asked myself. Why are they choosing to do this? It can't just be about making a shit ton of money, or working part-time hours, so why are we putting ourselves through this? Although it was alarming to see so many others in this predicament, my desperation was starting to be replaced with a quiet feeling of confidence. Reassured by the fact that this was not just me. I began to ask myself more resourceful questions. What is it that is making this so hard? What are we doing to ourselves that is causing so much struggle? What are we pretending not to know? What are we choosing here? And the question that was to ultimately inspire me and my business and lead me to this point in my journey ... Does it really need to be this hard?

DROP KICK PROCRASTINATION

So, that was the day I attended my first ever networking meeting. I have been to many since then and continue to attend them as a little dose of sanity and a fast injection of joy and motivation. Procrastination had been like a monkey on my back for so long, I couldn't remember what it felt like to get some shit done. I'm a world class organiser, and while I no longer seek to punish myself through over achievement, I get shit done. I love a to do list, or as I now call them "will do list", and the feeling of accomplishment when I can tick a task off my list is addictive. Creating that connection again with other likeminded people seemed to kick my core behaviours back into gear.

I have always had jobs that require me to serve in some way. Sounds a bit archaic, but customer service, training manager, customer support adviser, administrator, PA, and now coach. Always serving others. My motivation is triggered by a simple need or request. Abbie, can you unjam the photocopier? Abbie, can you order the tea and coffee? Abbie, can I talk to you about something that is really bothering me? Abbie, can you help me?

Sitting at home alone, there was not much of that, so my core behaviours were on permanent shut down. Until I walked into that pub and joined a network of other start-ups. "What do you do, Abbie?", they asked. "Oh, wow that sounds amazing; I could do with some help". Or they would just want someone to talk to or someone to listen. I was useful again, and at the same time they were helping me. And that is how it works. This has been my core motivation though my entire coaching business. I am the coach I am because of the clients that I meet. Every day is a school day, and helping them helps me to satisfy my core values for growth, purpose, connection, and consistency. So, being in that room, and many more like it, is how I stay motivated, focused, and productive. Who knew that all I needed to do was find a pub with a few mates in it, and I could have avoided so much anguish? I have no regrets; I honestly believe that those months of struggle are what have made me who I am today. They are what has shaped my business and my purpose. The journey is far from over, but now I know what I need to do, what I need to help me to stay focused: people.

Having a regular source of connection meant enormous shifts in my motivation, clarity, and confidence. Feeling reassured by having others in my corner meant that I was able to begin to take steps to get stuff done. Up until this point I had been swimming around a barrel of confusion and getting nowhere. I was distracting myself with tasks that helped me to feel busy, but that weren't actually achieving anything. Isolation leads to low self-esteem, which in turn allows self-doubt to creep in. Procrastination is then inevitable. We end up in a loop of unresourceful behaviours and indecision, either working too hard on the wrong things or never finishing anything.

> At the start, I could have been sat in a room with Sheryl Sandberg offering me free advice on how to grow my business, it would have fallen on deaf ears. There would have been too much noise in my head to be able to hear any of it. You must quiet the noise before you can hear the good stuff. I love being in a room with clients and feeling the energy and watching the subtle changes in facial expressions and body language, as a moment of realisation appears. Lockdown and social distancing meant that I could no longer do this, and I had no choice but to move online. Honestly, I had been wanting to move online for many months at this point and just never managed to build up the courage or motivation to do it. Suddenly, I had no choice, and remarkably, I wasted no time in shifting straight over to Zoom to host both group and 1-1 coaching. I mean literally I wasted no time. The second social distancing was announced, even before lockdown came into play, I had completely shifted my business and my mindset. And all it took was a global pandemic to quiet the noise of judgement to let me get on with it. Thankfully, I was already heavily supported at this point. I was already a part of several fantastic networking communities, as well as a member

of an amazing business mentoring programme. This meant that I already had all the support and expertise I needed in place to make this shift. Had this not been in place, I am certain my business, like many others, would have folded.

I had been told for over 12 months, "Abbie you need to get online", but I couldn't hear it. I procrastinated and distracted myself with excuses as to why I didn't want to do it. The story I told myself was that it didn't meet my values ... I can admit now, that was bullshit. It was because I was afraid of failure. Afraid to compete and terrified of allowing myself to be vulnerable. So instead I procrastinated. Connecting with others who understood this enabled me to see through that fear. To call myself out on it and eventually act.

When you *find* connection

GET PERSPECTIVE

Connection offers a multitude of benefits. It really is an essential part of being alive and feeling alive. We find joy in the company of others and passion in the art of conversation. In a business sense, this conversation plays an important role in how we navigate both our emotional and physical challenges. For me, people mean perspective. I crave the clarity and perspective that comes from a conversation with clients, colleagues, and other coaches. I love a bit of coach on coach action, and I purposefully seek out opportunities to network and collaborate with those who share my passion for facilitation. Losing perspective hit me hard. I had no way of processing my thoughts without others around me, and I started to go a little bit crazy. I often picture Tom Hanks on the beach in *Castaway*, giving birth to his only companion Wilson, by drawing a face onto a volleyball – being stranded on a deserted island can't be fun and I wouldn't last a day. I'd probably lay down and die the moment I had to stalk my own food and kill it, go in search of clean water, or do an 'outdoor poo'. I think I would probably just make myself comfortable and wait for rescue or death, whichever came first. It's strange when we think about what we will and won't fight for. How important things are to us and the lengths we'll go to, to survive. If I were alone, I'd probably give up quickly, but if I were stranded with my kids, or my friends and family, that would be a quite different story. I would be delegating, organising, and strategising like a boss. Everyone would have a task, and I'd be focusing on short-term tasks and long-term survival. We would have meetings and skill sharing assessments. I'd be fighting with every ounce of my strength to ensure we all survived. See that is the difference. When we include others in our goals, make them a part of our why, we increase our motivation, priorities, and perspective. We have something to fight for. Working alone doesn't mean you have to feel alone. Connection offers perspective and ignites passion. Passion that in times of struggle will save you.

Perspective helps to keep confusion and overwhelm to a minimum, and in order to achieve perspective you need facilitation, which means talking to someone who will challenge you when you get in your own way. You need perspective so that when your brain starts to throw all sorts of avoidance strategies at you because it thinks that asking for a client testimonial is going to kill you, you can recognise what's happening and respond rationally. Your brain can't tell fact from fiction. It has no idea if a threat (asking for a testimonial) is real or imagined;

therefore, you need perspective so you can tell it the right things and give it the right instructions to help it power through.

Connecting with other start-ups gave me the perfect opportunity to talk things through. Listening to how others have tackled their challenges, what they have learnt, and mistakes they have made, all served to offer me a way to sort fact from fiction. Setting up a website and plugging in a Facebook Pixel to it is just one example of things that my brain thought would kill me; it was saying: *No. No, you don't want any part of that; you're going to make a mess of it; only people with a degree in IT or anyone under the age of 30 knows how to do that stuff. Stay back or you'll get burned.* I pushed through, followed the instructions – which, I might add, were no harder than any home hair dye kit I've ever bought, and I did it.

Regaining my perspective was an enlightening time and let me tell you that with the right advice and guidance, plugging in a Facebook Pixel is not that hard to do. Without connecting with the right expertise my business would still be a hobby, sitting on the Life Coach Directory hoping someone would see it. These days I seek connection in a variety of ways. From networking and interacting in Facebook groups, to working with clients who inspire me and getting out for the occasional coffee and cake. As well as my new online offers, I still run a regular Meetup session for a small audience of local businesswomen. This serves to help them through coaching, and it offers me a perfect opportunity to top up my energy reserves by being around amazing people.

BECOME ENERGISED – INNIES AND OUTIES

Connection gives us energy. I would challenge anyone who disagrees, even for the most introverted among us. You just need to know what your version of connection looks like. I learnt a lot about introverts and extroverts through reading amazing books such as *Quiet* by Susan Caine and through my diploma training. A quick-fire way to tell which way you swing is to ask yourself, what energises me? It's all about where we refuel. In a room full of people chatting and conversing or in a good book or focusing on a task. My daughter Ellie is a textbook introvert, and for many years I couldn't understand her map of the world. I used to think she was moody and aloof and couldn't understand why she'd get so exhausted by family activities and being around crowds. With what I have learnt and now appreciate, I am better equipped to notice what works for her and get perspective on where I too get my energy and where I become fatigued and withdrawn.

This book is not a place to go deep into the ins and outs of introversion and extroversion, and despite what I have read, learnt, and experienced, I'm no expert. I will offer you this: find out who you are and go with what feels right. If you're the person at a party standing in the kitchen or seeking out a quiet place, then you're probably an introvert. If you're already planning your escape before you even get to an event, then you're probably an introvert. If the thought of being in a room full of other business owners at a networking event makes you sick to your stomach, then you might well be an introvert. Be sure that it is your introversion and not self-doubt that is at the root of this dread. I sit somewhere in the middle. Although I will admit that some of my introversion can be attributed to small snippets of low self-esteem and fear; I find writing to be my solace, my comfort zone, and it's where I find my flow. It's where I feel most content. Therefore, I often favour sitting alone at home creating, over rooms full of people. While I do gain energy from being around people, it comes with a caveat: they must be the right people. If I'm talking about coaching or self-development, or helping someone to facilitate their thoughts and act, then I am an extrovert. Since I need both quiet and connection, after a few hours of coaching or networking my biggest realisations come on the drive home, where I can reflect.

Introverts will often hesitate from attending events because the thought of it is exhausting. So, find what works for you. Is an hour of people connection worth the effort? If it means that you can learn and grow from the experience and then use the time after to reflect, then this is a way to find balance. Understanding what works for us and noticing when it works is a great activity and coaching tool that I encourage all my clients to take the time to do. Extroverts will maybe find the answers and connection in the room, but its ok to find them on the drive home, too – or about 2 days later when you least expect it, while walking the dog or listening to a great audio book.

Mindset determines how we absorb information. Choosing the right mindset through which to view your surroundings means that you get to choose the stuff you want and need and ignore the rest. Choosing information and activities that energise you will offer endless motivation, maintain resilience, and help build confidence. If something makes you feel like shit, then you're not going to do it, at least not very well and not for very long. If you come out of it feeling energised, happier, fulfilled, empowered then your brain's going to want more of that. Happiness and fulfilment are practices that bring with them energy. It becomes a cycle: external information viewed through a mindset and met with curiosity – energy is gained – action is taken – repeat. This may sound a little woo woo but seriously when we are disconnected our energy plummets, almost immediately. Find those who top you up and keep you going and avoid connections that drain you. If too many triggers are being pulled through online interactions, limit them. We don't have to interact with huge numbers of people, just the right people.

BECOMING MORE PRODUCTIVE

When we're energised, we're motivated; and when we're motivated, we tend to get stuff done. For many of us, that productivity comes in peaks and troughs, so it's important to have strategies in place to help make productivity consistent. Procrastination is rife when you're not able to find the right way to tap into your productivity. Procrastination can be trigged in so many ways: fear, overwhelm, confusion, and doubt are the obvious culprits. However, it may just be that you aren't connecting with the solution. Productivity is a behaviour, so the solution to procrastination is introducing new behaviours. I am inspired by audio books, learning, and connecting with actual people, and my productivity is sent into overdrive when my pragmatic behaviours are activated. What helps you to be productive? When and where are you at your most pragmatic? Sitting alone at home is not where my productivity is ignited. I can certainly be productive while on my own, but that productivity needs a trigger and that trigger is found through connection when my value to help others, for example, is aligned with my goal.

Many, if not all, of my clients will have shown up struggling with procrastination at some point. Lethargic, can't be arsed, lack of concentration, and good old displacement distractions are rife, and 'not knowing where to start' is often how they describe their predicament. Developing motivational cues is a simple way to train the brain that it's time to begin. We start with simple behaviours that eventually become habits. Some of us will have grown up around motivational cues that are a natural way to maintain motivation, set goals, and develop resourceful behaviours that lead to long-term rewards. Others won't have been so lucky and are, therefore, less able to 'self-motivate'. So we need to introduce strategies that train our brains to act. We'll be exploring strategies around time later in the book, but one of the first things I suggest to a client who's struggling, is to attend a group coaching session. Isolation means we ignore a lot of our core values, such as kindness and generosity to others; so in connecting with fellow business owners, we are both inspired and motivated.

This book has a link to download a variety of exercises and mindset building tools that will enable you to create habits that help kick start motivation and become more productive. The exercises are simple yet effective, but action is where the magic happens. So, before you get out your workbook and dive right in, make a connection. Book a place at a networking event. Call a colleague and meet for a coffee. Join an online group. Meet a friend. It is not enough just to think like an entrepreneur, you also need to act like one. Regular, repeated behaviours are the key to building a business, so introduce a daily practice that connects you to others and build up your energy.

> During the Covid19 pandemic a lot of horrible things happened. Thankfully, most of the responses within the business world were positive, and many companies, small businesses included, stepped up to meet the new challenges. One of the great things to come out of this time was virtual networking. Most networking was done face to face and Portsmouth has more than its fair share of networking events – ranging from 6.30am breakfast clubs to events for working mums and female entrepreneurs to chamber of commerce and social enterprises. Getting people out of their homes to network is always hard, and for those who dedicate

> themselves to facilitating networks like this, it can be an exhausting undertaking. So, when everything went online, it was for many a golden opportunity to take part in networking events that they were previously unable or unwilling to attend. Switching to online coaching meant a huge rise in the number of hours I was able to commit to coaching and the luxury of being able to put in a load of washing one minute and then be sat at my computer in my slippers, ready to coach a minute later. Not only was I responding to the increased demands of clients, but I also became much more proactive. I was able to plan in multiple coaching sessions throughout the day with no financial outlay.
>
> Previously, I'd meet my clients at their homes or in another location, and this was time consuming. I thought nothing of jumping in my car and driving to Winchester for a networking event at 10.30am and not getting back home until nearly 2pm. My day was gone. The shift was, I guess, imposed upon me initially by the pandemic; however, it demonstrated very clearly where I'd been going wrong. Seeking connection – but in ways that were unproductive. My new way of working has meant a huge uptick in productivity for me and even more importantly more time for creativity, myself, and my family.

One of the reasons I chose to work for myself is that I value my home life. I love keeping house and being around for my kids. I love having autonomy over what I do each day and the freedom to pop to the shops, do some gardening, and go for a walk between coaching clients. Having a business is not just about the service you offer. Much of your time, probably 50% of it in the beginning, will be spent on your business: marketing, admin, accounts, planning *etc*. And you need to find time for all of this in addition to offering your service. So being productive and using time well is essential. Finding opportunities for connection that are timely is great; remember to decide what you need from your connections and be sure to give as much as you receive.

WHERE ISOLATION SHOWS UP IN BUSINESS

Isolation shows up in all sorts of ways. I waited too long to figure out that lack of connection was what had sent me spiralling into depression. It causes such powerful and debilitating mindset blocks, and yet, it is possibly the easiest problem to fix.

Reach out to those who share your values. Isolation tends to be a problem at the start your business journey because of the immediate disconnection from work colleagues and normal day to day routines. The employee mindset is challenged almost instantly, as we must suddenly become our own boss. Accountability is a problem, as most of us are not particularly good at being accountable to ourselves without at least some kind of involvement from others. And time – it takes time to build a business. It takes time to build connections and relationships, and it takes time to work out what we need to do. Patience is not something we can channel easily when feeling confused and afraid.

I took on a new client only weeks before the lockdown. Becky came along to one of my face to face group coaching sessions. I was overjoyed when she booked, as she was one of the first ladies to attend a meetup whom I'd never met before. Becky had recently left her part-time job and had plans to offer her services as a virtual assistant. Becky is my perfect client: in her 40's, she's passionate and ready to work but simply unaware of the enormity of the tasks she'd taken on. Unfamiliar with social media, Becky had struggled with visibility and had very quickly become isolated. I saw the signs immediately, and I empathised so hard with the story she shared: confusion, brain fog, self-doubt, and fear. "I get so far and then the voices start", Becky said to me during a 1-1 session. "I know what I need to do, but I can't seem to stay focused long enough to get anything done". As with all new clients, I had sent Becky a brief questionnaire to complete in preparation for the session. I asked her how she felt answering the questions: "Like I am finally doing something to get out of my own way and really beginning to make progress. Just answering the questions, I can see what the challenges are now, and I already feel more confident about tackling them". At first glance it would appear Becky had picked a pretty unfortunate time to start a business. And in some ways, yes, she did. Having made that brave step to come to a group coaching session, that option was then swiftly removed again as soon as lockdown came into effect. Without a large audience of connections in online platforms, Becky was once again isolated. Busying herself with tasks that felt safe and comfortable, none of which were helping her to connect with the outside world.

An employee mindset will guide us to work hard. It will push us towards staying busy; it will not, however, encourage us to question: is this really what I need to be doing? When stuff feels hard or scary, we simply default and do something else. Choosing to reach out and work with a coach meant that Becky was able to introduce accountability into her daily routine. She was able to question her decisions and push past the self-doubt and inner voices telling her she shouldn't be doing this. She was able to begin to identify her audience and become far more purposeful in her efforts to reach out. Just as I had done myself a few years earlier, simply reaching out and connecting had triggered a huge shift in Becky's mindset. She went from confusion and self-doubt to courage and determination.

Top tips summary – Isolation to connection

If you do only one thing after reading this chapter, please, get out and connect. There is a lot to achieve in a business, and connection is not the only thing we need to do. It is, however, the first thing we need to do. Without it, our passion, and our joy for what we're doing will fade, and without that, what's the point of having a business?

If we're lucky, we'll have friends and family who support us. This is sadly not always the case, and I often come across clients whose families do not support their decision to leave a perfectly good job and "go it alone". There are many reasons for this, which we'll explore in detail later, but the most common one is they just don't get it. Those who love us don't want to see us suffer, so when we struggle, they don't get it. To push past this, we must engage with others who do "get it". Those who understand our passion and drive and who are unaffected by the struggles that we need to endure to succeed. We can be surrounded by friends and family and still feel isolated because our values are being ignored.

So, when we think about isolation think not only about physical people and energy, think also about the energy and satisfaction you get from feeling heard, being understood, and feeling like you belong. We all want to be a part of something bigger than ourselves. Being an employee can meet this need. So, when we are working alone, our need to belong is ignored.

Finding a tribe is the business definition of belonging. People who have your back, share your values, and will support you through your journey. My tribe have been my saviour, and I invite you to join us. There are details at the end of the book of how to join.

Here are some tips on ways to get out of isolation and to create behaviours that help you to stay focused and productive, while meeting your core values and need for connection:

Where Isolation Shows Up	Top Tips to Beat Isolation
You are disconnected from your peer groups and seek reassurance from family and friends.	Our friends and family want to support us, but unfortunately, they rarely understand our struggle. Connecting with others through networking and group coaching offers effective support and helps build confidence.
You experience long periods of uncertainty which can lead to increased anxiety and/or depression.	We are by nature drawn to connection and without others to bounce ideas off we can quickly begin to feel anxious. Find groups of other business owners either online or face to face where you can interact regularly, ask questions and share experiences.
You lack focus and are distracted easily.	Maintaining focus can be difficult if we are working alone Accountability is a fabulous tool for keeping us on track. Join groups or engage with a coach to help you stay accountable.

You regularly make mistakes, but you aren't learning from them because you have no frame of reference.	Confidence and growth come from a consistent process of trial and error. When we operate alone, this can be hard to do and fear will kick in. Share your ups and downs with others in your network, which will help you to be less afraid of failure and more willing to learn from it.
You end up firefighting challenges instead of planning and preparing.	When we work alone it is easy to keep our head down and power through. Meaning we don't see a problem coming until it is right on top of us. Sharing tips with others helps us to be more proactive and less reactive
You miss good opportunities because they're clouded with negative self-talk, hesitation, and judgement.	When fun or interesting opportunities arise, we can often hold back as fear or negative talk kicks in. Grab a business buddy and take them along for the ride. There are no extra points for turning up alone. Business can be fun.

BOOK RECOMMENDATION

The Storyteller's Secret by Carmine Gallo

I took the quotation at the start of this chapter by Sheryl Sandberg from *The Storyteller's Secret*. I love this book for so many reasons. It helped me to write this book and has taught me that it's ok to own my story. The book is a compilation of stories about Ted talkers and inspirational business owners who have leaned into their stories.

Many are tales of struggle, tragedy, poverty, and overcoming adversity. Now my slightly weird reckoning with childhood limiting beliefs doesn't really constitute tragedy, and my rumble with depression can't really be classed as adversity. Growing up in the 70's, eating a lot of fish fingers, and wearing clothes your mum made from curtains (true story – we were like the bloody Von Trapps) doesn't really count as poverty. However, this book, and many of the others I've read, has shown me that it's not just ok to own my story, but that my story may in fact help others. We all tell stories every day in our businesses, and I encourage you to grab a copy of this book to see just how your story can be told.

Networking and building an audience are perfect places for telling a story and there are experts in business now who offer professional training on how to tell your story: from a 1-minute intro pitch at a local networking meeting to a 1-hour pitch to a potential client. Telling our story is how we make friends and how we connect. It's how we get people to know, like, and trust us. For micro business owners, networking can look a lot more like making friends. We get to share our story. We stand up to do our pitch and the first thing we share is why we do what we do. There is always a reason, and we are compelled to share it. Most of us don't come from a generation where "being an entrepreneur" is a career option straight out of school. Many of us will have enjoyed a chunk of life before making our move and telling our story is how we connect. And I love it.

CHAPTER 4

Big 7 No. 3
Confusion to *Clarity*

*"If confusion is the first step to knowledge,
I must be a genius"*

LARRY LEISSNER

Confusion

***Uncertainty about what's happening,
intended, or required.***

Experiencing confusion can be a bit of a mind fuck if you don't get a grip on it right away. It can consume you in ways you never imagined. Confusion leads to overwhelm and once overwhelm has engulfed you, energy and focus are sucked into a void and it can be hard to regain your balance. In business, when it comes to confusion and overwhelm, prevention is much better than cure. Once we start to spiral into uncertainty, it can be a big hole to get out of, and it seems the more we claw away at the walls, the lower we sink. It's exhausting; so being able to notice as soon as confusion is showing up is a great mindset tool. There are so many reasons why we get confused in business.

For example, The introduction of new technology can stir up all sorts of unsettling feelings like embarrassment and low self-esteem. We start to question our abilities because this new thing is outside of our comfort zone and pushing forward feels uncomfortable and unsettling. Our brain dislikes confusion with a passion and will work tirelessly to solve the puzzle. Unfortunately, when our values and beliefs are challenged through this process, confusion emerges. Conversations in our head start to sound a lot like this: "I know I need to do this but …" Once this starts, decision making becomes nearly impossible because our logical brain has basically thrown its toys out of the pram and declared, "I'm out; your emotional hormones are just too exhausting; you sort it out". You can hear it, can't you?

So, when confusion shows up, we want to nip it in the bud as quickly as we can with practiced mindset tools that keep our logical brain in the game and our emotions to a minimum.

Confusion hits hard, particularly at the start of a business journey. We tend to look outside of ourselves for help, seeking answers to our problems instead of trusting what we already know. Though we do require expertise from outside sources, we run into problems when we question our own abilities and knowledge. Then, we allow fear of failure to cloud our judgement and struggle to choose a way to move forward.

Clarity

The quality of being coherent and intelligible.

Gaining clarity is a core coaching behaviour. The facilitation of a conversation that allows a client to hear and feel their inner story. Mindset coaching is an excellent way to swipe away the distractions; through Socratic questioning, it shines a light on the path ahead. This is often referred to as a 'light bulb moment'. I have experienced this moment many times, each following a period of calm curiosity. To gain clarity and find the solution to what's causing our confusion, we must first calm our brain down. And breathing is the simplest and easiest way to achieve this. Just breathe; your brain needs oxygen to function. When in panic, our brain starts to batten down the hatches to conserve energy to fight, and our logic is the first casualty.

Confusion shouldn't mean panic, but I know first-hand that when we are really in a hole, panic is inevitable. Clarity comes when we slow down the panic and start to think logically again. Every problem or situation has an answer; we might not always like it, or we might question if it's even possible, but there's always an answer. Usually there is more than one, and this is when confusion kicks in.

Some problems do have a right or wrong answer. These tend to be the boring bits like accounting, bookkeeping, or tax returns. And when we experience difficulties, we don't hesitate to reach out for expertise to help solve the issue. Another good example is IT. Many of us have struggled with technical problems; however, it's never long before we succumb to the pain and reach out to an expert. We tell ourselves it's ok to not understand the tax code or know how a website works.

Confusion occurs in less clear cut, less easily outsourced situations, especially when there are multiple answers. In these situations, we need coaching, which is a process of facilitating clarity. It helps you sort through the information and gain clarity to find the answers to take the next step.

First, we just need to calm down long enough to see it. When several triggers are in play and there are a multitude of possible options and answers, I encourage my clients to break everything down into small manageable pieces. Get a piece of paper and get everything out of your head. Lists, brain dumps, journals, and mind mapping are great tools for gaining visibility on confusion and generating clarity. Things are much easier to process when they are out in front of you. And this is a where I begin with each new client. Once they begin to get stuff out and onto paper, I can sit beside them, with the information in front of us, and we work together to find a solution.

My Struggle with Confusion

WASTING TIME AND MONEY

My big rumble with confusion began around the same time as isolation was taking a firm grip on my mental health. Even once I had started to address isolation and started to reconnect with the outside world, I was still experiencing a vortex of confusion; in fact, it became worse, because now I had something to lose again. Connecting through networking and realising that I wasn't entirely useless meant that my dream of being a successful coach was again a possibility. At the depths of isolation, I had almost given up on it. Now it was real again. The problem was that I was now painfully aware of what I didn't know. Ignorance about the complexities of starting a business had meant I was wasting time and money on quick fixes and solutions – like paying for advertisements in places my clients would never see them.

In every learning process there is a point at which you don't know what you don't know. Once you start to become aware of what's required, it can suddenly feel like you've taken a big step backwards. I had been working so hard on the things I thought would help, except none of them were what was required. Networking showed me what I needed to do, and that was going to take time and money. But now I was out of both. I could see very clearly that setting up a business is not something that happens overnight. There really is no such thing as an overnight success. Except maybe for X-Factor contestants and a few of the participants of Love Island. And we know how some of those turned out. Trying to fast track success might work in the short term; however, in the long term, it will come back and bite you in the arse.

What I know now is that even if I had had all my ducks in a

row from day one, I still would have needed time to build up my client niche, to learn about who I am and what I want from my business, and to imbed that learning.

By the time I reached out to network, we were about as skint as we'd ever been. Dave and I had been married only a year. We had a new house, big mortgage, and a growing family. While many of my friends were starting to enjoy the feeling of passing the halfway mark of a 25-year mortgage, Dave and I were starting again. Not to mention the fact that I had spent most of our wedding fund and all our savings on gaining my diploma and Train the Coach licence, so guilt and frustration were now showing up big time. Fear of making any more mistakes and panic over money meant each time my mind came up with a possible solution, the fear and uncertainty would rugby tackle it to the floor. It was like being stuck in a maze. Every time I thought I was finding a way out, I came up against another dead end.

Confusion is frustrating and exhausting. Feeling desperate meant that I would have done almost anything to get out of this maze. I battled on, thinking that if I kept running around the maze, I'd find a way out sooner or later. Occasionally an opportunity would pop up. Usually in the form of a phone call from a marketing agent offering to raise my visibility and get me an endless stream of clients; all I had to do was buy advertising space or sign up to their directory and all my struggles would be gone. I cannot tell you how much money I wasted buying in to that bullshit. When money is tight, but you go ahead and waste more of it – that's a feeling like no other. Stupidity, shame, and blame were now my companions in the maze. *WTF is happening here? Why am I the only person struggling? All I want to do is earn a bit of money and help people. That's it. Why is this so hard?*

LILY PADDING

Guilt and desperation from having spent all our money were causing me to spiral. Every day seemed like *Groundhog Day*. I would wake up with butterflies in my stomach and an ache in my chest. For a split second each day I would have a moment of wondering, *Was this all a dream? Are we ok now?* And then as quickly as the thought came, it would disappear only to be replaced with the noise of fear, judgement, and confusion.

I can't tell you how many times I wanted to just shut the whole thing down and run away, which would definitely have been an easier option. But then the nagging voice of "What if…."? Would then join in, and I'd be even more consumed by the anticipatory heartbreak that comes with giving up.

I have run away and given up on a few things in my life, most of them ideas that never even got off the ground. Did I tell you that I was the one that had the idea for Uber and Uber Eats and for cleaning wipes and doggie costumes and don't get me started on Mrs Hinch. Oh my days, I could have been an internet sensation back in the day, if they'd had Instagram back then, and, you know, if I could've been bothered! Each time I came up with an idea, my brain would block it almost instantly: *That's not what people like us do. We don't invent things. We work for the people who buy the stuff other people invent*". Looking back now, none of those ideas were my passion. My point is that I was now aware of how powerful my inner thoughts could be at persuading me to take the easy route – to stop, avoid, and run away.

This time, I was determined to fight to the death. I was not giving up on coaching. Instead I was doing a great impression of a big fat frog, lily padding from one idea to the next. Today I will focus on life coaching, the next day weight loss coaching, the day after that business coaching, because that was where the money was. Each day I would go through a process to jump to the next thing that would save me. *People pay loads for weight loss coaching. What about coaching for kids or relationships? Maybe I'll try group coaching.* Chasing ideas but not thinking it through. Confusion about time, money, and what I really wanted to do was causing me to lily pad. I was looking too far into the future, trying to invent a business that would last in the long term and pay out in the short term. My focus was too far ahead, and my crazy inner voices were telling me keep moving forward, but my gut was telling me to stop and take stock of the situation. Conflict, confusion, shame, blame, judgement, and desperation were my *Groundhog Day*.

When your mind is working to problem solve, occasionally it will spit out an answer. Your mind wants to fix the problem, and it will keep going until you tell it to stop or give it something else to think about. This is where mindset tools come into their own, and we can control and divert our inner thoughts to go to places of resourcefulness. Mindset tools act like a companion – a driving instructor so to speak – and they keep our thoughts going in the right direction, rather than swerving and changing direction like the cars in a TV police chase. For most of my early years in business, I was driving without an instructor, chasing down every side street, hoping to find a way out of confusion. Every search on the internet sent me to a new conclusion. *Today, I'll be a life coach. Today, I'll teach coaching. Today, I'll find someone else to work with. Today, I'll stay hidden. Today, I'll create more materials. Today, I'll offer workshops. Today, I'll help people in relationships. Today, I'll help other coaches. Today, I'll try to find a job. Today, I'll be a business coach. Today, I'll pretend that this was all a bad dream and distract myself with cleaning.*

STOP BEATING YOURSELF UP

I spent months beating myself up for being a failure; no matter what I tried nothing seemed to work. Every time it seemed as though I was finding a way through the fog of confusion, another internal struggle would appear. "What if you go get a job?", I said to myself one day. "But what about Jack?", I asked (my then very elderly Labrador who was needing more and more attention). The last 10 years of my life had been dictated by Jack, an epileptic, food-focused Labrador, who was so loving and giving, and expensive. Due to mistakes in the early days and choosing a crap pet insurance company none of Jack's epilepsy or joint related medication was covered. So, every month brought a bill of over £180, plus food and the incidentals like surgery to remove a growth or a swallowed a stick. Jack passed over the rainbow bridge while I was writing this book. I loved him and having him taught me so much about unconditional love and the joy of being in the moment. He was also the reason that I used for many of the decisions I made in life, and the decisions I made at this point in my business journey were no exception. I couldn't get a job because I needed to be home for Jack. I couldn't get a job because what if the coaching thing does take off and a client wants to book an appointment; I couldn't get a job because people won't take me seriously as a coach. I couldn't get a job, so I must endure this misery and hope that things work out.

I thought, I'd just work even more hours and do more and more, then it'd have to work in the end, right? I was terrified of deciding. Every time I came up with a possible solution, my brain came up with 20 reasons why it wouldn't work. So, I just kept going round and round and round in circles, getting more overwhelmed and exhausted with every new day. I was so consumed with blaming myself and feeling guilty that I forgot how to solve a problem.

We solve problems by talking about them. By breaking them down and ultimately by trusting ourselves long enough to decide. Trust the process, trust yourself. Have faith that by following your own path, you will find the way. When we blame someone, even ourselves, we're not owning the problem. If we don't own it, we can't fix it, and for so long my struggles were on the outside. The moment came when I finally admitted in a telephone call to a networking colleague, "I feel like I need to get a job just so I can calm the fuck down; having no money is messing with my head, and everything I try is going wrong". The reply, "Abbie if you need to go and get a job then go get a job, loads of start-ups have part-time jobs; it's not an either or situation" ... *Oh my god. Are you kidding?* I thought to myself. Suddenly, I could feel the breeze coming through the exit to the maze. I began to run towards the fresh air; finally, I'll be free of this self-imposed captivity. Finally, a way out. It's not like I hadn't thought of getting a job. Honestly, for weeks it was all I could think about; the problem was I wasn't stopping still long enough to consider this as a realistic option. Each time my mind came up with the "idea" fear, shame, and confusion shot it down. You must deal with the struggle before you can hear the ideas, have the courage to stop and re-evaluate, or give yourself permission to consider the possibilities.

My problem wasn't money or finding a job. My problem wasn't my skills as a coach or my expertise. My problem wasn't passion, determination, or commitment. My problem was that I was looking at the wrong problem. I was so busy beating myself up and listening to voices of fear and judgment that I forgot how to coach myself. Had I reached out to a business mentor back then to help me to process what was happening, instead of beating myself up for not having the answers, I would've come to this conclusion a lot quicker. Being a coach doesn't make you immune from struggle, as I'm sure you've gathered by now. Being a coach should mean that when struggles occur, we're able to navigate our way to the solutions – faster and with minimal discomfort. All good coaches engage in regular supervision or mentor coaching for themselves. My problem was I was trying to solve this all on my own. I wasn't getting the problem out in front of me, and I was avoiding the discomfort that comes with asking for help. I allowed my belief that asking for help meant failure to drown out the logic. What a dick.

How I found clarity

BEGIN TO QUIET THE NOISE

When writing this chapter, I was reminded of a story I read about a troop of soldiers fighting in the jungle. This tale has been repeated over time, and its origin is unclear:

> After days and days of hacking through the jungle with machetes, the exhausted troops were almost at the point of giving up. They were trying desperately to find a way out, and at every turn, the jungle seemed to get deeper and harder to cut through. Finally, one of the soldiers decided to climb a tree. The tree was high, and he was afraid. Yet his determination to find a way out of his current predicament was more powerful than the fear of falling. So, he kept climbing until, eventually, he could see out across the tops of all the trees. He stopped for a moment and enjoyed the silence. The noise of the jungle had disappeared. He could feel a cool breeze brushing

over his face, and the warmth of the sunshine was a welcome break from the humidity below. He paused for a moment to enjoy this feeling of rising, and then he looked around. He looked east, he looked west, he looked north, and then he looked south. Taking in all the information, finally he descended back down the tree and revealed to his eager companions ... "Yeah, we're in the wrong jungle", he said." Shut up", came the reply from his fellow soldiers, "we are just starting to make progress".

The noise from all my failure and no money was deafening, and hard as I tried, I couldn't shake off the guilt of having been the one to put us in such a difficult financial situation. All the long hours, missed family time, and frustration would possibly have been easier to bear had I been able to put money in the bank to pay for a holiday or, I don't know, food! My family were unwavering in their support, but they were not going to stand by silently and watch me burn myself out. No matter what options I explored, everything hinged on us just being able to survive. I was exhausted and missing the consistency and connection of being at work. There was no way I was going back to my old job, and the thought of writing a CV and going for job interviews just sent me even further into a hole. Finding a job is a fulltime job, and by this point I was so low I just couldn't face it. I distracted myself for a while, and then the light bulb moment. I could sign on with an agency. They do all the crap bit for me, and all I'd have to do is turn up. No expectations – that sounds like a safe option. Then the confusion. What if they want me to work weird hours? How can I explain I have a sick dog that will shit on the floor, if I am not home on the dot of 3.30pm? And so the excuses started again. I did this little dance for about 3 weeks, till finally I thought sod it I can but ask. I got in the car, drove downtown, and walked into Office Angels. I had worked in lots of offices over the years, and every time we had a temp, they came from Office Angels. I will just tell them I want filing and answering the phone. That way they won't find out I am shit at IT, and I can't count for toffee. I walked in. The young girl who greeted me was polite and friendly. After a brief explanation about how I was looking for some very short term and very temporary work just to keep me busy while I build up my client base, she showed me to a meeting room, and I filled out the forms. When she came back a few minutes later, I somehow felt the need to explain again that this was just temporary and ask whether they had anything short term. Oh, and I can only do around 15 hours a week. That way, whatever hours it was, I was sure I could fit that in around Jack's eating and pooping schedule. "As a matter of fact", she said, "I saw a lady this morning in Lee-on-Solent that is looking for admin support. It's only 12 hours and it is in Lee-on-Solent. Most people will not want to drive all the way out there". "SOLD!", I shouted a little too quickly. "When can I start?" "Well, you have to go for an interview, but I think you are just what they are looking for", she said, a little surprised. I had no fear of driving the 8 miles to Lee-on-Solent. I would much prefer that to trying to park in the centre of town. I used to live in Locks Heath, so commuting backwards and forwards up the M27 was nothing new to me.

 The interview was arranged for a couple of days later, and all I needed to do was go back the next day with my passport. I could literally feel the fog of confusion lifting as I walked away that afternoon. "Why did you wait so long, you idiot? Of course, they have contracts for 12 hours a week. FFS what have you been dilly dallying about all this time? You idiot". Ok, so I quickly reframed *idiot* and decided it was the universe telling me that I'd been waiting for the right opportunity, and today was that day, and I wasn't wrong. The next day was yet another challenge, and I questioned again whether I was making the right decision when, on the way to dropping in my passport to the agency, I stopped to pick my daughter Maya up from school. We pulled away and before we got 20 feet down the road, I had a flat tyre. *"Seriously – does the universe want me to give up or what!* I frantically phoned Dave, who dutifully skipped the gym and came to fix my tyre. We made it to Office Angels only minutes before they were about to close. They photocopied my passport while I relayed the whole flat tyre saga. Pretty sure they couldn't give a shit, but I love to talk, especially when I'm nervous, so they got the long version. The young lady handed me back my passport and confirmed the interview for the next day. I breathed a sigh of relief, and for the first time in months I felt in control again. It was a moment I'll never forget.

I arrived for the interview with little expectation. I just kept telling myself, *this is just admin. This is easy; you're a temp – no one even talks to temps, so you can go in, do your stuff for 4 hours and get out of Dodge. I can probably hold a wee for 4 hours, so if the loos are horrible, 4 hours isn't long. What if the people are weird? What if they don't talk to me? Its only for 12 weeks. If they're insane, I can just leave. Nothing to lose; nothing to lose.*

I met with Penny, and we hit it off right away – we're now the absolute best of friends. She's my person when it comes to keeping me motivated and grounded. I have maybe 6 ladies in my business life that I can call "my person". Any *Grey's Anatomy* fans out there will know what I mean when I say, "my person". For those unfamiliar ... the lead character, Meredith Grey, strikes up an unlikely friendship with Cristina Yang, the moody and abrupt but lovable sidekick. They share many experiences over the seasons and throughout they refer to each other as "my person". In one of my favourite moments, Cristina passionately exclaims in defence of Meredith, "If I murdered someone, she would be the person I would call to help me drag the corpse across the living room floor". Penny is "my person".

I didn't know at the time just how fundamental this job would be to my growth as a coach and business owner, and to my sanity. The first wages arrived into my bank account at the end of the following week. £102 – not a fortune and we had a long way to go before we were out of the woods, but oh my days the feeling was priceless. Confusion, Guilt, Blame, and Fear disappeared that day, and Purpose, Growth, Consistency, Connection, and Choice returned. Now there was still a way to go. But when we deal with the confusion, everything else is just stuff to get done.

START TO BREAK IT DOWN

My biggest fear. The story I told myself. The root of my confusion was that no one would take me seriously as a coach if I went back and got a job. It would mean admitting I had failed as an entrepreneur, and those people who were just waiting for me to fail or give up would be right. This messed with my head so much – it drove me crazy. Despite the heartache I experienced, I believe those months of struggle are what truly define me. Who I am in business, who I am as a coach, who I coach, and why. I wouldn't change it. Instead, I'll dedicate the rest of my coaching career to making sure no one else has to struggle like I did. Yes, we need to work shit out for ourselves. Yes, we need to make poor choices and make mistakes; and yes, probably we need to waste some money along the way. We do not, however, need to push ourselves to the point of depression. And we absolutely, categorically do not ever need to give up on our dreams. Does it really need to be this hard? No, it absolutely does not. I am here and I see you, and you never need to feel alone, confused, or afraid again. To my clients I am 'their person'.

Taking a step backwards does not mean failure. Taking a step back is what we do when we need to get a clearer picture or perspective. We look at a painting, we step back; we look at our daughters in their prom or wedding dress, and we step back. We have to, to get the perspective to soak up every single inch of what lies in front of us. So next time you think that going backwards is a sign of failure, picture this: the Eiffel tower looks like a pylon right up close. The best place to experience its beauty and magnificence is from a distance, a place of clarity and perspective.

This is exactly what I was able to do when I took the job at Atlantic Refrigeration. The noise had started to get quieter. I was connecting and feeling useful again and I had others around me who needed me. The job was easy enough, so my confidence grew. And the tasks were challenging enough that I didn't get bored. It really was a great place to work. Penny and I became friends very quickly, and her unwavering support of my "Coaching Business" was heart-warming. "We know this is just a temporary thing for you Abbie; we love that you are following your dreams. Whatever you need, we are here for you. If you need time off to see clients, just let me know." Oh my god, had I fallen on my feet or what?

Overnight I had gone from a quivering psychotic mess to almost the old Admin Assistant PA Abbie. Calm, in control, and useful. Home started to feel like a much happier place too, and I know that Dave was quietly relieved to have his nicer, calmer, in control wife back. Dave is by far the head of our household and I love him unconditionally for that. It makes me feel safe and feminine. He is however very good at delegation and is more than comfortable with the fact that I 'run' the household; so while I struggled every day, things got missed. So when things started to get back to normal, I know he was relieved. He had remained courageous and supportively quiet throughout my melt down, and I am grateful to him and to my girls for their support. They knew I would get there eventually and that I just needed to work it through.

Going back to work was nothing like the step backwards I thought it would be, and so many benefits I hadn't anticipated were starting to come up. Less available time meant that I used the time I had for coaching far more efficiently. Feeling useful triggered my motivation to get stuff done on my business, and now that I was engaging in networking, I was starting to understand more about what those activities might look like. The support and encouragement I got from Atlantic Refrigeration meant my confidence was growing too. I got to practice my coaching skills every day. Now some days my Socratic questioning went down better than on other days, for sure. I mean sometimes a guy just wants to eat a burger and not be asked "what other food choices could you have made today Garry"? Most days we had such fun and the benefits just kept coming. Paige, another coworker, is the same age as Ellie and another Instagram wizard. She would regularly share with me tips on how to post better content and share my expertise. I was treated like a VIP in that workplace and after the 12-week contract was up, Penny had no hesitation about asking me to stay on, and I had no hesitation accepting the permanent position. Even though it meant a hefty pay out to the agency – they wanted me that badly they were prepared to pay. What this did for my confidence and my soul I will never forget. When in summer 2019 I decided to trial a new workshop version of my group coaching programme, Penny was the first to jump up and offer the conference room at Atlantic to host the sessions. She even joined in on the 8-week course, and by the end of it our tribe was born. Penny, Dee, Pauline, Vicki, and me. The original Mindset Tribe. Friendship, connection, and conversation are how we hold back confusion. Whenever I feel myself becoming confused or struggling to make sense of a situation, I call on my tribe. They help me to talk through my confusion in a way that is curious, kind, and restorative. My tribe has grown, and I now share the support of many awesome and amazing women. I would not be here today, however, if it were not for these ladies. It brings a tear to my eye just to write this chapter. The love and support they showed up with is something I will never forget.

DEVELOP YOUR ENTREPRENEURIAL MINDSET

You don't know, what you don't know. When I started my entrepreneurial journey, I had no clue what setting up a business would entail. No idea about the process of navigating social media, building relationships, or what to expect. I had a picture in my mind about what I thought working for myself would look like, and to be honest it was based mostly on the Avon reps and workmen I had encountered over the years. To sell their products and get clients, an Avon rep would hand out leaflets and people would sit comfortably at home, tick the box, and order their stuff. I thought I could offer my coaching services in the same way. So, I had 1000's of leaflets printed, but no one to give them to. I thought about workmen, electricians, and builders – they do ok. They just pop up on websites like Check a Trade and customers find them that way. So, I paid hundreds of pounds to directory websites, but without a clear message about who I was and the clients I wanted to help.

This is not how entrepreneurs operate. And whilst Avon reps

and workmen can be very successful, there was a lot more to it than that.

Coaching requires belief and commitment. It is something we have to work for and trust that by putting in the work it will pay off. We have to be open to it. We have to want it to work and believe that it will. We almost have to believe in its potential before embarking upon it. Many who train as coaches will themselves have already experienced a journey of self-discovery. It is those very processes that inspire and motivate us to share our newfound wisdom with others: 'I have seen the light and you can too'. It can be a little evangelical, and this is where selling coaching becomes problematic. Perceived as a bit 'woo woo' and almost cult like, people dislike being preached to and until you've experienced it for yourself, it's a tough sell. This is also why many coaches struggle to charge for their services, seeing it as a calling rather than a career.

Thankfully, these attitudes are changing; however, for my target audience, demonstrating the value and the purpose of coaching was still a tough sell. So, publicising what I did felt like a struggle. It was my interpretation of "what I did" that was creating the confusion. I had to go back to the drawing board, dismissing everything I had grown up believing about hard work and reaping rewards. I now had to stop asking permission to join in and just get out there. Stop seeing my coaching as a calling, and start seeing it as a product that can benefit others. I had to demonstrate value, and not compromise on price. Be bold in my offer and speak to the right audience. Now, not only did all this feel like an assault on every value and belief I had grown up embracing, it also conflicted with everything that I had learnt about coaching; so the negative self-talk started: *I can't do this. I'm going to look and sound like an arsehole. People will think I am arrogant. If that is what I must do, then sorry I am* out; it's not worth it.

Then, in true Facebook algorithm fashion (I swear my phone can hear me), I magically started to see posts and ads popping up all over my news feed. I spotted one that said, "How to Think Like an Entrepreneur" – dismiss your old beliefs blah blah blah. I was scrolling aimlessly at the time and so thought sod it and clicked. It was an E-book, and from there on in the penny dropped. Employee Mindset vs Entrepreneurial Mindset. *Wow was this really a thing! God, I'm naive.* It still felt icky. So now I know what I don't know, but how? Seriously, how can I be that person? I was picturing Deborah Meadan on *Dragons' Den* and thinking, do I really have to be her? She is probably a nice person when you get to know her, but I seriously could not be that bold. She has no fear of being disliked or controversial, she is incredibly successful, but surely there is a price to pay. I can't relate to that. I would be unrecognisable to my friends, family, and clients. The few clients I had that is.

Then, in a split second, I started to see where my limited beliefs were getting in the way again. Now that I knew how I had to behave, it was easy to see the obstacles I was creating that were stopping me from doing exactly that. Who says I can't be Deborah Meadan? I then began to feel a scarily familiar feeling. Confusion was creeping in again. My behaviours, values, and beliefs were being challenged again, and it was starting to pinch. Nope, no way; I'm not going there again. And that's the difference. I still struggle, and every day is a new challenge; the difference is now I know how to beat it.

So, what do I need to do here? There must be a way to learn this shit without compromising who I am. Of course, there was a way. There is always a way. A combination of understanding my why, identifying my core clients, perfecting my message, and believing in my offer were just the start. We can absolutely learn how to think like an entrepreneur, once we understand who we are and who we want to help.

This process of realisation is the foundation of my group coaching programme and the reason for this book. See it's one thing to be told 'think like an entrepreneur': *this is what you need to do – follow this plan, and I guarantee success.* But if your mindset isn't in tune, you'll never be able to follow those plans; so I'm helping you with your mindset. If I gave you a guaranteed 6-figure income plan for success, but your core beliefs of "rich people must be miserable", "money can't buy you happiness", and "I don't deserve success" are stuck front and centre of your brain, then no matter how much instruction you're given, you'll never be successful. You need to do the work on and for yourself first, and the rest is easy.

WHERE CONFUSION SHOWS UP IN BUSINESS

Confusion shows up in so many ways, and if we're lucky, it's temporary. We just need to step back and take some time to work it out. Confusion indicates that there is a need to find a solution to a problem, unlike overwhelm or overthinking which can happen even when we know exactly what needs to be done. Confusion costs us time and money and chips away at our energy and our self-esteem. So, we want to notice it as soon as it begins and get cracking to find the solution as quickly as we can.

When describing her rumble with asking for help, Brené Brown writes in her amazing book *Rising Strong* (2015): "I was so afraid of my own need that I couldn't look need in the eye" (177). In this powerful and emotional chapter, she describes her own hesitation to ask for help; it must be heard or read in its entirety to be deeply appreciated. The point I offer here is that we must accept asking for help to grow stronger. I have both empathy and frustration when it comes to people who refuse to ask for help or those who constantly ask for help and then refuse to accept it. I love to help people, and I absolutely do not hold back from seeking help for myself. It literally defines who I am. You must be able to accept help to truly be able to offer it, kindly deeply, and sincerely. If you won't accept help, it means you see it as a weakness; therefore, you see those who need help as weak. So, to find your way out of confusion in any situation, especially in your business you need to both ask for and accept help. Find your people. Build your tribe.

Confusion can be triggered through isolation, self-doubt, and fear; left unchallenged it will inevitably lead to overwhelm. Confusion feels like a never-ending maze of U-turns and dead ends, and it is exhausting. Instead of keeping our processing in the logical part of the brain, fears, panic, and emotions force us to start digging into our subconscious and the solutions become less clear. Conscious thinking then becomes overthinking, and this begins a cycle of confusion.

We are consciously aware of this endless cycle of overthinking, as our brain works tirelessly to solve problems. The trouble is we don't always know what problem we're trying to fix, and here in lies the problem. If someone asks you a question, like 'what did you have for breakfast this morning?', Your brain will easily seek out the answer and produce it. We don't encounter doubt or fear and are confident in our response. If I were to ask you who won the 1981 Eurovision song contest with the song "Making Your Mind Up", Even if you can't instantly recall the answer – you'll probably know if you know it or not. Your brain either says, 'yep, I know that – it's Bucks Fizz', or it will say 'I have no idea' or 'I do know, but I've forgotten'. Either way, we can usually access an answer with little or no stress. Your mind might trigger a few memories and possibly a fear of giving the wrong answer, but we can quickly decide and give our response.

If, when goal setting, I were to ask a client, "what could happen as a result of making this decision?" Their mind is going to start searching for the answer. In a coaching context, this is exactly what we want as it allows a client to tap into their subconscious, and a skilled coach will help facilitate the client towards a solution. Without help or facilitation, this can be a fruitless pursuit. And even those of us who are trained to facilitate, can come a cropper when we start to dig too deep because then even the simplest of options become confusing and vague. This leads to procrastination and other unresourceful behaviours. Our brain wants to please us. Unfortunately, if the answer is not instantly accessible it starts to dig deeper which can trigger all kinds of unconscious responses: self-doubt, fear, guilt, hesitation, judgement, possibilities, options, pros and cons, and of course confusion. A business journey is littered with questions like these. Some we can answer instantly, and others will trigger a response that sends us spiralling into uncertainty. Having a coach along for the ride helps us gain clarity.

During the Covid19 pandemic uncertainty was rife. We were trying to plan and make decisions based on what ifs, maybes, and who knows. We had to be patient and pre-empt what we needed to do to meet the needs of our family, ourselves, and our business. *Shall I do this? Or that? What if I try this, or buy that? I need to do this, but I do not know how. But what if I ask that question, and then I do that? Is it going to be the right thing?*

Thankfully not all situations are as utterly mind blowing as Covid19. However, working for yourself and wearing all the hats will often feel like this. So being able to tap into the facts and building a regular practice of asking for help reduces confusion. So too will developing effective mindset tools that help you eliminate the noise from self-doubt, confusion, and fear.

Top tips summary – Confusion to clarity

The entrepreneurial mindset is developed through practiced behaviours. We don't just decide to think like an entrepreneur; we have to become one. Behaviours help us to build confidence and make progress, when we can let go of the negative thoughts that are keeping us from finding clarity.

The first step is to pay attention to the trigger. *What is the thought or story that is going around in your head? What triggered that thought. Who or what was present at the time?* Choosing the mindset through which you take in information will help you build confidence, so ask: *What is true here? Am I working with facts or am I operating out of fear, shame, or judgment?* When we have clarity on what the problem is, we can then begin to create the behaviours that will bring the best outcome.

Mindset works a bit like a washing machine. It is a constant process of opening the door, putting the dirty washing in then choosing the right programme to get the washing clean. The more we practice, the easier it becomes, and we know instantly which programme to use.

I have an amazing washing machine. I mean an actual washing machine that is amazing. It has so many programmes on it, it took me a week just to work out how to do a fast wash. I don't know about you, but I only ever use 3 maybe 4 of the functions available. The rest felt unnecessary and too confusing. Colours, fast wash, whites, hot wash, fast spin, rinse, and repeat. At first it took me a while to work out what buttons to press and where to put the fabric softener and discovering all sorts of additional functions I hadn't known were there. Now I can do it with my eyes closed. Literally with my eyes closed. And that is how we create the behaviours in our lives and businesses.

Curiosity, practice, repeat.

Making decisions is at the heart of every business. Every day is a series of choices. Some are easy to make and others more challenging. Some days we're on the ball and others, we struggle. It's often our energy that dictates how effective we are in making constructive choices. I had an episode recently that later turned out to be hormone related and symptomatic of the dreaded menopause. Brain fog, anxiety, and confusion were a daily occurrence, and yet I couldn't explain why. Nothing seemed to make sense. I had started to doubt myself and very quickly began to feel as though I was back in that maze. It was a scary time for me, and I'll share more about it later in the book.

The point here is that this time, I was determined not to get lost. I began reaching out: talking, starting conversations, asking for help. Finally, a conversation with a friend and a trip to the doctors and my symptoms found an explanation. So, to be clear, explore all options if something doesn't make sense; reach out and talk about it.

One of my biggest struggles has been mastering the world of social media and learning how to make it work for me. I had to learn how to engage with an audience and how to sell myself, when all I really want to do is hide. There is a reason why we pay digital marketing agents and VAs a small fortune to help with branding and raising our profiles – because it's really fucking hard to do. I remember during a conversation with my daughter Ellie, I was asking her how to post on Instagram. After about half an hour of conversation about relevant hashtags and examples of 'this person knows how to post and therefore this works', Ellie sighed and said, "Mum, honestly you will never really get it". "What? Why?", I said, feeling both hurt and relieved by this statement. "Our generation grew up with this. We see it and use it in a way you will never really understand. It's not just about how to use it to sell a business; it's like a language you haven't learnt". Wow, so my kid is cleverer than I thought. "Ok so what do I do then?", I asked. "Well, you could start by just letting me do it for you", she replied. "Ok" I said, "I can do that".

When you face confusion, use this check list:

Where Confusion Shows Up	Top Tips to Beat Confusion
You are unclear about what the problem is so waste time seeking the wrong solutions.	If you're not sure what, exactly, the problem is, start at the end goal or outcome and work backwards.
You are trying to fix too many things at once without success, leading to feelings of desperation.	Stop, step back, make a list and prioritise. Don't try to be a hero. Multi-tasking problems is a recipe for confusion.
You procrastinate continuously, which reduces productivity and leads to low self-esteem.	Confusion is often a trigger for procrastination, and once that kicks in, productivity and self-esteem will take a nosedive. Is there a recurring pattern that triggers procrastination i.e. certain tasks you dislike or don't understand? If so, outsource these tasks or ask for help.
You actively avoid situations where you might appear stupid.	Decide what looking stupid means to you. Reframe feeling stupid into being curious, willing to learn, and brave.

Your confusion means that you stop trusting your instincts or trusting others.	Take some time to sit and breathe. Try to relax and let the noise die down. Logical thinking will then return, and solutions begin to appear.
You market your product or services to the wrong audience or lily pad from project to project trying to find what will sell.	Without seeing the results first, it can be hard to know if we are selling to the right people. Before embarking upon marketing activities, make sure you have worked through identifying your niche and ideal paying clients. Find the people and the problem then create a product to meet those needs.
You consume copious amounts of content, trying to learn your way out of confusion.	Confusion can indicate that there is something that we don't yet know. Before embarking upon another online course make sure you are not forgetting what you already know. If imposter syndrome or perfectionism are popping up, a quick checklist of credibility skills can put them in their place.
You hold unrealistic expectations which leave you feeling unaccomplished and demotivated.	Goals are achieved 1 step at a time, and this helps keep expectation in perspective. Take some time to define your goals as Specific Measurable Achievable, Realistic and Timely. Break everything down and keep track of your progress.

BOOK RECOMMENDATION

How to Be Fucking Awesome by Dan Meredith

I love the book *How to Be Fucking Awesome* by Dan Meredith for so many reasons. 1) it's not too long; 2) it has the word fucking in the title; and 3) it's written by someone who knows the struggle. It's refreshing too, to read a book from a very male perspective. My ideal paying clients are women and, let's be honest, women of a certain age. This means I read a lot of Brené Brown and my network and mentors are almost entirely female. So, to see and hear something from a perspective that is way outside of my normal perspective was great. Let's face it when I first pictured an entrepreneur, they were male, smartly dressed, and a bit of an arsehole. Dan isn't smartly dressed or an arsehole, but he is an acquired taste. His book is totally on point when it comes to demonstrating what an entrepreneurial mindset entails. He describes clearly, and without hesitation, the process he worked to build his business and earn a sizeable income from it. There is no confusion. It is plain, simple, concise, and to the point – just what I needed.

He could be described as the kind of person I would've turned my nose up at in the past. He looks like an overnight success, made his money by schmoosing with the big boys ... blah blah blah. Bullshit. The book is in truth an open, honest, and frank portrayal of entrepreneurship delivered in such a way as to enable you to ask very important questions: "What is my version of this? Where does who I am fit in with what needs to be done here?" It's a great book. Maybe not for the F-bomb phobes, and his Instagram should come with a 'WARNING', but through all the manliness and references to oral gratification is the real Dan Meredith. A kind, humble, generous, and sensitive person with the wickedest sense of humour I have witnessed in a long while. I laugh every day at his social media, and when we're laughing, we're learning. The book's a great read and a no-nonsense, straight-to-the-point demonstration of how behaviours and entrepreneurial mindset can make the difference between good and great.

CHAPTER 5

Big 7 No. 4
Fear to *Courage*

*"Whatever you fear the most has no power
– It is your fear that has the power."*

OPRAH WINFREY

Fear

An unpleasant emotion caused by the threat of danger, pain, or harm.

Fear. We have all experienced fear at some point in our lives. And if mental health statistics are to be believed, then more and more of us are experiencing it on a daily basis. But why? Surely the world is less scary now than it used to be. As humans, we are programmed to fear danger. To sense it and to avoid it. Most of us will be familiar with the concept of fight or flight, and if, like me, you have read anything about self-development, mindfulness, coaching, counselling, self-help, or wellbeing, you'll know exactly how this basic instinct is triggered. Last time I checked, a Google search of "What is fight or flight" came back with 577,000,000 results. Words like anxiety, depression, mental health, stress, sickness, overwhelm, and exhaustion pop up all over the first page. These are followed by mindfulness, meditation, counselling, and coaching.

So why are we so afraid in our businesses? Well we are the business and our business is part of our life; so if we have underlying fears or limiting beliefs, they'll come out no matter what the situation. One of my favourite sayings is, "Wherever you go, there you are". We basically carry all our shit around with us until we work to let go of it. The saying's origins are uncertain, but it is in the title of Jon Kabat Zinn's 1994 book. Zinn is credited with being the person that brought mindfulness to the masses. A medical professor, he worked with patients suffering from chronic pain; and through mindfulness based stress reduction, they were able to stop fearing pain and better manage their chronic illness and symptoms. Fear is something that we should only experience when faced with a clear and present danger;

unfortunately, society has become so confusing and fast paced, that we now have 5-year olds stressing about what outfit to wear. Teenagers are crippled with anxiety triggered by social media. Young adults are consumed with fear over not being good enough. And grown-ups live in constant fear of judgement, failure, and success. When our values and beliefs conflict with our goals, the fight or flight response become a constant. This is not good for our minds or our bodies, so we need to address this "First World Fear" now.

Courage

The ability to do something that frightens one, bravery.

I don't tend to describe myself as courageous or brave. I am utter shite in an emergency, and I have a list of fears that range from 'my fear of flying' – because I am scared the plane will crash into the sea and I will be eaten by a shark – to my 'fear of frogs' – because I think they are evil and have magical powers – to my 'fear of having too much'. This shows up in my reluctance to push forward towards financial success because I fear that something horrible or tragic will happen to someone I love as payback. Finally, my "favourite" is the 'fear of being disliked' – this one sits on my shoulder and rides around with me like a judgemental monkey pointing and saying: "There that person doesn't like you, and that thing you did, you've upset them now; they hate you and will never forgive you".

So, to be courageous I have had to make some choices in my life: *stop panicking and get on the plane you absolute dick* (I am still prone to the occasional burst of negative self-talk), *you'll sink and drown in 5 seconds flat anyway – you won't be alive when the sharks eat you.* I've come to accept that "if" frogs were magical and evil that they would probably not be all that interested in me. And there are always butterflies and bees, who I believe are also magical and good, so they will reverse the spell. I've decided that despite the icky, painful, discomfort that I experience when I am talking or even thinking about money, that my gratitude and humility will protect my family from payback. And the hardest one of all, I am courageous enough to be vulnerable. I trust that by being good and kind that my intentions will shine through and that monkey is not a part of me. Therefore, I can choose to carry him around or leave him at home. Courage and bravery are the actions we take when we feel hurt, exposed, afraid, and vulnerable. If you're not experiencing fear, then you can't be courageous. Courage can be running into a fire to save a family or standing on the front line on a battlefield. Or it can be as simple as deciding that being yourself is enough, and with support, we can all do that.

My struggle with fear

UNMASK THE FEAR

"Mum, are you ok – you look like you've been mean girled again?" Ugghhhh don't you just love those moments when you realise your kids are way cleverer and more insightful than you are? I brought my girls up well. Despite a few hiccups in the early years (the practice years), I am a good mum. There, I said it; I am a pretty awesome mum, and my kids are proof of that. I mean I'm not perfect, I still fuck up, but I own it when I do. I brought my girls up to see themselves in the world. To be brave and take responsibility for their actions. They have been my rock, and I look forward to leaning into them and their lives as they grow up.

When she asked if I'd just been "mean girled", I'd just picked Maya up from school. Something I do quite a lot, as I love our time together in the car. She tells me about her day, and I tell her all about my day too. It's funny because she is so wise, and when I am feeling particularly hurt or vulnerable, she always knows the right thing to say. We facetime Ellie too so she can join in or do a group FB chat, and I always end up feeling much better.

I realise now why their guidance and support has been so effective in these particularly low moments: they get it. Because my real fears and sadness, the ones that actually make me cry, come through the situations that send me right back to my childhood and to school. If something upset me that day it wasn't a piece of writing that didn't go well or a printer with an inbuilt desire to wind me up. It is when I've been "mean girled" or think I might have "mean girled" someone else – that horrible sick feeling in your stomach that makes you run to your bed and hide under the covers.

For anyone not familiar, *Mean Girls* is a film about teenage girls. Cady Heron (Lindsay Lohan) joins a new school after living in South Africa. This is Cady's first experience of proper school, and her naivety and values are challenged when she's introduced to the cruel tactics and strategies employed to facilitate the laws of popularity. The hierarchy is apparent, and her fellow students are hiding in tightly knit cliques for safety. She unwittingly finds herself in the good graces of an elite group of cool students dubbed "The Plastics", but Cady soon realises how her shallow group of new friends earned this nickname.

I loved school. I mean, I didn't do particularly well at the stuff school is supposed to help with like, gaining an education. I was, however, very good at having a laugh and avoiding all the things that I didn't fancy, like science, maths, and French. I am blessed to have the same friends now as I did when we left school over 35 years ago. So why then do I find it so hard to operate in situations where the school playground tactics are so prevalent? Because my strategy for survival at school was humour, servitude, and avoidance. I was great at making people laugh; I was the fat funny one who didn't bother anyone. I was the kid who would lend others money and never ask for it back. I was the kid who avoided all opportunities to stand out and spent my entire childhood blending in, people pleasing, and making myself small. I remember one summer I got a cool boyfriend and had lost weight. The backlash was unbearable. The popular girls would look at me with curled-up noses and the others avoided me. WFT? It wasn't long before that boyfriend disappeared, and I was back to being the funny fat kid.

All these behaviours have been replicated time and time again throughout my life. First in my personal life – choosing destructive and unhealthy relationships that allowed me to duck and weave, stay small, and keep pleasing because I didn't know how else to be. Then in my business for fear – that there would be a price to pay, or fear of not being liked, standing out, failing, competition, or upsetting others. Every time there was a chance for me to grow and lean into who I am, I held back, stayed small, and repeatedly shaved pieces of my identity away so as not to bother anyone.

Letting the mean girls win worked. Ok, to be clear, there have been very few, if any, actual mean girls in my journey; the problem here is my perception of the hierarchy what I think people might be thinking or saying about me, and my perception of how others are responding to my behaviours and intentions.

This is how mean girls and bullies stay in control. They use your own fears to control you. Apart from the real bullies who will beat you to the ground, the tactical bullies control through fear. So, we allow our own fears to control us. And this is where I was that day in the car with Maya. No one had bullied me. I had simply fallen into a self-fulfilling prophecy of perceived rejection. "Mum what is it? Who has upset you?" "No one puppy", I replied, "I think this one's on me".

School was a tricky time. I was never really bullied at school, and I have certainly not experienced bullying in my business. It's simply the trigger of a belief story that I carry around in my head. Actual bullies might have been easier to deal with, and this is the learning. If the bully is in your head and you are choosing to listen, then choose again.

CO-DEPENDENCY OR COLLABORATION?

Collaboration is something I adore. Probably because of my life as a twin, I'm sure there is a collaborative gene that sits somewhere in my body, but also because, well it's just more fun. It has, however, caused me to come a cropper on more occasions than I want to think about. In both my personal and business life. Collaboration in relationships was more like co-dependency, which meant I supported and nurtured everyone involved except myself. Feeding into their narcissistic addictions, placating their ego, and sacrificing myself and my own needs.

As we know, with any new challenge comes a moment of uncertainty and pain. The discomfort of leaning into the unknown and waiting for the wave to wash over us. I love a new challenge, and in business every day brings a new test of my mental resilience. Some lessons and situations pass relatively unnoticed, while others can take months or even years to work through. In her book *Rising Strong*, Brené Brown refers to the second act. She is referring specifically to the part in a book, play, or film where all the hard work happens. That's where we play out the tragedy or triumph. The beginning feels easy and the end is hopeful and happy. The second act is where the story plays out. The long drawn out, nitty gritty where the lead character struggles to win the girl or the villains outsmart the police. It's where the information is. Without it there is no story. "We can't skip the 2nd act in life", Brown says, its where everything happens.

My second act in business is still playing out. While I have made progress, closed a few chapters, and definitely had a few wins, my second act is far from over. And I'm ok with that. I think one of my biggest fears is what it will feel like when the struggle is over! We need pain to feel alive. And right now, I feel happier and more alive than I have ever felt before. The core struggle at the start of my second act was fear. I had no idea at the time just how powerful those core beliefs, values, and behaviours from my childhood would be, or what an impact they would have on my perceptions. They really did block me at every turn, and I am frustrated to think about how much time I wasted being afraid to be alone.

I never quite feel comfortable when I am alone. That is unless I am tapping away on my computer writing blogs or pottering around at home cleaning and tidying, then I am incredibly happy to be alone. I relish the quiet space during the week when everyone else is at school or at work to tidy and sort as these activities relax me; they are my meditation. At these moments, I have nothing to fear – pretty much everything else in business leaves me feeling vulnerable, and this is where fear creeps in. I imagine being an identical twin has left me in constant need of reassurance and connection. Kate and I have a weird energy between us, one that a lot of twins will testify to. We are not quite mind readers, more emotion readers, and while I go many days or even weeks without seeing her, my body notices when she's not there.

I grew up always having someone to hide behind or share the blame with. A constant source of protection and confidence. Today I operate in the world extremely well without my sister by my side, until vulnerability appears, and in business this is pretty much a daily occurrence. Without Kate in my business, I miss the energy of having someone by my side, fighting my corner, and protecting me should things get ugly. We've worked together many times in the past. Over 70% of our working lives have been spent working in the same office or company. This was no accident, and I missed the safety net, so, I went in search of replacements. Always feeling as though I needed to have someone else there to share the burdens and the triumphs. I thought I was seeking collaborations, to make things fun and interesting. After many disappointing and soul-destroying attempts, I realised it wasn't collaboration I was seeking but co-dependency.

Overcoming my own fears and low self-esteem felt easier and more achievable if I could share the burden. I gain courage from helping others; it triggers an instinct in me that builds belief. Therefore, if I am "doing this for someone else", I could sidestep my own procrastination and limitations.

Collaboration should be equal and consensual. It should be a process of joining forces with others that share your values and common goals. If collaboration is something you're considering because it feels like somewhere you can hide, then I invite you to take a step back and ask, Why do I need to hide? What am I pretending not to know? What do I bring to the table? What do they bring to the table? Collaboration is just one of the ways I have missed out on or mistaken opportunities because I was not coming at it from the right mindset. Because I was letting the 11-year-old me call the shots. No more. My girls get it. They remind me every day how brave they are, and they also remind me every day of how brave I can be too.

LEARNING TO FAIL

Fear of failure is usually top of the list when I ask clients what stops them. No one wants to fail. When we experience failure, it's almost always because what we're trying to achieve has meaning to us. We don't fail at stuff we don't care about or haven't tried to do. "Oh, I failed to walk a tight rope or swim with sharks today" – err, no. I don't care for either of those things, and so far, I've never attempted them. We fail at what we love, just as we fail in love. But Tennyson was right, it is "better to have loved and lost / Than to never have loved at all" (*In Memoriam* 27, ll. 15–16). Bang on. I would rather lose Dave now, knowing how amazing and completely loved I have felt in our relationship, than to have never experienced what true, unconditional love can feel like. It's worth it.

Like love, business is always risky. We do everything we can, and often we succeed, but just as often we fail. Nevertheless, we must try. "What is the cost of not trying?" I ask myself that every day because a coaching diploma and 1000s of hours of reading does not immunise you against the practice of growth and the struggle it brings. Being a coach meant I judged myself quite harshly for not already knowing how to get myself out of these situations. For a while, I would beat myself up, "come on Abbie, you should know this". And believe me, it was said to me several times too by other people. "Shouldn't you know what to do then? How can you help other people if you can't help yourself? Comments like this broke me on more than one occasion. And to this day I still hear the echoes of those words, when the days are dark and the struggle is particularly exhausting. What I have come to realise now is that it is through those struggles that we learn and grow. Curiosity is a powerful practice, and it comes with pain and discomfort. Coaching has taught me to maintain my curiosity and to stay focused on the learning. It has helped me to grow my mental resilience to such a level that I almost welcome failure as a tool for enlightenment.

While there are, sadly, people out there who would love to see you fail, pay them no mind. They are not a part of your journey and deserve no space in your head. Those close to you can bring you down sometimes – they don't want you to fail; they're just afraid to see you struggle, and to them it makes more sense to avoid and abort than it does to endure.

Let me fail so I can learn is what I chant to myself when the naysayers are around. It is better to try and fail than to not try at all; that really would be painful. At the start of my journey, I admit I lily padded around from project to project for so many reasons. Confusion, self-doubt, inexperience, and of course fear. When I first set out to be a fulltime coach, I made one promise to myself: to offer my coaching skills in the same way as Lisa offered hers to me. Now, we were friends and no money ever changed hands. She openly offered herself and her skills to me as an extension of our friendship and to help me through tough times. She helped me develop my mental resilience rather than jumping to my rescue or simply piling on. This is not a business model I would encourage, not if you have chosen coaching as a way to earn income. However, the values and the ethos of this have stuck with me. I continue to this day my pledge to "walk beside" my clients as we make our way together on their journey.

Believing that many of my potential new clients would benefit from this same approach I went with affordable and accessible. Make it relatable. Make it easy. Make it every day. Make it so that those who would not or could not normally engage with coaching can; make it so they can benefit too. I was on a mission to convert the whole of Portsmouth to the amazing magic of coaching.

In the early stages I focused too much on the offer and not enough on the audience. I set up Support for Change, which I honestly believed would be the answer to every ordinary person's problems. Can't lose weight, come for coaching. Crap at sticking to relationships, join our group. Struggling with anxiety or stress, you came to the right place. It was woolly and vague. I had a Facebook group and a monthly meetup group. Not only did I not do my research, I had no clue how to reach the right people. I spent months perfecting learning materials and making up folders, printing leaflets and business cards. I hired a venue that cost me £37.50 a month. I hired it for 3 hours instead of the 2 I actually needed so I could satisfy my 'be prepared' driver just in case someone wanted to chat afterwards; I needed to 'be accessible'. I naively decided upon the price of £5 per session. People will absolutely pay £5. They dish out more than that to go and sit in a circle at a slimming club to be told stuff they already know. My thing is way better than that. Coaching is amazing and life changing, and they will get so much from it. It's great; I'm great; what a bargain! I paid up front for the venue and printed all the flyers; at that point I was around £200 down. As the date drew nearer, I could feel myself hoping no one would come. The fear of failure combined with fear of success, which meant I was destined to be right either way. My self-fulfilling prophecy came true. It sounds crazy, but the weight of expectation was so enormous – when no one came I was broken, and also a little relieved.

The second time I tried, I was a bit braver. I hired the room for only 2 hours and decided to charge £20. In the time since the first attempt, I had done a lot of work to build up my

Facebook group – as I had seen this model work in other groups. Have a warm audience, give away free coaching then hit them with an offer that you know they need. The first evening was exhilarating and disappointing at the same time. Two ladies came. Karen, whom I had coached previously and who had been to one of my vision board workshops, and Rayo, a delightful lady who had seen the advert on my website. What black magic was at play that day I have no idea. I think that Rayo was the only person ever to have actually found my first website! We had an amazing session, and over the months, the groups grew and shrank randomly. One month I had 4, the next 2, the next 6, and the next 1 person. I was haemorrhaging money. Now, I made some great connections through Support for Change, some of whom are still my clients today, and I learnt a lot about what not to do – as well as what does and doesn't work when it comes to sticking to your morals in business. Thankfully, I met Rico in the summer of 2019, and he knew exactly what needed to be done. "Abbie who are your audience? What is this group for? Who is it for? I am confused, what is the purpose of it?" This was another body blow of realisation. What was the point? Who was I trying to help? Why did I ever imagine that offering anything that vague was ever going to work? In August 2019, I ended Support for Change and closed the Facebook group. It was not an easy decision, yet it was, in reality, far easier to do than I anticipated. Working with Rico gave me the focus I needed. As a digital marketing expert, Rico guided me through the process of discovering my unique selling points, identifying my niche market, and defining my offer. He also created a pretty slamming website for me, too. I owe my business identity to working with Rico. He is, without doubt, the kindest and most supportive business partner I have had to date.

So, was Support for Change a failure? No absolutely not. Did

I fail to do my research? Yes. Did I try to set up a business based on hiding my real skills and trying not to bother people by asking for so little money? Yes. This isn't the only time I've attempted things and failed. I've set up countless workshops and had no takers. I've created and paid for ads on Facebook that never got the reach because I don't know how to do this properly and asking someone to do it for me would have meant taking myself seriously, and we couldn't have that.

Things can and will go wrong even when you do everything right. These are the failures that offer the biggest learning because when these things don't turn out right, if we can avoid blame, what we are left with is some real information to work with. I recently advertised a vision board workshop and only 2 ladies came. There were a variety of scheduling clashes with other groups in my network that couldn't be predicted, so my potential target audience was reduced quite dramatically. Now I suppose I could have gone all out to push my agenda over theirs, but I chose not to. My two daughters also came along, and they had the best day. "Mum I want to do your vision board workshop", Ellie messaged one morning, "Can I do it"? "Hell, yeah you can do it"; I was so proud. We had the best day. The 2 ladies who did come got their money's worth from me 10 times over, and I had a blast. The biggest learning for me was that I can be entirely present in a room with only 2 paying clients and give them the best experience possible. I was in my element. Building relationships and reach takes time and no matter what marketing tactics you employ, nothing replaces the feeling of connection and rapport when you coach 1-1. Not once did my brain huff at the lack of attendance. Not once did I feel less inclined to coach because I wasn't earning big money – until the drive home.

Now whilst this "feeling" of accomplishment was energising

and I did love every moment. I couldn't ignore the fact that I was actually out of pocket. Not only did I not make money, I had spent more on room hire, equipment, and a buffet than I had earnt. A great day for personal growth and energy, a very bad day for my business and personal finances. *FFS Ab this is not a hobby WTF are you doing?* I muttered as I drove home that day. A ping pong conversation began to ricochet around in my head:

- It was such a fab day.
- Only two people came.
- They loved it and I feel amazing.
- Why did you hold back from promoting it more?
- I will be able to use the lovely photos to put on social media so everyone will see what a fantastic coach I am.
- You spent more than you made Abbie, is this a business or your own personal wellness hobby?

Failure works when you take the time to learn from it. Not just power past it. After spending hundreds of hours over the last few years, reflecting on my journey, noticing the wins and obsessing over the losses, I came to one rather startling conclusion that day. "Am I afraid of money?", I asked myself. "Yes, it would appear so", came the reply. Could this explain my constant bungie type behaviours when it came to pushing forward? Bungie behaviours are how I describe the feeling of clawing my way into the stretch zone, like I have a huge piece of elastic around my waist. Every step getting a little harder until eventually the cord becomes so tight that I get catapulted back and end up on my arse.

Fear of money? Is that a thing? Fuck, I bet it is. And sure enough – one quick Google search and my fear was justified. Financial fear and fear of success. I had been so determined to meet my value of affordability and accessibility for all, that I hadn't realised that this value was in fact hiding a fear of vulnerability that came with financial success. This was huge. "Oh my god that's it! I am deliberately limiting my own progression. Hiding my fear behind a façade of philanthropy". By sticking to my values to deliver my offer in the same supportive and charitable way it was given to me, I was unknowingly supporting an underlying fear.

This was a huge lesson for me, and the process of learning from my failures is for sure how I reached this startling conclusion. Ironically, it explains pretty much everything that was wrong in my business to that point and was a problem that everyone around me seemed to have noticed way before I did: "Abbie, clients won't see your value until you do". WTF. Failure works for us when we choose to reflect, evaluate, and learn. Fail, learn, do better. So, what can I do better here? I asked myself. How can I meet my value to help those "like me" and still earn money?

What does "like me" mean? What am I struggling with? What am I willing to pay for? If I am willing to pay, then others must be too. What do I need to do to help those like me and still earn money? What is behind this fear of success? What can I do to move past this?

I have included in the workbook download an exercise that I undertook to begin the process of overcoming this fear. I built confidence in myself and my offer by building behaviours that enabled me to overcome that fear and pursue income as well as self-fulfilment.

I still employ the same model of affordability and accessibility in my business today. The only difference is that I know who my audience are, and I value my own journey as much as I value theirs.

Where I found courage

BUILD YOUR TRIBE

Nowadays I make sure to charge for my services, and if I'm ever in any doubt about a person's ability or willingness to pay, I do one of two things. I'm either courageous enough to let them go, or I go all out to demonstrate the true value of my offer and the transformation that is possible from working with me. By defining my niche and aligning my financial goals and behaviours with my values, I'm able to work confidently and purposefully towards financial rewards. This has not been a quick fix for me. Reframing my beliefs around money and learning to use it as a tool or steppingstone towards my actual goal has been a useful and enlightening exercise. Money was controlling me. I thought money was the goal and because that felt icky, I avoided it. I was wrong.

So here's the thing, money is not the goal. The goal is what you get to have, do, see, and experience when you have money. Its why we often go to work in jobs we hate, because the ends justify the means and we need money to put food on the table and support our family. Our money pays for holidays, uniforms, treats, and it can also pay the mortgage, top up our pension pot, and build a solid financial foundation for us and our family. I had the privilege of achieving this in a job I loved … so WTF was wrong with me?

> The money conversation is one I regularly facilitate in group coaching sessions, and it came up time and time again during COVID19. "Everyone is struggling, how can I charge for my stuff when the world is in pain, Abbie?

> I can't charge for an online Zoom session; it's not the same is it? If I charge, people will think I am ruthless and greedy, Abbie". Now to be clear a lot of people suffered financially during the pandemic, and I believe those ripples will still be felt for many years.

The fact is though that not everyone was suffering, and when we begin to break down the word "everyone", we start to see where polarised thinking and low self-esteem are popping up.

I encouraged my clients to look at the facts. Who are your clients? What do they need right now? How can you adapt your offer to give them what they need and still feel confident to charge for it?

People still need to eat, and I have yet to see a supermarket giving food away. A person's values don't change when money is tight, their priorities do.

What about you? Where do your clients benefit if you can't pay your bills? What happens when this is over, and they call you up for an appointment and you're no longer in business? When we feel vulnerable, or lack confidence in our offer, we can easily allow these excuses and limiting beliefs to trigger hesitation and procrastination. Justifying why we can't do something and avoiding the discomfort.

Working a process to focus attention, build confidence, and shape behaviours requires accountability. We are unlikely to be able to reconcile these beliefs without at least a modicum of input from others. This is just one of the many reasons coaching works – these are the struggle my clients experience.

I found the courage to sell, to compete, and to be me, when I found my tribe. Tribe is a word that kind of made me twitch at first. "Tribe"? Are we even allowed to say that? I soon discovered that tribe is a term used in business to describe social groups linked by a leader that share a purpose or goal, common culture, or organisational boundary. Tribes can be super powerful, and when they act together for a united purpose, they can be unstoppable. "Ok, so I need to get me one of them sharpish", I thought. Good news is, being a tribe builder is actually my superpower and something I do quite naturally. Getting other people to join in is what I'd been doing for the first 3 years of my business. Linking people together, sharing experiences, and building friendships that were strong and purposeful. I already had "my people", so rallying them up to form a tribe would be no problem.

For once, something that was going to be easy. And it was. While it took time to get the numbers up, it felt effortless and natural to be joining these women together. Safety and support. Accountability and connection. Friendships and fun. Who knew getting together with my mates would be how my business would finally start to work?

A Facebook group with a dedicated purpose. Marketing strategies that meant I was speaking to the right customers with the right message. Trusting that my own skills and unique selling points would get me in front of the right people. Finally, things started to shift, and it felt great.

The great thing about a tribe is that you care a lot less about trying to fit in and please other people when you have friends around you. Like school, I guess we do migrate to those who share our taste in clothes or sports or hobbies, and later in life, our values. I've been lucky enough to have received excellent tribe-building training from the very brilliant Lauryn Bradley. Her book *Grow Your Tribe: How to skyrocket your business by loving your audience* (2019) is amazing. Simple, no frills, full of facts and top-class advice, this book is a must read for anyone in the business of building a business. If you need an audience or client base to sell your product or service to, then I recommend you get a copy right away. This is just one of the many books I recommend that contain all the facts and advice you need to be a success. Once you have gotten out of your own way, that is. And you're already well on your way to doing that.

Once I began to focus on who my business was for and what problems they needed help with, my tribe began to grow and so did my audience. Other coaches were noticing me, in a good way, and congratulating me on my skills and expertise. Offers of collaborations started to happen, and I accepted them with the appropriate mindset. I even stopped to ask myself a few times – "What do I get out of this"? If it wasn't right, I moved on. Operating inside of an audience that I could relate to felt amazing. It also allowed me to truly lean into me. To be myself. To stay curious and willing to grow, but with the confidence that I called the shots. Trusting your authenticity is a message that has been sent to me loud and clear for as long as I've been on this ride. You have to be authentic to build a strong foundation for yourself and your business.

There is a reason we focus so much on building: building a business, building a tribe, building your confidence, and building a life. Building these things, like building a house, takes time; it won't happen overnight, but if you do it right and focus on building your tribe first, you can have so much fun in the process. Whatever kind of day I'm having, I'm certain to be surrounded by people I love and who love me back. I've been building tribes since I was at school. While I was avoiding work at all costs and just hanging out with my friends keeping everyone together and organised and entertained, I was developing what would become the core principles of my business – too bad my teachers and parents didn't realise that then!

A final word on building your tribe. Tribes are an amazing, safe space when you invite the right people in. There are rules, especially for a business tribe, such as boundaries and acceptable behaviours, common goals, and values. And the golden rule of building a tribe is you absolutely must be the truest version of yourself within that tribe to really make it work. False tribes don't work, and your tribe members will find you out in an instant.

So, before embarking upon this activity to help in your business, be sure to embrace your authenticity. Ask yourself what you want from the group and what they will want to see in return. If you don't compromise your values, tribe building should feel comfortable and easy. Your tribe won't always agree with you, which is great because healthy debate and conversation are helpful to all involved. But the key is always to keep the communication flowing two ways. My tribe see me, just as I see them. They understand my needs just as I understand theirs. They help me as much as I help them, and it is my relentless pursuit of this two-way interaction that has enabled me to grow as a coach and as a business owner. We must accept help in order to offer it, and I am so incredibly grateful for the help and support I receive from my tribe.

QUESTION YOUR INSTINCTS

Competing, selling, and asking for money are still things that trigger fear stories in my head – like trailers for a scary movie and I hate horror films and scary movies. My imagination, if you haven't guessed by now, is eclectic and irrational to say the least, and 3 seconds of a trailer can haunt me for weeks. I'm still terrified of the dark and will always check in the back seat of my car before getting into it. I had a super traumatic experience many years ago and I am not afraid to admit that I weed my pants. Not completely, but enough to make it uncomfortable for the ride home. I was sat in a dark car park waiting to pick Ellie up from Guides. It was quiet and no one was around. I was sat flicking through my phone, as you do, and suddenly a furry creature caught my eye. It was leaning over the back of my car seat and was about to go for my ear. Oh my god. I screamed. Jumped and peed all at the same time. My brain said werewolf. Not dog or cat. Werewolf. My heart was pounding I swung around with such force I tied the seat belt around myself and was then wedged between the seat and the steering wheel. Panicking now because I couldn't move to escape, I turned to see nothing there. Then as quickly as I had seen the werewolf, I realised it was in fact the fur lining on my hood that had caught my eye. Oh, ffs seriously. I breathed a sigh of relief and embarrassment and as soon as Ellie jumped in the car, which made me jump again, I told her what had happened:

"You peed yourself mum?", she asked with a curled-up nose.

"Well yes but that's not the point, the point is I imagined a werewolf not a cat or bunny rabbit, werewolf! Don't you think that's hysterical?"

"Not as hysterical as you peeing in your pants; I can't wait to tell Maya."

Instincts are an essential component for survival. Without them humanity would not have lasted this long. Our now, highly intelligent, and sophisticated brains have not, however, kept up with our surroundings, and they still rely heavily on the basic core behaviours of our distant ancestors. The world is a scary place, but we have far less need to fear wild animals than our brains might have us believe.

Instincts trigger a response that is immediate and based on learnt patterns and information. So, if our instincts trigger fear and we retreat or run away, our brain will inform us immediately that this is what is required. Instinct doesn't need our input and requires no explanation. It's a feeling that rises from your stomach to send you a message to act. We experience this often in our lives and our business journeys.

Our instincts alert us immediately if our values are under attack. This can be experienced as a feeling of dread or confusion; the thought of pushing forward suddenly begins to feel laborious and icky. Our values are important, and when they're challenged, we know that they are indeed the right values. This doesn't mean, however, that we must stick to them so hard that we resist perspective.

When asked to collaborate, for example, my value for not letting people down and my driver for perfectionism will be the first to make an appearance. They can overpower logic, and my immediate response is to find a way to say 'yes'. To please, to placate, to serve. Nowadays, thanks to my more entrepreneurial mindset approach, I make sure to check in with myself before committing to something that I may later regret.

What are my instincts telling me about this opportunity to learn something new? Can I pursue this opportunity without compromising my authenticity and just simply apply my skills in a way that fits with my needs, rather than feeling compelled to collaborate only I don't let someone else down, or to satisfy my need for protection? Basically, I ask myself what's in it for me? My go to question for any new opportunity. One I wish I had been more inclined to use in years gone by. Using this new structured mindset approach, I'm able to make sense of the values that my instincts trigger, leading to far more productive and satisfying collaborations.

In summary, listen to your instincts, and then apply logic. Your instinct is alerting you to potential danger or conflict. A basic human survival technique. Useful in a jungle or battlefield, not so important when sat at your desk debating whether to email your clients with a flash sale or join a Facebook live. In business, we must notice these sudden impulses and then take a deep breath. We need to use our mindset tools, and follow up this warning with perspective, curiosity, and logic. Doing so will break our past patterns of procrastination and avoidance through perceived fear and enable us to think rationally before deciding what action to take. Through mindset, we have the power to challenge our instincts and use them to trigger a new response. The moral of the story is ... when you see fur think hood not werewolf. You'll be far less likely to pee your pants.

COURAGE TO ACT

"I want to feel more confident" is a pretty standard response from clients when they come for coaching. No matter what the scenario, confidence, either the need for it or the lack of it, is almost always what a client will respond with (quickly) when I ask them what they want. When I ask clients what they need to be able to feel this way, the response is slower. They'll hesitate and look up searching for the answer. "I need, support; yes, I need support", one said. "I need to learn to be confident", another said. "I need to start earning money", yet another said.

So, when a client says I want to be confident, I ask: "When was the last time you had confidence?" It is almost always following a time when they chose to take action – *When I turned up at the meeting and did my presentation. When I asked that girl out or applied for that job.* I follow up with, "So, did you wait for the confidence? or did you decide to act and as a result, you experienced a feeling of confidence?" Most will say they just decided to do it. Something inside said just do it. Many will say they were terrified at first, but when they got there it was nowhere near as bad as they thought it would be. Some say they were just sick of holding back.

If fear is holding you back from competing with others, either on social media or in person, then waiting until the fear disappears will leave you way behind the rest. If you are fearful of compromising your values by upping your sales pitch or marketing programmes, then holding back will leave you resentful and cash poor. If fear of compromising your core behaviours means that you dig in so deep that your behaviours become overdone and unresourceful, you're going to struggle and get exhausted and overwhelmed very quickly.

Fear of competing held me back and derailed my purpose so many times. Every single time I went to write a post on social media I'd be consumed with conflict and internal conversation. *What if this annoys someone?* The more confident I tried to sound in my posts the more I worried that those who weren't yet reaping financial reward would resent me and feel bad. Spoiler – at this point I had £0 in the bank and was just about scrapping together enough cash to stop all my direct debits from bouncing. Why was I worried about upsetting someone else, when by holding back I was only hurting myself and my family? The hesitation and fear about being visible online was exhausting and fuelled all my other anxieties around being a failure feeling guilty for causing our little family to suffer. I was hurting myself and my family. "Right you need to get over this Abbie" – and eventually I did.

Entrepreneurs don't fear competition; they use it as fuel. They understand that a market with competition in it is a market worth being in. Steve Jobs lost no sleep when he launched the iPhone. Even though there were already smartphones on the market, he didn't sit there worrying if other mobile phone manufacturers would think he was an arsehole for having such an amazing product. He was driven by the need to launch a product that he knew people wanted and needed. He focused on the end game, the consumer.

Competition is an arena, and it is the mindset we take into it that determines our success. If you are there battling with the competition in a way that is honourable and courageous, then you'll survive. Your clients and customers want you and many will need you too, even if they don't know it yet, so you must let them know who you are. And you can only do that if you're brave enough to step out of the shadows.

When it was first time for me to step into the arena, my struggle was fuelled by strong values and beliefs about fairness, honesty, and integrity, as well as my need to be liked, my need to fit in, my desire to support others, and my belief that I wasn't good enough to go it alone. I also added to that my story about a "price to pay". It's really hard to push yourself into the arena to sell your stuff for actual money, if in the back of your mind you're terrified that if someone pays you, the devil will appear and want his cut.

I grew up listening to a lot of Chris de Burgh. The songs "Don't Pay the Ferry Man" and "Spanish Train" haunt me to this day. In my map of the world there is always a price to pay. If, like I did, you believe that to do something good means that you're hurting or taking away from someone else, then being in business for yourself is going to feel like a horrible and unresourceful place most of the time. Fear of money and fear of success can be hard to overcome. Old beliefs that you should 'know your place' and or never try to be better than 'average' can prevent us from fully committing to a process and even cause us to snatch success away just when things are starting to look hopeful.

The moment I began to reframe 'that' was when my entire

approach to selling, marketing, and entrepreneurship shifted. My fear wasn't competition. My fear was competing. Because competing meant that someone else had to lose. I don't like losing, but I also don't like upsetting people, so for me I would just opt out and not enter the arena. Or I would enter in such a way as to look weak, apologetic, and needy. When I began to focus less on what other people were or were not doing and concentrated on getting my own shit together, I started to make progress. Instead of hiding behind my principles of fair play and using them as an excuse for my mediocre attempts at selling, I chose to focus my attention on what money and success would mean for me, and for my family, my business, and my clients. I read a nifty little tip online somewhere that said, 'think of money as the vehicle to get you to where you need to be'. Money is not the end result; it's what you do with it that matters. If success is feeling like a block to you. If you're avoiding competition because you've decided that you already have enough, I invite you to look at what it is that you have enough of. If you love your home, your family and your life, and you're settled and content with your hobby/business, how amazing would it be to have even more of that? Now I am, I hope, still honest, kind, authentic, and transparent in the way I conduct my business. I just choose to think differently about what I'm doing and what the outcome will be.

Rico showed me how I could stay true to myself and compete. Reading books like *How to be Fucking Awesome* and *Grow Your Tribe* taught me that being an entrepreneur was a framework for application not a persona to be worn. And beautiful Brené Brown – why are we not teaching her books in every school around the world. Sod Shakespeare he's had his time; this is the stuff we should be teaching our kids. Brown has taught me that my crazy map of the world is not quite so crazy after all. My fears and my beliefs are a part of me. Curiosity and growth are what I practice going forward, and this is how I do better. It's how I keep going and where I find courage. So now when my clients say, "Abbie, I want to feel confident", I reply, "then you need to find courage".

WHERE FEAR SHOWS UP IN BUSINESS

Fear will stop us in our tracks every time. If we fear failure, we won't try; if we fear success because we think there is a price to pay, then we'll avoid acting. Fear is natural and is useful in small doses. Prolonged fear becomes anxiety, and that's never helpful. When operating in and around our businesses we need to be mindful of where the fear sits. Sometimes it's there right in front of us like a tiger about to pounce, and other times it feels more like being followed down a dark street by a werewolf lurking in the trees. A state of fear, even mild fear, isn't great for you or your business, and it'll show in everything you do. Fear causes avoidance tactics, and if we don't keep an eye on what's happening, we can very quickly find ourselves with an entire armoury of self-defence moves, strategies, and behaviours. We avoid vulnerability at all costs, and offset triumph, success, and joy with a short sharp burst of self-sabotage. That said, if you ever do encounter a werewolf in a dark forest, you have my full permission to run away screaming.

Some of the examples in the table below may sound extreme or unlikely, and hopefully for the most part they'll be rare and only appear from time to time. Social media and beliefs around money are usually top of the list of triggers. Even if the fear or hesitation is mild, it can still restrict you in your business. Look again at the list, and ask yourself these questions: when was the last time I did this? What negative effect did it have on what I was trying to achieve? What could I have achieved or created if that fear was gone?

If a pattern begins to emerge then this is where your focus needs to be, and I recommend starting by downloading and using the exercises for overcoming the struggle with fear.

Top tips summary – Fear to courage

Our businesses should never feel perilous. Excitement and anticipation are what we strive for. Excitement and anticipation are motivators. Fear stops us in our tracks. Seek opportunities to become engaged and excited. Stretch yourself to practice new things.

Fear can be triggered in lots of ways, but it's unlikely you'll experience life or death situations during the day to day running of your business. Unless of course you're a deep-sea fisherman or lion tamer, in which case you'd better have your wits about you. For most of us, the fear is in our minds, and if we work hard, it can be managed. Don't let fear control you. If fear goes unchallenged it'll leak out over everything. It will morph into shame, resentment, jealousy, and anger, and these aren't helpful in any situation. So, notice it. Make friends with it, and soon it'll become a trigger for curiosity, and that always leads us to a solution.

Where Fear shows up	Top Tips to Beat - Fear
You experience feelings of anxiety when trying to move forward.	Shine a light on the path ahead. Break everything down so that each time you step forward you are always stepping into the light.
You fear vulnerability and therefore avoid asking for feedback.	Effective feedback offers us lots of information and so we need to be ok with exposing ourselves in order to grow. Seek feedback from those you trust and those who understand what you are looking to achieve. Avoid asking opinions from those who are not invested in you. Their opinions hold little value. So be brave and reach out.
Your fear of success makes you hold back from promoting your business.	If you are holding back from prioritising bringing income into your business, you may have a fear around money or success. Visualise what lies beyond the income. Money is a vehicle to get you to that place.
Your fear creates low-self-esteem, and you constantly judge yourself and resent it when others succeed.	We see others doing what we feel we can't, and we become jealous and resentful. These are not useful feelings. Most people will happily share how they overcame their own fears. They only seem to be fearless, in reality they were just as afraid, but they found a way through. Ask them how they did it.

Your social media is inconsistent and weak because you're trying not to bother anyone.	Posting online is a battlefield when we try to avoid judgement or rejection. Practice is a great way to desensitise yourself. Put posts out there; be ok with getting no response. Be as true to who you are as you possibly can. Authenticity builds resilience.
You avoid spending time reflecting on your results following a failure.	Reflecting on our progress means looking at the hits as well as the misses. Fear feeds on uncertainty, so the more you know the less afraid you will be.
Your fear of failure leads to hesitation which starts to show in your business.	We have to fail in order to move forward. Make it a daily practice to make notes on what you have learnt and where you can make improvements. It's all about doing better next time.
You are unable to get clarity or perspective on your successes for fear of appearing smug and avoid celebrating.	This is a fear we can eliminate easily as it only actually exists in our heads. Decide if you are compromising your values by being a success? If success meets with your values, then remove the judgement.
You try to bargain your way out of situations by making excuses for your behaviours or inaction.	What advice would you give to a friend who was making excuses and avoiding taking action. How would you help someone to feel less afraid? Sometimes the solution can be as simple as listening to our own advice.

You numb the pain of fear by self-medicating rather than addressing the cause of the fear.	Self-medicating to distract or numb the pain of fear is common. Often it is harmless; however, some behaviours can have devastating effects on our health and wellbeing. Take some time to notice all the ways in which you avoid or distract yourself. Start by replacing a bad habit with a good one. Swap out the wine for a good walk in the fresh air. Self-medicating can become self-care.

BOOK RECOMMENDATIONS

Daring Greatly; Dare to Lead; Rising Strong; and Braving the Wilderness – Brené Brown

No one does fear, judgment, shame, blame, or vulnerability better than Brené Brown. I was a little late coming to the party and only recently discovered these incredible books. They've completely revolutionised how I approach my journey through life and business. I can now see where I made and created mistakes, and where I was strong. Where I was prepared to be vulnerable, and how I could be proud of my determination to remain curious and grow from my experiences.

I adore the process of questioning, why does this have meaning for me? Where is the learning here? What is on the other side of this discomfort? Reading is a habit of successful people. The busiest and most successful entrepreneurs in the world, read every day. If you think you don't have time to read, I challenge you to think again. I'm an audio and podcast junkie – I literally cannot get enough of other people's wisdom and how it inspires me to work harder to own my story. No one has inspired my determination to grow more than Brené Brown. Making peace with your fears and the ridiculous yet effective avoidance strategies you create is ground zero for a process and practice of change. So, if there is something you need to let go of, change, adapt, or make peace with, I promise the way to do it will be in her books.

Fear is not a problem in business or in life. We need it, and we're built to deal with it. The problems come when we allow fear to control us. When we walk into a dark room, we instinctively tread carefully and try to feel our way around. Switch on a light and everything looks quite different. Courage and purpose return instantaneously, and we go about our business unaware of the burden of fear.

CHAPTER 6

Big 7 No. 5
Guilt to
Forgiveness

"Who you are is defined by what you are willing to struggle for."

MARK MANSON

Guilt

The fact of having committed a specified or implied offence or crime.

Guilt is a powerful and subjective word. It can hold a deep and compelling meaning when we apply it to situations of wrongdoing, crime, and hurt. Committing a crime or causing harm, is, I hope something very few of us will truly experience. But we have, I'm certain, all felt guilty at some time in our lives. *I feel guilty for leaving my friends at work to pursue my dream of owning my own business. I feel guilty for not spending more time with my family while I concentrate on my business. I feel guilty for succeeding when others around me are not. I feel guilty when I am invited to go out with my friends, and I don't have the time or the money to go. I feel guilty when I fail.* These are all things I've said to myself at some time or another.

Feeling guilty and being guilty are clearly not the same thing. We impose guilt upon ourselves to somehow lessen the pain of what we're experiencing when we're struggling or feeling vulnerable. When we are overwhelmed and when we are exposed. Guilt in any form requires evidence in order to convict. So, within this self-imposed guilt, where is the evidence? Choosing to feel guilty as a way of numbing the real pain leads to more misery. Because when guilt gets a grip on us, we lose all power to solve the problem. We are driven to blame ourselves or others for something that is not right or not working. This drains our energy and our focus, and the real problem or mystery goes unsolved.

Consider what would happen if a real crime were committed, let's say a painting is stolen from an art gallery and the security system was old and unreliable. If the police spent all their time berating the owner of the gallery for not updating their security and the owner felt miserable and blamed themselves for being so remiss, the crime would never be solved. Just as our hypothetical police and gallery owner must stop victim blaming and start looking for the real criminal, we must look at the real baddy in the situation when we feel guilty. Our values, as amazing as they are, can sometimes get in the way, as can our drivers and beliefs. They trigger feelings of guilt when they're challenged or ignored. In this chapter, we'll explore how guilt shows up and how a simple process of investigation can reveal who the real culprits might be.

Forgiveness

The action or process of forgiving or being forgiven.

Seeking forgiveness is what we do when we know we've done wrong. We try to make it right. But in business it is rare that we've actually committed a crime or done something to hurt or harm another person, so it's our perception of wrongdoing that creates the guilt. Guilt is an emotion most of us understand. We've all eaten the last biscuit in the packet or found a fiver on the floor in a pub and popped it in our pocket. *Abbie did you punch your sister? Abbie did you wear my jacket and spill gin all over it? Mum, did you eat my last Easter egg while I was in bed asleep.* Yep, yep, and yep. Sorry is usually enough when we've hurt someone else. But when we are the culprit, the victim, the judge, and the jury things start to get tricky.

When we experience feelings of guilt, acceptance and forgiveness for our perceived crime is how we begin to move past it. We have to accept that sometimes we'll have to do things that others may not fully understand. We need to accept that in business there is room for everyone to succeed but achieving your own version of that success requires sacrifice and commitment – sacrifice and commitment can trigger guilt.

Acceptance of what our values, beliefs, and driver behaviours mean to us is our first "crime" scene. For example, I have a core value as a homemaker. I love to tidy my house, I love cooking nice meals, I love looking after my family. I value my role as the person who keeps all the other shit in check. This doesn't have to be my role, but it is a role that I want, enjoy, and value. So, when I embarked on starting a business and my attention was taken elsewhere, the shit started to hit the fan. Questions like "what's for tea mum?" were interpreted as a full-on attack:

"I haven't had time to shop; I've been busy today. There's a pizza in the freezer, can't you have that?"

"We had pizza yesterday."

"Oh my god, seriously, do I have to do everything around here?"

Guilt is what made me react in that way because I was't meeting my core value as a homemaker; I was failing, and it was because "I" was choosing to have a business. Forgiveness and acceptance of the fact that it was my core value that was having a tantrum and not me was a lesson I learnt the hard way. During my time of isolation, guilt consumed me in ways you cannot begin to imagine. Discovering how to navigate my values beliefs and behaviours is how I learnt to accept the process and start to forgive myself.

My struggle with *guilt*

THE STORIES WE TELL OURSELVES

I hope to keep this chapter short and to the point. Guilt is not something any of us need or want to dwell on. It's a shitty, fucked up emotion that has no meaning other than to make us feel bad. So, I plan to demonstrate here where guilt was showing up for me and then offer you some quick and easy ways to kick that shit to the kerb, *tout suite*. First, I want to reiterate that this is not a helpful guide to how to deal with actual guilt. In our lives we may be unfortunate enough to bear witness to real pain and guilt. I add to this grief. Grief is a process we will all go through and when guilt and grief buddy up, then we need professional help to work through that. I have my own story with grief. Thankfully, I learnt how to hold that grief up high and well away from any guilt that was lurking down below. This took a lot of work and professional intervention, so if you're experiencing guilt and grief please seek support.

Ok that is the heavy shit out of the way, and now let's look at the stories we tell ourselves that lead to mixed emotions, over reactions, and exhaustion.

Guilt makes you defensive. Your instinct is to point the finger. When my sister and I had taken our bickering and fighting to such a volume that my mum would come tearing into the room shouting, "who started it?" We'd dutifully point the finger and blame each other. My mum's response was to punish us both; she had little tolerance for our constant bickering and no time for a lengthy trial that would simply end in stalemate. Me and Kate are tight when it comes to battling a common enemy. So, she would simply hand down the punishment, which was usually either separation and solitary confinement, putting us each in a different room to ponder our behaviour, or she would take away whatever we were arguing about and leave us both pissed off. I used to like the solitary option. If I were the lucky one, I'd get to go to our bedroom where I could sit quietly and play with the toys that were in there without competition or annoyance. The less fortunate twin got put in the bathroom. I spent a lot of time in the bathroom playing with loo rolls and turning shampoo bottles and after shaves into characters for my games. We never learnt to keep the noise down or stop fighting, and we rarely said sorry to each other. This was what guilt and punishment was like in the 70s. At least in my world. Nowadays, we reason with our kids. We placate them and try to encourage them to work out their differences. Sometimes, anyway. I didn't do this very much with my kids either. I opted for the just pick one and punish them approach, which was just as ineffective for long-term growth and self-awareness. I would walk into the room and just start yelling at one of them (usually Ellie), "you're old enough to know better, leave your sister alone". So here we have it. My story with crime and punishment. I remember getting blamed for stuff all the time and having no clue what it was I had done wrong. Punishments came hard in our house. Not physical ones, but my mum was consistent with carrying out her promises. It normally ended with isolation, disconnection, and no due process. It didn't matter if I was the one who started it or not. The punishment was the same. So, I didn't really learn how to deal with guilt.

Later in my life, this became problematic. Anytime something went wrong I accepted the blame instantly and without question. In relationships, difficulties and arguments were always my fault. When people treated me badly, I blamed myself. When things were unfair, I convinced myself I didn't deserve them anyway. This led to a long list of dysfunctional, co-dependant relationships and some great material for my later journey of self-awareness.

I am grateful for my past because without it, I wouldn't be who I am. And I'm certain I wouldn't be in the loving relationship that I find myself in today. Dave is my reward for doing the work. He is the gift that keeps on giving, and I remind myself every day of how grateful I am to share my life with him. And I'm proud of us both for the work we put in on our relationship, every day, to enjoy this beautiful life.

Our relationship is not without its ups and downs. But this time there's no blame or self-deprecation. Only conversation and connection. Curiosity and forgiveness. My newfound guilt management skills have, however, been put well and truly to the test since starting my business. This has to date been the biggest test of our relationship and I am pleased to say so far, we're winning.

SELF-SABOTAGE

As you've come to realise in the previous chapters, it's my understanding that our drivers, values, and beliefs shape us. They're a constant pop up of questions, responses, fears, and subconscious behaviours that determine how we respond and how we operate within our lives. Understanding them is vital and when it comes to struggles such as guilt, it's imperative that we know what we're dealing with. Learning to understand my values, behaviours, and beliefs and when they were helping and when they were hurting me was a life changer. I had, as you'll know by now, spent much of my early years in business battling and struggling. Questioning why things were so hard and suffering when things didn't work out.

Low self-esteem and limiting beliefs created in our early years will influence our values in later life. Negative experiences at school, sibling rivalry and comparisons, and lack of encouragement mean that we can hold values that aren't entirely our own. Or at least not ones that serve us well. I grew up thinking that college and university was something other people did. Working hard, having a job, keeping house, and being a wife and mother was a good and honourable thing. And it is. Trouble was, I thought this was all I could be. So, I never challenged myself to do more. Each time life offered me an opportunity to grow, I'd hesitate, avoid, and self-sabotage my way out of it as quickly as possible. Deliberately underperforming at school is one example. Embarking on and pursuing shitty relationships and staying in them, despite my own better judgment, is another example. And passing up life changing opportunities such as promotions, because it meant elevating myself to a level of achievement that I didn't believe I deserved, is yet another example. I used the excuse that I wanted to be a homemaker as a barrier to becoming more. Believing that I didn't deserve anything more became a self-fulfilling prophecy.

So, what does this have to do with guilt? Well, here's the thing – if we prioritise and hold on to values without context, they quickly become shitty values. Ones that no longer serve us, ones that lead us to make poor choices or procrastinate. Guilt shows up as a way of preventing us from being curious about our values and stops us from letting go of the labels we have, over time, assigned ourselves. I labelled myself as average at a very early age. Constant comparisons to my siblings, friends, and classmates meant that my level of ambition was set pretty low. The family script plays a huge part in dictating our ambition, and for me that script meant I was not expected to excel. My early belief that one bright kid in the family was enough kept me small. Parents, teachers, and peers play a significant role in making us who we are. The whole nature versus nurture debate is not one I feel equipped to explore in depth, so suffice it to say that we all, not just me, we all are affected by our upbringing in both amazing and positive ways, and on occasion, some rather strange or limiting ways too. My mum and dad were affected by their parents and theirs before them. It's what family is all about. I know my values, beliefs, and behaviours have had an enormous impact on my parenting style. The hope is that with each generation we learn to adapt and grow and in time, do a little better. Guilt was the feeling of disappointing my family script. I had lived with this identify of 'average' for so long that to let go of it seemed cruel.

The dynamic between my twin sister Kate and I had been engrained from the womb. She was the protector; the one who cleared up my mess. Her identity was formed around her role as the elder twin. As I have mentioned in previous chapters, this was not without its advantages for me. I regularly got myself into situations that required intervention or rescue of some description, from picking a fight at the local skate park, only to have Kate take the punch that was destined for me, to finding myself homeless, depressed, and desperate, arriving on Kate's doorstep with two carrier bags and a 10-month old baby who refused to sleep. Kate, as she had many times before and many times since, rescued me from my own fucked up decisions and put me back together again. It wasn't until I met Lisa that I began to understand the role I was playing, not only in my many co-dependant relationships but also in my family. I was playing the role of the victim.

Embarking on a journey of self-actualisation doesn't come without its pitfalls. There's a long process of re-adjustment, and it comes with consequences. Changing a dynamic within an existing relationship is hard. Those around us, who love us the most, can become confused by the change. Used to having their part to play, suddenly we're the one ripping up the script and asking everyone to improvise. No one likes improv, do they? Letting go of my limiting beliefs and victim mentality was liberating; however, I struggled to let go fully of the role I had played so well. This brought up feelings of guilt, and for a long time, whilst working to build mental resilience, I was still silently sabotaging any real progress. Thankfully, I was able to overcome the struggle and let go of those old beliefs when I began my counselling training. Soon after, when I met Dave, I was at last able stand on my own two feet in a relationship that was functional, loving, and healthy. Years later, this could not be said for my business, and I wasted a lot of time at the start, self-sabotaging my own progress. Just as things started to go well, procrastination and guilt would pop up and send me sideways. Self-sabotage happens when we're reluctant to let go of something or fearful of what the next step might mean. Guilt is a common cause of self-sabotage, as is low self-esteem. For me letting go of my label as the needy twin brought with it guilt and fear, as it meant having to brave the wilderness all alone. Starting a business brought this all flooding back. The guilt came from having to make choices this time. Having to give up time with my family and with Dave to work on my business. Guilt began to creep in as I worked to relabel myself as a 'Female Entrepreneur'. I was out in the wilderness again, and instead of being brave and pushing forward, I sabotaged my progress through guilt and low self-esteem. Working purposefully towards success, while secretly sabotaging my progress from within.

KNOW WHERE YOUR WEAK SPOTS ARE

When our values are challenged, it can be exhausting. The struggle comes when we're under constant attack from our own judgements. Trying to ignore or adjust a value to fit with what's being asked of us is nearly impossible.

Let's step forward a few years to the moment I qualified as a coach. I signed up for a 24-week course. It was delivered over webinar, and at the same time I was also planning a wedding. My brain was in overwhelm, while I navigated the process of learning as well as trying to be present in my life. The life I had dreamed of. It was all going so well for the first month, and then as the wedding was fast approaching, I began to sink into overwhelm. I couldn't cope with trying to divide my metal energy and myself between this incredible yet challenging learning and thinking about wedding dresses and flowers. The diploma won. Our wedding was amazing and simple and wonderful, but by the time I got to the wedding day, I was completely and utterly mentally drained. The day went by so quickly, and I felt like I was barley there. My core driver to commit to others had taken over. I was apparently more prepared to fuck up my wedding, than I was my studies. Because I love and trust my husband without question and he loves and supports me, somehow, I think I decided that whatever went wrong, he would forgive me. I didn't have that level of confidence in my ability to pass my diploma, so that had to be my priority.

The wedding came and went, and we managed to carve out 3 days away for our honeymoon, which was and still is one of my happiest memories. It was only 3 days because not only did I refuse to go away for longer because of my studies, I had spent half our wedding budget on the diploma, so money was tight. Dave, bless him, was so supportive of this, and when he said, "babe your dreams are bigger than just one day", I fell in love with him all over again. But the moment we returned, I was straight back into it, and a week later I handed in my coursework. Neat, tidy, organised, and complete. On the exact date that it was due. It hadn't even occurred to me that this date was fluid. That's the date, so that's the date was what I kept saying to myself. Why would you need to change that? How weird. So, when others on my course were asking for extensions, which were freely available by the way, I was confused.

After handing in my folder I questioned my driver. "Why did I have to comply? I could have asked for an extension and made things a lot easier for myself and relaxed more during the wedding". Well I think we know the reason for that, my core beliefs, values and drivers that said, "do as you are told, deliver what is asked, don't let people down, follow the rules". Why am I telling you all this? Because I want to paint you a picture of where my mental resilience was at this point.

Already mentally exhausted, I had also, 6 weeks prior to finishing my diploma, signed up for the Train the Coach programme. Another 6-month training programme that would give me the skills and the opportunity to teach other coaches. So, the moment one training ended, another began. I was addicted to this amazing roller coaster of learning and discomfort. It was awesome. And in January 2017, I gained my training licence. It was a dream come true. Not only that, I was asked to co-host the webinars, the very ones I had been so petrified to attend. I was elated. Exhausted, but elated.

I remained in fulltime employment and struggled to juggle my new coaching responsibilities and my existing commitment. Terrified of letting my new coaching community down, I willingly began my journey of becoming a professional coach, the only problem was that by this time, I was already experiencing depression and anxiety due to the immense pressure I had put myself under. It was as though my poor brain was like – "seriously dude we need a break, go watch some telly". I couldn't; I kept going with devastating consequences. Fast forward 9 months.

The first time I decided to leave my job, in September 2017, and go it alone as a fulltime coach, I was ill prepared. I had no clue how to run a business, and as I have pointed out in a previous chapter, I hadn't anticipated just how long it would take and how hard it would be. We were skint, and it was my fault. Guilt was creeping in, and despite Dave's unwavering support, I was beating myself up daily with guilt and frustration. "It's ok" I would say to myself, "I'll just keep working harder and harder and harder, something will start going right sooner or later surely." But as we know, it didn't, and guilt finally consumed me.

I'd spent all our money and now I couldn't pay it back. I was the reason we were suffering. Dave never said a word. His painful glances said it all. When I was upset or clearly spiralling, he would look at me with so much love and fear. He wasn't afraid of being skint, he was afraid of what was happening to the lovely woman he had just married, the one who loves to cook dinners and keep house, who sorts all the bills and organises the family events, who tells him when his kids are coming for the weekend, who was easy to be around – kind, funny, and forgiving – he was terrified that she had been possessed by the devil and was slowly turning into a crazy woman.

Guilt thrives when our defences and energy are low. It infiltrates our inner thoughts, and before long, this starts to show on the outside too. "Have I got any sandwiches made for tomorrow boo?", Dave asked one day. My outward response was to roll my eyes and say, "No I will do it now". In my head, the voices were screaming: *seriously can't you make your own sandwiches? Can't you see I'm drowning here? Oh, you think I have just been sat on my arse all day, do you? Well no, I have not actually, David, I've been slogging my guts out trying to find a way to pay back all our savings and make a living.* He couldn't hear those voices, but the words were written all over my face.

"Shall we have fish and chips as a treat tonight boo?", Dave asked one Friday evening after a particularly tough week at work. I replied, "Err yeah ok if you want them; we don't have any cash though; there is stuff in the freezer, and I don't mind cooking." In my head, I was dying: *Oh my god fish and chips that's going to cost at least £20 for the 3 of us we have no money I can't say no because then he will start to resent me even more because it's my fault we don't have any money.* Again, he never heard that, but he could see it in my eyes.

Guilt is not the problem; the problem is what it makes you do. My inability to process that guilt was tearing me down. It was consuming me. I felt guilty when Dave left for work; I felt guilty when we couldn't afford to enjoy Christmas without the strain of debt. I felt inconsolable when we had to start cancelling charitable direct debits and donations and cutting back on food shopping and bills and sacking our lovely window cleaner. It was humiliating and true to form – where there is guilt there is shame and blame.

Isolation, shame, guilt, blame, confusion, overwhelm, and exhaustion. And I couldn't process any of it. It consumed me. So yes, I did spend our money – with Dave's blessing. Yes, we were in a slightly sticky patch when it came to money – but we still had food, shelter, and each other, and most important of all, no one else was complaining. My self-imposed guilt was selfish. What I was inadvertently doing was playing the victim. I was drowning, and I needed someone or something to save me. Guilt loves a victim. Except no one came. I made bad decisions about my business. Guilt made me lily pad and question decisions; it made me desperate and needy and distracted me from actually finding a solution to our predicament. It leaked out over everything I touched.

How I embraced *forgiveness*

DIFFERENTIATE YOUR "WHAT" FROM YOUR "WHY"

My core values were forcing me once again to make a choice between being a homemaker and pursuing my goal to become a professional coach and business owner. By neglecting my desire for and my joy in being a good wife and mother, I was feeling like a constant failure. I had decided that to become a business owner, I couldn't do everything, and I had to sacrifice the part of my life that I decided was negotiable. Except the part of my life I believed was negotiable was the very reason why I chose to have a business in the first place. I wanted to fulfil my passion for coaching, absolutely. But I also wanted to be present at home. To be there to cook meals and enjoy family time. I was searching for work life balance, and yet I was choosing to tip the scales in favour of work. "They will love me regardless", I had kept telling myself. I suffered, and it almost destroyed me. This wasn't the only value I was ignoring; I had sacrificed time with my family too – not just feeding them and picking up after them. I had sold my fun time down the river too. Weekends were non-existent. Some weeks I hardly noticed it was the weekend, and evenings were a blur.

The result of all of this was, as we know now, for me to go get a job at Atlantic Refrigeration. So much of my joy and passion came flooding back. Not only was I feeling useful and occupied again, I was able to separate my time better and start to ringfence my family time as well as get my house and finances in order.

See here is the thing, when you have literally 24 hours a day and 7 days a week to get shit done, you tend to procrastinate, avoid, and slide. I had less time to do stuff, yet I was getting more done. It was magical. The guilt lifted because I was contributing financially, and the process of feeling useful again helped me to get perspective. I stopped feeling like the baddy in the story, and when I stopped blaming myself for our situation, it was so much easier to concentrate on meeting my values as well as achieving my goals.

So, when in January 2020, I chose to take the leap of faith again and left my job at Atlantic, I was determined not to make the same mistakes. Dave had started to get used to me being normal again, and we had some money behind us this time. Dave was also very aware of how frail Jack was becoming, and he knew that my being home was the right thing to do. He was able to relax more at work, knowing I was home.

I was determined to learn from past experiences, and so in December 2019, just before I left Atlantic Refrigeration, I made sure we were ready. This meant a process of reflection and gratitude. To see where the pitfalls were and to ensure we didn't drop back into them again. And in January 2020 I was once again officially a 'fulltime coach'. I gave myself 3 months to build a solid foundation. I would have time to work on the mentorship programme as well as networking and creating my online group coaching programme. I would get an ad done and get the blogs written that I had been putting off. I would focus my time on the tasks that I knew would generate income in my business and learn more skills along the way. I would also have time to write this book. Something I had wanted to do for so long. Three months was possibly a little optimistic and when in the May Jack was 'still with us', I was strangely grateful for lockdown as I was able to avoid the guilt of not getting it all done in time … as now I had lockdown to continue my work. To get the book done and be present at home, for me is one of the many positives I chose to focus on at this time.

January 2020 the time was right. "I need to get this book done", I said to my coaching friends. "I just feel like I have a lot to say, and when I've said it, then I can really move on, does that make sense?" "Yes, absolutely", they said. So, writing a book is a lot easier to do than I thought. At least when you work with a writing coach, that is. However, it takes time. You must plan it properly, decide on who it is for and why and you must write it. So, this is what my time would be spent doing.

The other thing I was determined to do was to stay true to my values, my joy, and my passion. I was not about to give those up again. I had in a moment of clarity realised why I wanted to train as a coach in the first place it was so I could have more freedom and enjoy my life. Not to work 70 hours a week. Remembering my *why* was a key moment for me. Separating my *what* from my *why* was even more fundamental. *What* I want to do is to be a coach, to help other women to navigate the journey and make it just a bit easier and less of a struggle for them. I want to earn money from my business, and I want to be my own boss. I want to write books and hold workshops and hang out with my coaching buddies and be home in time to cook tea. I want balance.

Work-life balance can mean a number of things. Separating work from home or managing the overlaps. When you work from home, separating them physically is not always easy, so separating them mentally is where we need to focus our energy. This is where the struggle sits for many of us. Working from home, as many discovered during lockdown, is not the easy option. Not only do we have actual interruptions, we also create a lot of noise in our own head. Unable to focus on one task without being distracted by the constant chatter of judgement and fear and the sound of time passing us by.

My *why* is very different: I want to be a coach so I can give back to others in the kind and selfless way that it was given to me. Why I want to do this is to honour the memory of a dear and precious friend who was not able to do that herself. She had the opportunity to continue to change lives taken away from her, so I chose to take the torch and carry it forward. My *why* will never appear on a FB post, and I struggle to write it now. My *why* has threads of guilt running through it. Lisa would be devastated if she thought for one second that I was doing any of this for her. Lisa never planned to use her skills in business. If she had, she'd be giving Brené a run for her money, I can tell you. She was so gifted and yet she stood by her why: "I learnt this all so it would help me, Abbie, not to run a business. I did this so I can grow as a person, be a great mum and a great wife. I love my life they are all I need."

Guilt, however well-handled, was driving me to push forward with something without really appreciating why. I needed to own this shit quick, and so that's what I did. I reframed my why and here it is: *My why is to continue a path of growth and self-awareness to use my new skills to pay it forward and enjoy my life.*

This new version of my why helps me to stay in the right lane when it comes to tough decisions in my business and when it comes to where I find my joy. I have approached this second stage of my business feeling much calmer. I have safeguarded my time and become far more productive. I enjoy every moment of my life and my business now. I am meeting my core values, and Dave has sandwiches ... most days, and I have let go of the guilt I was carrying and replaced it with purpose. My core values have stood me in good stead, and mindset tools have enabled me to ensure they are used to the best of my ability.

BE HONEST WITH YOURSELF AND HAVE THE CONVERSATION

There is still that little twinge of guilt when Dave's alarm goes off at 5.20am. Most mornings I was getting up with him, as Jack had inevitably pooped on the floor and I would hear Dave call up from the kitchen, "Ab your dog has done another shit". "Right, he is my dog when he shits on the floor, he's your dog when he comes trotting up to see you when you come home at night". Dave doesn't have a lot of time to get ready in the morning before he needs to be out the door. He certainly wasn't able to factor in picking up piles of dog poop and scrubbing carpets into his morning ritual, so I would go down and clean up the mess, and then go back and sit in bed with my coffee and wait for the time when Maya had to be up for school. "Have a nice day babe", he would say as he left. I felt my heart tighten. "He wouldn't be saying that if I was going out to work, would he"? He must really resent the fact that I am home, and he is working, I began to think. "No no no" I quickly started to say to myself; "Don't start feeling guilty again, don't let guilt back in," I whispered to myself to keep me from sinking to that place. Instead, I leapt out of bed the moment he left and started busying myself as a way of justifying still being at home while he had to brave the M27 on a wet and dark Tuesday.

One day when Dave came home and he was feeling particularly tired, he was huffing and puffing as he does when he is either cold, tired, or hungry. I started my normal daily justification run down of things I had completed, people I had helped, and conversations I had had. Not to mention if Jack had had a good or bad day. He sighed and said, "Well that's nice, I've been soaked through to the skin about 5 times and not had time for lunch."

No, no. Please don't do this to me. I cannot get dragged into guilt again, I thought to myself. "Oh, babe that sounds horrible, what do you fancy for tea?", I asked; desperate to dismiss my guilt. "I'm just going to have a pizza. I need to go to bed" (frozen pizza is the go-to food for whenever anyone in our house is feeling bored, sad, tired, miserable, or can't be arsed. And like many others, in our family we eat our pain.) "No, this cannot be happening again. Please don't make me feel guilty Dave. I cannot get dragged into that place again. If you are sad then that makes me feel guilty". I blurted out. "I'm not trying to make you feel guilty I'm just saying", he said, looking a little confused. "I know babe, I know, and I'm just letting you know that right now I'm on the edge. I can feel things starting to move, but I must stay focused and motivated I can't go back to guilt". "What do you mean go back to guilt?", Dave said, shocked at the idea that I could be feeling guilty. "Guilt consumed me last time Dave. It made me do crazy shit just to try to stop the pain. I swear to god its why I failed last time. One step forward, two steps back, every time. I feel bad when you leave in the morning for work. But the truth is I can't do everything; I can't work fulltime, run a business, and run a house. I can't". (Now to be clear there are women in my network doing exactly that, and if I found out they were writing a book at the same time too, I think that would finish me; but truth is I don't want to do it all. I don't want this to break me). "Honestly, if I could just ..." "Stop it's fine", Dave said, "I get it, I'm just tired babe, I know how hard you're working, and I want to help, I'm not trying to make you feel guilty".

"Cool, ok thank you", I said, feeling suddenly liberated from my self-imposed jail. "Awesome, so while we're on the subject, if you could make your own sandwiches and wash up tonight that would be great too", I said with a smile and a wink. I'm sure this irritated him slightly, as he usually does both of those things, but he chose in that moment to nod instead and say, "ok babe if that's what you need".

Being brave enough to share how I was feeling was a big step for me. This was probably the first time I had ever processed guilt out loud and stopped self-sabotage in its tracks. I had begun to learn how to notice it and what it was doing to me. I feel it's so important for us to have open and honest conversations with those closest to us when we embark on our journey. Resentment builds up when we don't process our feelings. If guilt, fear, confusion, isolation, overwhelm, or even lack of time is causing you to struggle, then it stands to reason that you'll need help. If you don't ask for help, then you can't expect to get it. When we push through and punish ourselves, we become a martyr to the cause. Really that's not how we want to feel, is it?

If we're not able to ask for help because we're placing judgements on it, then we're also placing judgment on giving help. Say what you need and be clear about it. Tell your family and friends what you need from them and give them the opportunity to give it to you. Withholding a request for help and then resenting others for their lack of support is self-sabotage. I have included a short exercise in the workbook download to help with this. For now, rest assured that having the conversation out loud with the people concerned is in no way as painful as the misery we can inflict upon ourselves when these conversations stay only in our heads.

Dave and our girls are my world. Some days it is as big as I want my world to be and other days, I feel an overwhelming urge to burst out of my comfy little bubble and make a mark on the world. A mark I hope will help others and one that will mean a better world for our girls to grow up in. I help so many amazing businesswomen to burst out of their bubbles and into the world. They have amazing products and so much passion. The world needs that. There is no limit as far as I can see for passion and kindness; the world is currently operating at a deficit, or at least that is what the media portrays. I avoid the news at all costs and get only snippets when my sister comes round, or something pops up on Facebook or Twitter. The snippets I see are sad and scary so the more women I can support to build confidence in their "why" and stop apologising for their dreams, the better the world will be. If that's not an antidote to guilt, I don't know what is.

IT'S A LEAP OF FAITH KIND OF THING

Before you take a leap of faith, you first need to be sure that you're jumping over the right gap and second that you're going to land where you want to be. It's not enough to power through regardless. Pain is not a justification for hard work, and we don't need to have the pain of guilt to drive us forward. Accepting that sometimes things will be good and other times they will be a bit shit is just part of life, and it's part of business too. Guilt drains us of our energy and makes us want to blame. So, find out what's causing your guilt – which of your core values is crying out for attention – and fix it. Aligning your goals with your values is how we grease the wheels. It's how we can be sure we're moving in the right direction. Do we need to be brave to take a leap of faith, even when we've done everything we possibly can to make sure that we're going to make it across the gap and the landing will be solid? Yes. Do we need to say a little pray or promise before we jump? Maybe. But the best way to ensure your leap is good is to put the preparation work in.

Don't try to jump with your arms full. If you're carrying guilt around like a sick puppy, hoping someone will come and save you, you're not ready for the leap. Put the work in and lay your guilt to rest. Will it pop up from time to time? Maybe, but this time you know what to do with it. I carried guilt around and let it dictate my path for too many years because I was ashamed to admit it was there, and I was ill equipped to deal with it. That's no longer true. And I can honestly say I feel so much lighter. I still struggle, I still stress, I still feel the pain of failure, only this time I don't let guilt join in. I have those struggles because I'm brave and trying to be better, and there's nothing to feel guilty about.

WHERE GUILT SHOWS UP IN BUSINESS

Guilt can show up in all sorts of ways. It sits underneath many of our struggles. It causes us to overthink and doubt ourselves and our skills. The simple solution to guilt is to look for evidence. If there is no evidence to support your hesitation or struggle, then there is little point in wasting time and energy sitting in the discomfort. Guilt is debilitating in business and can be tricky to overcome. But to be successful, we must deal with it.

Guilt is an unnecessary burden in business. Yet it is one that we do encounter. Having the conversation with whoever or whatever is at the root of your guilt is an excellent place to begin. Shining a light on the struggle can be all we need to do to unburden ourselves. If you're carrying around something that's weighing you down, drop it. Then ask yourself, "do I really need to be carrying this? Why am I choosing to take this with me? Who is telling me I have to take this with me?" Thoughts are powerful when we allow them to dictate our emotions and behaviours. Change the thought, change the behaviour.

There are Mindset exercises in the workbook download to help you begin the process of changing those thoughts and focus on asking the right questions to engage your mindset to identify the behaviours, values, or beliefs that might be triggering your guilt. These exercises will help you take back control over how you process these things more positively and productively.

Top Tips Summary – Guilt to Forgiveness

Guilt is a struggle that we are choosing to endure. Emotions will sit in guilt until we give them somewhere else to go. Guilt means we care. If a person or situation is triggering guilt, it's probably because we love and care about them. We don't feel guilty about stuff we don't care about. Trust that the person or situation we care about probably cares about us too. And they will not want us to struggle. So, get a hold on what the story is you are telling yourself and work a process to make peace with it. Our business journey has enough struggles. Real struggles, like working out how to include VAT on an invoice or how to edit content on your website or which events to go to or simple stuff like how much coffee can one person consume in a day before they start talking like Speedy Gonzales.

Here are a few of my tips for managing guilt triggers and repurposing your emotions into more positive and future focused solutions.

Where Guilt Shows Up	Top Tips to Beat Guilt
You feel shame or as though something is eating away at you each time you try to move forward.	Begin by taking a few moments to explore what might be going on for you. If pushing forward with something feels exhausting, then there is a chance that guilt is weighing you down. What are you guilty of? Who will suffer if you do? Who will suffer if you don't?
You spend too much time on tasks that keep you safe and hidden, instead of pushing towards those that challenge you to step outside of your comfort zone.	Understanding your WHY is essential for gaining clarity on what drives you. Be clear about what you've set out to achieve and why you want to achieve it.
You start to experience feelings of resentment, leading to self-sabotaging behaviours.	If you're still struggling to make sense of what's weighing you down, then you may need to get some help to process. Coaching offers excellent tools for clarity and perspective and can help you to work through current emotions and create a more positive mindset moving forward. Ask yourself what ultimately drives your guilt?
You want to stop feeling guilty and start to blame those around you for your struggles.	If there's a person or situation that repeatedly triggers your guilt, then you need to talk about it. Share your feelings and what it means to you and what you're experiencing. This is not about blame. If you need help to have this conversation, then seek support from a professional. Otherwise, a simple, relaxed conversation is usually enough.

You question the cost of what you want to achieve, believing there will be a price to pay for your success.	Guilt can also be a result of positivity. Something great happens, so we need to redress the balance. A belief that for us to win someone else has to fail. Is this true? Can we all be winners? Who actually loses when you win?
You're distracted and overwhelmed by trying to keep everyone else happy.	Running a business takes a lot of time and energy, and there will be times when we have to make a choice between family time and work. Guilt can mean we exhaust ourselves trying to keep everyone happy. Have a conversation. Be clear about the time you need for your business and commit to making time to step back too.
You make a mistake and instead of forgiving yourself you feel guilty, which leads to anxiety and confusion.	Building mental resilience enables us to bounce back from a mistake or set back. Commit to a regular daily practice of acceptance and forgiveness. Over time this will replace any feelings of guilt that may creep in.

BOOK RECOMMENDATION

The Subtle Art of Not Giving a Fuck – by Mark Manson

Mark Manson is an extraordinary writer. He has a huge social media following and a website just full of blogs and downloadable resources. His books the *Subtle Art of Not Giving A Fuck* and *Everything is Fucked* are essential reading for today's world. Manson has a unique and incredibly amusing way of exploring some of the more serious sides of life, society, and the world by making sense of the struggles that lead to so many of the world's social and economic issues. I particularly enjoy his take on holding shitty values and how we can become our own worst enemy by sticking to principles and values that are in fact not our own. They are borrowed or learnt from those closest to us. Most enlightening is his take on the pain we choose. Pain is a natural part of life. No matter who you are, what you have or don't have, you will always experience pain. We need it to motivate and to drive us. Choosing to set up a business by yourself is choosing pain and struggle. It will absolutely be a roller coaster of emotions. But if you choose the right business, the right why, and the right destination, it's a journey filled with so much joy that the pain becomes bearable and the result is life changing. Not giving a fuck, as Manson says, is not about not giving a fuck, it's about choosing what you want to give a fuck about.

CHAPTER 7

Big 7 No. 6 Time **Fatigue** to Time *Management*

*"Time is free but it's priceless.
You cannot own it, but you can use it.
You cannot keep it, but you can spend it.
Once you have lost it you can never get it back."*

HARVEY MACKAY

Time Fatigue

Time is the indefinite continued progress of existence and events in the past, present, and future regarded as a whole. Fatigue is generally defined as a feeling of lack of energy and motivation that can be physical, mental, or both. The dictionary doesn't offer us a clear definition of *time fatigue*. Time is a complex and unexplainable concept. We all have time and understand what it is, yet we can't really explain how it works without science, like in Stephen Hawking's *A Brief History of Time* (1988). My brain explodes the moment anything scientific comes up. Conversations about how the stars we can see in the sky are already gone because it took so long for the light to get here that they are now in fact not there anymore – boom mind fuck.

So, let's be clear, I am not offering any kind of scientific explanation here. Time fatigue, in my opinion, occurs when what we do with our time doesn't meet our expectations of what we hoped we would achieve. For example, if our mind is consumed with following a path of creativity and we spend hours upon hours writing blogs to promote services, yet we have done nothing about finding clients to buy those services, then we can quickly become exhausted. As Mackay explains, we can't own time, but we can use it, and that means turning what we can't see, hear, touch, or taste into something tangible. When we fail to use time in a way that energises us – completing tasks, meeting deadlines, and feeling fulfilled – we can become demotivated, stressed overwhelmed, and exhausted. Those who manage their time well seem to have it all sussed out. Their lives seem less complicated and more complete.

Going to and from work can be mundane, but it offers a framework around which we structure our lives. A beginning, middle, and end to the day. Lunch breaks and of course weekends and paid holidays. When it comes to starting a business, we're still operating with the same number of minutes in our day as everyone else on the planet, but our days seem endless and blur into the weekend. We check our phone to see what day of the week it is or even what month it is. If we're lucky and our kids are still at school, we can at least be held accountable to term times. Without imposed structure, we procrastinate, become isolated, and burn out. We berate ourselves for not having a regular income, and yet we have no way of knowing how much time and effort we're putting in to getting clients. Routine becomes a distant memory – like an old boyfriend, one you are kind of glad isn't there telling you what to do and where to be anymore, but you also kind of miss having someone to get dressed up for.

There is of course the underlying fear that we all live with: time is always running out. But we can't live like that; we can't operate always feeling like today could be our last day. If I did that, it'd be an exhausting day of hugging, eating, and breathing deeply. Followed by a catatonic state of ambivalence. Be grateful, be authentic, seek joy, but I say live each day like its ok to be your last. For me that means no regrets and getting my head around time to be as productive as I can be, so that my days aren't filled with empty regret.

Time Management

The ability to use one's time effectively or productively, especially at work.

Time is a tool that helps us to be productive. We each have 24 hours in our day. We each have 7 days in our week. What we chose to do in that time and how we use it and manage it is entirely up to us. If we fail to make time tangible, it will run away from us. It will simply exist as a thing that puts pressure on what we want to achieve and cause us stress. How we experience time can vary. There are, I believe, two types of time travellers in this world: *through time people* and *in time people*. I'm a through time person, which means I plan, prepare, and think long term. Through time people stay mindful of the passing of time. We rush to get tasks competed, and we always meet a deadline. In time people are more detached from time. They don't feel its pressures in the same way that through time people do. An in time person will sit and be mindful for hours while working on a task and be completely unaware of the clock. Finding out which you are and how you experience time is a great exercise that I share in the workbook download. Whichever you are, good time management is a skill that can be learnt and developed.

Ever wonder how the big business people manage their time? How does a billionaire run a huge multinational corporation with only 12 hours of daylight? They have other people doing shit for them all the time, that's for sure, but really what do they do? How do the big entrepreneurs of our time seem to be so accomplished and yet so chilled out? They control time. Time does not control them. Later in the chapter we'll be looking at ways you can implement behaviours into your day that will enable you to take control of time. Use it well. Be productive and motivated in order to avoid stress, overwhelm, and burnout.

My struggle with *time fatigue*

TAKE ALL THE TIME YOU NEED

Time is the most important factor when running a business. If we aren't purposeful and productive with time, it is unlikely we'll ever be the best we can be. This is true too for life. When it comes to business, we need to be doing what's necessary without creating overwhelm or exhaustion. Being overworked is not effective nor is being lazy or unproductive. I thought when I left my job in 2017 that all I needed to do was work hard at being a coach, and that would get it done. I had no idea what tasks to do to build a business. I just knew I needed to get shit done. I have always been a busy person and pride myself on my organisational and planning sills. I am reliable and always on time. I have, for the most part, had jobs that require methodical planning and organisation. And I have also chosen to use these skills in other ventures, such as event organisation and charitable activities.

On reflection, these vocations and activities all had one thing in common. They all involved other people and a desire to serve. Each of my jobs, right from my first job at the Sea Life Centre at the age of 14, meant directly reacting or responding to a need, want, or desire. I am a problem solver and solution focused person, so when faced with a challenge, I step up. As an employee, we are constantly fed a steady flow of requests. Can you order this? Can you do this for me? Can you find me a … whatever please? Some requests are not even spoken. We can sense that there's something that needs to be done, and we get on with it.

When I left my job to be a coach the first time, I didn't realise just what an impact that employee mindset would have. This affected me in all areas of my business and caused numerous struggles, such as isolation, fear, and overwhelm; time was a huge underlying factor. The thing that I couldn't see, hear, feel, or touch was quietly sabotaging my efforts and causing me anxiety.

Having "all the time in the world" to focus on my business sounded like a great idea. "I've worked hard for this", I said to myself; "I deserve to focus on what I want now". The problem was that I don't do well with too much time. As a through time person I'm compelled to fill the gaps in my day, and as a "semi introvert" and "creative", I also get lost in the moment: writing learning materials and creating courses that I had no one to sell to. Guilt kicked in because I was failing; I had all this time, and yet I was getting nothing done. Confusion started to cloud my mind as I lily padded from one task to another, each one failing or being left incomplete. I panicked about time constantly. I had no idea how to be productive. So, I sought out ways to add structure to my day; however, these were also mistakes. As we know now, collaborations work well when we come from a place of equality. When we seek to collaborate as a lifeline or rescue, it rarely ends well. I was also missing out on things that might have been useful. Such as going to networking events or meeting with other coaches and business owners to share ideas and struggles. I avoided committing to anything because I constantly felt like I should be doing something else, and worst of all, I neglected time with my family. I refused to take a break, ever, and this resulted in exhaustion, overwhelm, anxiety, and depression. All because I couldn't plan my day. Well there was a little more to it than that, but truth was that time was becoming yet another enemy I had to battle against.

As I discussed in Chapter 4, How I Found Clarity, it took a long time for me to make the decision to go back to part-time work. Managing my time was becoming another struggle. What about Jack? I can't leave him for more than a few hours. What if I get a client and they want to see me while I'm at work? What if I don't have time to do what needs to be done in my business? What if I can't keep up with work, home, and business? This was exhausting, but I did eventually make that decision and wow what a difference it made. Immediately, I had structure to my day and to my week. I was able to visualise my week and compartmentalise my tasks. If a client wanted to see me, I simply said, "I can't do 2.30 but I can do 3.30". I had purpose and motivation because my mind was back to being an employee again. This was my comfy place, the place where I thrive and excel. Being useful, managing and organising, being connected again. It worked like a dream. And what I had not expected was that these skills would transfer directly back to my business. Unexpectedly, I became more organised there, too.

Having an entrepreneurial mindset is key to success; however, this doesn't mean giving up on who you are or what makes you tick. It just means finding what works and using it to your advantage. If structure and time management worked as an employee, find ways to incorporate that into your business. If you respond well to time, then use that too. If you are an in time person and like to concentrate or get lost in a task – set a timer or ringfence that time so you can still get other things done.

When the day came to leave my job for the second time, I was determined to keep up these behaviours – to maintain the structure to my day and be even more productive than before. Things were changing for me. I had signed up to a mentoring programme, I was launching my group coaching programme and writing this book. I was now painfully aware of the things that I needed to get done to make my business a success, and these were going to take time. This was a leap of faith. I have seen many fellow women in business be afraid or unable to take the leap. To go from employed to business owner is not a decision anyone should take lightly. Even if you aren't weighed down by the burden of maintaining a level of income. Setting up a business costs money, so you need to be sure this is what you want. Many women in business do both: they have steady jobs and projects or side hustles. This is a great way to fulfil your passion, while earning extra income without the pressure or panic that comes when you have bills you can't pay. There are so many ways in which to have a business nowadays: multilevel marketing, affiliate links, side hustles, and passion projects. Find what works for you. Each venture will, however, require excellent time planning, as making time tangible is a way to survive and thrive.

WHAT TIME DO YOU HAVE?

Time can play tricks on you, and time fatigue was certainly the cause of much of my struggle when I gave up work to become a coach the first time. When I went back to work part time, I joined a business mentoring programme called the 80/20 Club. An online platform with an affordable monthly fee that offered learning materials, video tutorials, live calls, and expert advice and accountability. Oh, my days I was in heaven, and I immediately immersed myself into this awesome game changing process. It was like opening the door to Willy Wonka's chocolate factory. Everywhere I turned there were tasty treats: offers and insights of things that felt familiar and yet enlightening. I was experiencing what I maybe already knew on some level, but this time I heard it. I saw it. I smelt it. I tasted and felt it. There were a few surprises, and I hadn't realised how much I'd been ignoring my value for growth and missing the learning process.

Created by the brilliant Lauryn Bradley, the 80/20 Club is not only a buffet of business expertise and wisdom, it's delivered in a simple no-nonsense time savvy way. Lauryn's superpower is time. Controlling it, using it well, and making income from it.

This was not all entirely new information to me. I had been introduced to a variety of time management tasks, and yet few had resonated. Lauryn's approach forced me to challenge my beliefs around money as well as my use of time. I'm a busy person. I'm organised and I get shit done. However, and this is where our mindset needs to shift. Though I was busy, I wasn't prioritising the tasks within my business that directly led to income. I was so fearful and confused about looking pushy that I inadvertently avoided all opportunities to sell myself. I had stories in my head such as, "you're a coach, this is your calling, your passion, you can't appear to be selling your skills". I was doing everything necessary to be a coach and help others, everything except value myself enough to charge for it. I was getting in my own way and sabotaging myself. I was invisible.

So, I sat alone at home, creating materials and offers that no one would ever see, trying to learn skills I thought I needed and spending way too much time being busy with stuff that never earnt me a penny. I was allowing my beliefs and my values to dictate my behaviours and actions, and I was getting nowhere.

Built upon the Pareto Principle of 80% return from 20% output, when I opened the door to the 80/20 Club, it felt like I'd discovered a secret room. It was as though it had stayed hidden all this time until I was ready. The programme is for female entrepreneurs and small business owners. Had I found this back in 2017, I wouldn't have been ready. The learning would've been perfect and exactly what I needed at the start, except my mindset was so distorted with struggles that I wouldn't have been able to use it well. Thankfully, I got my mindset shit together, and the opportunity to join came just at the right time. Suddenly, all the good things I was doing were validated and the realisation of where I was failing were blatantly obvious, I had no choice other than to dive right in. I confess I did succumb to my previous pattern of learning, and completion compulsion hit hard. I was so curious to find out what was in there that I watched every video and looked at every exercise. I spent days in uninterrupted absorption, just taking in all the amazing stuff that was there. Any time we are ready to take a step up to the next level, in my experience is a double-edged sword. The feeling of excitement to finally be making progress and the undeniable weight of awareness of just how much work is involved in order to make it a success. I was now painfully aware of what I needed to get done, and my first thought was: "I need to make time for this".

I leaned into the learning and gave myself up to it. I followed the steps in the order in which it was suggested. Luckily one of the very first exercises in the programme was the "Priority Picker". A simple diagram or flow chart that encourages the user to filter each of their daily tasks through with the goal of prioritising the tasks that earn income. OMG, I love this tool. It took some purposeful practice before it became a habit, but now I use it every day. It's helped me get my head around time and perspective on where I was failing to manage my time and my energy meant a straight swap over to time focus.

While I'm acutely aware of the time around me (through time person), my core driver to complete things would often override my panic and awareness of time. The uncomfortable feeling of running out of time was, at that moment, more attractive than the feeling of leaving stuff unfinished. I worked hard to reframe this, and when 1 behaviour needs to change, we don't destroy it or ignore it; we replace it with another behaviour, one that with practice can feel comfortable. A good way to swap a behaviour that isn't working is to find one that still meets the same value. For example, I love to complete things, make them neat, and meet expectations. If I swap the joy of completing a task with the joy of meeting an expectation (i.e. a time limit), I can feel joyful about that too. I use a combination of time management strategies to help me to balance my driver behaviours and avoid procrastination.

As we know now procrastination encompasses a wide variety of avoidance and distracting behaviours that impact our productivity. I love the Pomodoro Principle of time blocking or boxing. Working in blocks of 25 minutes on a specific task or tasks, and then taking a break. This fits in well with other habits, such as keeping hydrated and getting up from your desk to move regularly. It also helps when you have to go downstairs and let your senior dog out into the garden for his 5th pee of the morning. I create a plan for my week and for my day. I have timetables for posting on social media, for example, and also time for admin and writing. This helps me to make time tangible, to make it work for me and not the other way around. Through time people can become enslaved by their own awareness, but through time blocking we get to make time our bitch. Whether you're an in-time or through time person, this will enable you to gain structure and build in good habits around your productivity. Those who procrastinate often haven't developed the motivation cues or triggers to 'get going' again. The Pomodoro Principle – you can look this up on Google – is a popular method used by many successful entrepreneurs. Time is a big factor in this process, so if you aren't getting done what you hope to each day, I encourage you to check out this exercise.

TIME IS A GREAT EQUALISER

I'm an early riser. I never thought I would be, but since meeting Dave, I've had no choice other than to work to his body clock. He's an industrial electrician and has for many years had jobs that meant getting up early to travel. A normal alarm in our house goes off around 5.20am. So, I am now a morning person. My inspiration kicks in too first thing in the morning, and since I stopped trawling through social media notifications at 6am (nothing good happens on Twitter or Facebook at 6am), I use that time to make notes and plans for the day.

I've also learned to work with my own internal clock. My brain likes to schedule conference calls with itself, often around 2am, which can be exhausting. To counteract this unconscious attack on my REM sleep, I have a note pad by my bed to jot down the brain farts. I call them brain farts because they happen in your head without warning at the most inappropriate times. Trying to suppress them doesn't work, so you just have to let them out!

Nothing is a bigger equaliser than time. So, in order to stand out from the rest, you need to understand your own strengths and core behaviours and use them effectively. My core behaviours and strengths are reliability, organisation, and process thinking. I pride myself on always knowing where everything is. I have a razor-sharp memory for the mundane stuff and an acute ability to see the big picture. Time appears to me like a day planner, and I can visualise everything that needs to be done. I can hold huge amounts of data, such as whose birthday is coming up, what date the school trip is, how long I have to spend cleaning and still fit in a trip to Aldi's and school pick up. I'm a walking talking productivity machine; ask me anything and I'll have or find the answer quickly and efficiently. Work colleagues, bosses, friends, and family have long relied upon my skills to get them where they need to be. Like an annoying little speaking clock, they could rely on me to tell them where they needed to be and what they needed to have with them. I can remember coaching conversations from weeks ago without the need to write copious notes. I always know what my client's goals are, and I often remind them of the intensions they have set.

Awesome yeah? Well it was until summer 2019. When perimenopause hit. I thought I was going insane. Anxiety and overwhelm were consuming me and my brain was failing. "Now what?", I asked myself. "Why is this happening to me? I've got all this shit under control, why am I suddenly feeling anxious and demotivated?" I'd struggle to find words during coaching sessions and my mind began to drift while a client was speaking. I was exhausted again. Like overwhelmingly exhausted and started to yawn during sessions and workshops. For weeks I slowly slipped into a funk of can't be arsed, only to then be overwhelmed with anxiety and paranoia. Hand on my heart I thought I had early onset dementia. This all came to a head when I was giving Jack his breakfast one morning. At this point, he was having 3 different types of tablets, plus a liquid, and each was meant to be given at a different time of the day. Not easy for anyone to remember, but at that point I was struggling to even remember if I had fed him or not. I had dished up his food as always and then around 5 or 10 mins later, I started to wonder if I had put his tablets in. The more I tried to recall the previous 5 minutes, the blanker my mind became. I couldn't even picture giving him the food. Wtf? It was a feeling of sheer panic: "How will I know if I have given him the right medication? What else will I forget? What is happening to me?" I remembered a friend describing her mums' dementia: "It's like finishing a puzzle and then throwing all the pieces back in the box. The picture is still there, only you have no idea what went where. She can remember taking me to Brownies, she recognises my kids, but doesn't know who they are or where they fit".

I was starting to wonder if this was to be my fate. This went on for weeks. I bought a pill dispenser with the days of the week on and started to write everything in my diary. Notes and lists everywhere. Should I record my last will and testament on the computer today in case tomorrow I forget who my kids are? I thought one morning. Ridiculous, I know, but together with the anxiety, overthinking, and unexplained paranoia, I felt like Superman carrying around that necklace of kryptonite. My powers were fading.

Then, just before Christmas I was due to attend an open evening at Maya's school. "You're not going to leave me, are you?", I asked Maya. "No not at all", she said. "It's just I can't face being sat there alone. I feel anxious, and I don't want to have to make polite conversation with anyone. Can we just go and get out as quickly as possible?" "No worries, momma" she said, "I will not leave you". Ok so she did leave me, but not for long, and while she was gone, I did start to chat to one of the other mums. A mum I know well. She showed me a text she had; it was an apology from her boss for being a bitch that day

"She is up and down all over the place right now", the mum explained. "I'm guessing it's her hormones".

"That's how I feel", I said. "I really didn't want to come tonight and I keep getting overwhelming anxiety. It's ridiculous because I'm supposed to be the one who helps other people keep their shit together, and right now, I just want to curl up and hide", I blurted out for the first time.

"I know exactly how that feels; menopause caused me to have to seek counselling in the end".

"What?", I said, "Menopause. This is menopause?"

"Yeah definitely", she said. "Sends you crazy", she said with a sigh.

"Oh my god but I don't have hot flushes and all the other stuff is still happening".

"Yeah that sounds about right. It starts a lot earlier than we realise. Perimenopause can last years, and anxiety and brain fog are often the first sign".

"What the fuck" I said, then as I remembered I was standing in a school hall surrounded by kids and their posh parents. "Oh my god, it is all making sense now".

Having that conversation was the starting point for me to regain my powers. Understanding what was causing my brain fog and low motivation meant I was then able to kick start some strategies to regain the skills and mindset I was once so proud of. I also had to start eating better, sleeping better, and getting more exercise, and over the next few months things started to get better. I still have moments of extreme fatigue and brain fog, and my middle is a bit thicker than I would like it to be. But now I have the information to create strategies to combat these moments when my powers fail.

Why am I telling you all this? Because life is constantly unpredictable. Stuff happens that we can anticipate, and stuff happens that we can't. If we allow unpredictable challenges to derail us every time, we'll accomplish nothing. So, getting your head around time means being ready. It means having the behaviours in place that allow you to stay focused, shift a few things round, and make the most of your productive times. My energy and clarity are not what they used to be. And I still have a long way to go with drinking more water and feeding my body well. I do, however, safeguard my time. So, when a "can't be arsed" moment appears from nowhere, or I'm lost in brain fog, I can still show up in my business and with my clients. Who knew that doing less would mean achieving more? Crazy yeah?

Entrepreneurs operate with the time they have. They choose their tasks wisely for maximum reward with minimum time and effort. Sounds easy I know, and when you have teams of people, these things appear more achievable. However, behaviours start at the top, so even if you are yet to assemble a team in your business, you can still behave like a boss.

Learning to manage time like *a boss*

TIME DRIVEN NOT TASK DRIVEN

I can get super lost in a task. Whether it's creating materials, scrolling through social media, or cleaning out my fridge, I'm a completer. So that means that if I start it, I must finish it. No matter what the cost. This makes me a great employee, one that bosses can rely on, and a great colleague too. If I'm on your team you can rest assured, I will do everything I can to make sure we win! I have in the past been called a 'pit bull' on more than one occasion and also referred to as a Monica. I love the episode where she cleans the bathroom while waiting for Chandler and Phoebe to finish wooing each other and the one where she offers to go clean up the apartment for one of Ross's girlfriends. And my favourite is the one where she does up the boys' apartment when they lose the bet and she and Rachel have to move in there. She goes at it non-stop, and she doesn't rest until she's so exhausted that she falls asleep while everyone else celebrates what a great job she did.

This is me. I close doors as I walk past. I have even numbers on the volume in my car, and when I start a box set, I will not come up for air till I have binged the lot. I do this with big bags of crisps and family packs of Mars bars too. I must get to the end! I don't have OCD. I get a little annoyed when people refer to themselves as "Having OCD" because they like their books in height order on the shelf. OCD is a compulsive medical disorder that can only be contained with medication and therapy. The rest of us, who simply suffer with completion compulsion and organisation drivers, have a choice.

I first became aware of how my completion compulsion was becoming unhelpful when I was studying for my coaching diploma. A new and scary learning situation had triggered all my defensive behaviours, and I was struggling to stay afloat amongst the overwhelming waves of realisation and self-awareness. I felt myself getting drawn into a vortex of compulsive strategies, and self-reflection was one of them. Self-awareness, actualisation, and reflection are amazing and life changing. We start to focus less on those around us and ask ourselves, "What is my part in all of this? What does this mean to me?" It can be addictive, and if we aren't careful, it begins to consume us. There is no bottom to the well of self-discovery, so we can be on that journey forever if we aren't careful.

I spent much of my time and energy overdoing the self-reflection and used up a lot of energy by constantly consuming new information. Just one more video, just one more exercise. It got to the point where I couldn't detach myself from it. Yes, I was organised and hitting every deadline, week after week. However, I was missing everything else. My kids, my husband, my friends, my life, and this was never what the learning was meant to be.

I was task driven. Starting and completing like a robot with no end in sight. I repeated this exact behaviour when, in September 2019, I joined the mentorship programme, and this is when I realised that constant consumption was not the most effective way to learn. I was starting to question all the weeks I had spent creating course materials, even when I knew the course wouldn't go ahead. I thought about the ways in which I had put off more important tasks in favour of completing the writing I had started or the webinar course I was watching. I'd signed up for several Udemy courses. If you haven't done any, they are a great way to dip into a subject and learn without it costing a fortune. I'd come across several' including a CBT introduction course and an empowering women and group coaching course. I've already trained in all of these, but they looked fun, so during yet another bout of struggle and procrastination, I bought into my constant need for knowledge. I can remember now, Dave asking me if I fancied going for a walk along the seafront. The weather was warm but not too warm, and I'd been in the house for what felt like weeks. "No, I'm ok I need to get this done." No, I didn't, I just couldn't face walking away when I had 3 more videos to watch. That was when I knew I had a problem. A bit like when you find yourself chomping on the 4th Mars bar in a packet of 6 thinking, "well, I might as well eat them all now". What was wrong with me? I was overdoing my strengths. That brilliant and reliable completion driver was being pushed to the limits. *How was I going to stop? What can I do to take back control? Have I always been this way? Can I be another way? Do I want to be another way? This is me. No, it isn't.* Our behaviours, values, and beliefs are information stored within a mind and body. That information can be tweaked, changed, overridden, enhanced, and replaced because humans have one incredible trait: free will. We can choose to question, choose to think differently, and choose to be different.

 I started to look at my behaviours around time a lot more closely. When I focused attention on the driving force, when I noticed what my brain and body wanted to do, I started to gather information. I began to see where I was experiencing compulsion, and where I was choosing to hold back.

I used to be a cleaning freak. I couldn't leave the house unless it was immaculate. I wouldn't let people round unless every inch was spotless and everything was in its place. When you live in a huge house with a dog and two kids, as I did back then, this was a big task. I realised when I started to work with Lisa that the reason I needed to do this was that everything inside of me was out of control. So instead of looking inwards, I focused all of my energy into trying to control the world around me: my environment, my kids, and my relationships. Picking up toys while the kids were still playing with them. Scrubbing the inside of an en suite shower before my friends turned up for a coffee. They weren't going to be asking to use the shower! I let go of that shit like a hot potato the second I realised what was happening, and as my self-confidence and esteem grew, my cleaning apparatus dwindled. I later learnt that my through-time driver was also very much in play here and trying to outrun time was pushing me to the point of exhaustion. My driver behaviours and low self-esteem were in control, and I was overdoing everything.

Having done the work to address my issues of low self-esteem, I am now back in control of my core drivers. I still keep a tidy house, but I don't obsess over things like I used to. So, if it were my low self-esteem that was causing me to do this with cleaning, then could it be self-doubt that was making me act this way in my learning and my business? Funnily enough the answer is yes. The solution is boundaries. Boundaries around time and confidence in what I want to achieve. I needed to control my core drivers instead of trying to control time. Time is not negotiable; a minute is a minute. What we choose to do in that time is negotiable, so this is where our efforts need to be. Deciding what gets done and when; realistic expectations, boundaries, and perspective are how we make time tangible and avoid time fatigue.

MAKE TIME TANGIBLE

Ok, time was now my new challenge. Which of my core behaviours, values, and beliefs was going to help me here? I love the Marvel comics and movies, and I often choose my values, behaviours, or beliefs like I'm choosing a team of Avengers. "Avengers assemble", I would whisper to myself. So, who do I need for this? Organisation, planning, and prioritising: they sound like a good place to start. Ok, I need a visual on this – creativity can help there. Simplicity will be great; I can always see a simpler and easier way to do things. And finally, consistency, my awesome core value that drives me insane most of the time but is also the value that keeps me on a straight path.

Right, ok Avengers have assembled, what now? I need to look at what my goals are, to decide which values and behaviours are going to help, and to identify where I was tripping myself up. In the end, I concluded that focusing on time rather than tasks would be a good place to start. Dividing my day into chunks of time and planning to include all the things I need to do. I now have a spreadsheet with coloured boxes on it accompanied by a collection of various coloured post it notes stuck right above my computer. Daily, weekly, and monthly tasks are all inputted onto the sheet. I use the Priority Picker exercise as part of my daily routine. I also have an online tracking ap as well as my trusted diary as backup. I love paper and struggle to read information online – so having a diary keeps me feeling safe and comforted.

This works well for me, as my brain is constantly reassured by my surroundings. Everywhere I look, I have reminders that all of this is under control, and I can now dip into a task, complete an amount of work within that task, and then move on. I avoid lily padding from task to task, and instead I plan what needs to be done in advance, then work purposefully to do it. I achieve so much more this way and am still able to complete most tasks on time – I just have to redefine my definition of complete. Now, complete means, "you did as much as you said you would do".

Thinking long term helps planning in your business; you absolutely need to know where you are heading. Acting in the moment is how you get there. Consistent, often boring and mundane, tasks completed each day are how you build a business. If you are building a house, you must dig foundations, lay pipe, build walls, install plumbing, and put on a roof. You don't start with picking out what pictures you are going to hang on the wall. That can wait till another day. Looking at tasks and asking, is this a priority? Does this needed to be done now? Can it be done now? If the answer is no, then put it in the plan – do not try to do it today. What tasks bring money into your business? Do those first. For example, writing this book has been an absolute joy and one that, I have to say, could easily have become an obsession. But I had to keep my family and my business running at the same time. And although I hope this will help my business and bring income in long term, I had to make sure I was doing the other stuff too.

Engaging with a writing coach was the best decision I have made this year. I could never have built my belief up to even start this book without the awesome input from Jennifer Jones. Not to mention how the support and accountability from the Entrepreneurs' Writing Club members helped me to stay focused. It was a delight when I realised that being consistent, organised, methodical, and a bit anal when it comes to drilling down on detail was exactly how you get a book like this written. "Oh, wow I can do all those things no worries", I said when I turned up to the first workshop. "You need to plan Abbie. You need to self-reflect and ask questions about yourself and your audience. You need to break it down into bite sized chunks to get it done, not sit for weeks slogging away and writing shit because you're exhausted. Dipping in and out works well for a book", Jennifer explained. "OMG I am in", I said. Together with Jennifer's excellent coaching, the icing on the cake for me was Jennifer's book *There's a Book in Every Expert (that's you!)*. A simple no-nonsense account of exactly how to get it done. What to expect, what to do, and how to stay motivated. I had the privilege of BETA reading her book before starting to write mine, and it was certainly what made the difference for me. If, while reading this book, you're thinking "Jeez if she can do this so can I", first – Congratulations! Second – absolutely; you can and please send me a copy of your book. And third – go buy Jennifer's book before you start; you will save yourself a lot of time and procrastination.

So, this is me dipping in and out, writing and rewriting and incredibly happy to get up and walk the dog or nip to the shops or answer emails in between. Because now I trust my process. Getting stuff out of your head and onto a piece of paper or app is how you can make time tangible. I now know what I need to do and what time I have to do it in. While we can't actually control time (and if you do manage it, please let me know), but we can use it well. We can make it work for us and not against us. The top entrepreneurs have this sorted. They leave nothing to chance. They safeguard their down time as well as squeezing every possible drop of productivity out of the minutes they have.

Giving up my job this time was a decision based on multiple factors. Not least my poorly boy Jack. I was able to justify giving up work to look after him by installing the caveat that it would be time well spent: writing my book, building the business, attending events, and growing connections. Jack has taught me so much about being in the moment. Dogs live in the moment. They have absolutely no concept of past or future they live entirely hard wired to the present. Jack might have cost me a lot of money and worry over the years, but he has always been a delight to be around. Happy, relaxed, and content. I have worked hard to achieve this in my life too and am learning more and more each day that it is ok to be normal. Boring is the goal when it comes to my life. I do not need drama; I crave normality and balance. And I do this by being grateful and satisfied in the moment. As I wrote this chapter, Jack was getting frailer by the day – he was 12 ½ years old. Not bad for an epileptic slightly obese and unbalanced chocolate Labrador. He had arthritis, rotten teeth, and was covered in lumps. We think he had cataracts too, and he was going a little senile. Every decision I made while I had him, had Jack factored into it and this stage of my journey was no exception. I began the chapter talking about how we can't possibly live every day as if it were our last. I would get nothing done. Jack taught me how to live each day without regrets. To make the most of it, so if it were to be my last or his, then in the grand scheme of things, that would be ok. I am subconsciously setting a time limit to get this book finished before he is gone. At this moment I don't know if I will be successful. But I keep writing and hoping for many more days of peace and quiet. Just the two of us. Me writing and him snoring. (Reader, I met that deadline).

BE YOUR OWN BOSS

I have the sweetest clients. Lee, one of just a handful of male clients I see, has been a client for a while now, and he has, over time, become a close and trusted friend. I have high hopes for the incredible adventures that lay ahead of him. He is seriously a top bloke and with good looks, a cheeky smile, a cracking sense of humour and emotional intelligence by the bucket load, he is the full package. He's also handy to have around, as his skills as a roofer and all-round craftsman are enviable. Lee calls me boss. He calls me Boss and it makes me smile. "Hi boss when can we meet next? ... Alright boss, look what I have achieved today ... Thanks, boss, for a great session this week; I feel on top of the world".

Lee came for coaching to help with focus and productivity. He thrives on staying busy, and his mind is rarely sill. He was struggling to meet the demands of his new role as a project manager and still find time to pursue his passion for entrepreneurship. Balancing family and responsibilities meant his mind was in overwhelm. In our first session, I asked Lee if he used a diary. "No", he replied, "it's all in my head". "Wow. Ok, that makes sense", I replied in a rather 'un' coaching fashion. I quickly followed up with, "what would your head feel like if all that were on a piece of paper that you could organise and tap into when you choose to?" The next day I received this message:

Boss I've bought a diary and already planned my week. I have even written in have play time with Summer (his daughter). Already feeling better. Thanks Boss you're a star.

Top tip for successful goal setting ... write it down. This simple, yet life changing, behaviour can mean the difference between success and failure. Lee is nailing life; his wife just had another baby and he recently came third in The Real Forex Trader Challenge series 2, which you can find on You Tube. An 'Apprentice' style challenge in which contestants use their currency trading skills to win their way to the top. With an insatiable entrepreneurial streak, I don't think it will be long before Lee becomes his own boss.

I don't imagine I'll ever be anyone's boss again, except my

own; so to be called 'Boss', well it just makes me smile and it lifts my heart, because being a boss is something I truly admire. I've worked for many awesome bosses in my time. I've worked for a few crap ones, too. Having worked in a lot of places, you begin to see what behaviours lead to success and a happy workforce and the ones that don't. My own skills, talent, and expectations have evolved over the years, and while my personality has remained relatively static, my behaviours have matured. What I've come to realise with age and experience is that with the right boundaries you can work with just about anyone, deal with just about anything, and go home at the end of the day relatively unscathed. Some of my bosses have been horrors, and while I have no time for unfairness, dishonesty, unkindness, stupidity, or outright cruelty, I have at least learnt what works for me.

The only boss I want to be is the boss of me. So how do I make that work? Would I want to share an office with myself? I like to think I would. Although I imagine I would begin to irritate myself if I weren't prepared to install some good boundaries. When we work alone, we are everything in our business, and some days, depending on your business, you might be the only person you speak to. So, you better get to know yourself and like yourself or that can lead to a pretty awkward working relationship.

Giving yourself clear instructions about what's expected is a great way to be your own boss. Days without a Zoom call or client session are thankfully few and far between, but on the rare occasion I don't need to show myself, I get some great work done wearing my pyjamas and can be known to go all day without showering – swapping from admin or writing to hoovering and washing. Every day felt like a pyjama day at the start, so I try to keep unwashed days to a minimum, an occasional treat. Now I make the effort to shower and get dressed. This sets me up, and then when the postman knocks the door at 2pm, he doesn't start to think I am either depressed or extremely sick.

I operate working hours too, now. I generally work around an 8 hour day, between 7am and 9pm – with regular breaks in the day for lunch and exercise, of course. This varies for days when I am out and about and the days when I have clients to see. I try to plan my week and my tasks so that I have 1 day a week without client sessions. This means I have freedom to be spontaneous, which is particularly important to me. As much as I love consistency and routine and I hate surprises, I get bored very easily too. So, it helps to have a day where I can plan something a bit different. It's not normally anything super exciting and nowadays usually involves food shopping, a quick catch up with my sister, or a well-deserved shoulder massage to keep tension at bay. I need that flexibility to keep me sane. I safeguard my weekends too, though I remain active on social media and present for my clients should they need me. I make sure there's plenty of down time too. When you work for yourself and so do your clients, it's difficult to switch off completely at the weekend, as for many that's their productive time.

I've organised my workload. I'm far more energised, inspired, and creative first thing in the morning, so I try to get social media posts and ads out of the way early, as well as admin tasks and bits on my 'will do' list. I do my best creative writing before lunch, so I make sure I to block out all distractions, especially those from social media, to get this done. I've set some tough boundaries, and I close down notifications and put my phone out of reach.

Accountability is fundamental in coaching and in being self-employed because you're the boss now. One of the biggest struggles my clients present with is following through on the goals and actions that they have set for themselves. After an epic coaching session, I'll often visit a week or two later to be greeted with, "I have a confession to make Abbie, I haven't done anything since our last session". Ok so without going too deep on the ins and outs of accountability in coaching, let's just say that it's not me you need to apologise to. This is your business, your life, your goals – it is up to you what you choose to do. Accountability only works if a client accepts that they are responsible for keeping themselves accountable. This is true for all single business owners, especially when you are the product. This is on you. And the best and most expensive coaches in the world aren't going to come do this shit for you. We have VA's for that, and they are awesome. So, if you can afford to pay to outsource everything that bores you, then crack on and good luck. If you can't quite yet justify the expense, then you're going to have to do it for yourself at least for a while. As soon as you are able to, outsource all the activities that drain you, not necessarily those that challenge you, but the ones that literally suck the life out of you. For me, this looks like having an accountant to do my tax returns and someone to do my Facebook ads. Algorithms are the work of the devil!

Accountability works like a boss who is not around much. A boss who you know is keeping tabs on you, a boss who you know will at some point ask you, "have you completed the report I asked for"? A boss who sits quietly in her office looking like she's not doing much but who, at a moment's notice can come charging into the room with a pile of paper shouting, "I need this all by tomorrow".

Thankfully, you don't have to endure that any longer. One plus point about working for yourself. However, you still need a boss, so be your own boss. Set deadlines. Delegate tasks. Hold yourself accountable. Have a start to your day, a middle, and an end. Set rules for distractions, like personal phone calls and social media interruptions. And plan your day. Set times to get things done and make sure you do the priority stuff first. And for small business owners, this means the stuff that brings in money, the stuff that helps you plan, and the stuff that will encourage you to be the best you can be. Remember to have a laugh too. Of all the jobs I've had, whether I loved or hated them, I always had a laugh and made friends.

Connection is the thing our soul craves, so make time for it, and if your behaviours and talents are dwindling and your energy is being sucked away like Superman in a pair of kryptonite pants, make time to recharge. Give yourself time off. When we go to work for others, its usually to fund the life we have outside of work. Even if we love our job, hopefully we love our life too. Simple, consistent, boring behaviours are the easiest way to keep moving forward. When we get our head around time, these behaviours become less burdensome and we get more done.

WHERE TIME FATIGUE SHOWS UP IN BUSINESS

Time is a biggie. Such a complex concept to get our head around. Too much and we procrastinate. Too little and we panic. Everyone has 24 hours in a day. EVERYONE. So how come some people can get stuff done and some can't? In business, time is a resource that's sometimes even more valuable than money. We can make more money, but can we make more time? Not really, but we can use it well. For this we need to get perspective on it. We need to understand how we operate within it and make it a tangible resource. This means streamlining procedures like onboarding and marketing. It can also mean outsourcing tasks we hate or don't understand, and it means staying connected to time.

We all experience time differently, and while we all have the same 24 hours, we each have unique lives, businesses, and responsibilities. What I've learnt throughout my journey is that developing consistent behaviours and applying them through a framework of time blocking has been where I have seen the biggest changes in my productivity and my energy. Time and energy go hand in hand. There is no benefit in having a load of free time, if you're too exhausted to use it. Equally, if our energy levels are dipping and we haven't planned our time, then reaching targets becomes almost impossible. Good, consistent behaviours and planning is how great entrepreneurs succeed. We can all find our place, or our version of this.

Top tips summary – Time fatigue to time management

> As I write this chapter, we are in a global crisis. Corona virus is gripping the world and causing widespread panic, anxiety, and fear. Stock piling loo roll, pasta, and paracetamol seems to be the latest trend, and while the government seem to be attempting to keep us informed, panic is setting in. And why? Time. None of us know how long this will last. We don't know how much food we need, because we don't know how long we will have between visits to the shops. And for many of us, we're terrified because right now the usually suppressed fear about dying that we all live with each day is being rammed into our brains on an hourly basis. Feeling like an unwilling extra in a disaster movie, my brain is battling to balance images of people clapping in the streets, nurses bravely leaving their family at home to go save others, and 100-year-old veterans walking around

their garden raising millions of pounds, with images of widespread death, misery, and suffering. All while trying to stay focused on where I can do good today. We panic because our mind is being forced to think too far ahead, and that never works because we don't have the facts. So, our brain spins into overwhelm, trying to find solutions for problems we don't yet know we have.

By the time this book is published, I hope the world is a calmer and healthier place. I hope the businesses that I wrote this book for are still operating, and that many more new ones have sprung up as a result of our time under lockdown, as more and more of us decide to use our time on earth to be joyful and fulfilled and to follow our dreams.

These are a few quick takeaways:

Where Time Fatigue Shows Up	Top Tips to Beat Time Fatigue
You panic that there isn't enough time, and this means you make mistakes, miss deadlines, and avoid activities that help you grow.	To use time effectively we need to understand where we are using it. Make time tangible.
You think you're multi-tasking and staying on top of things, but you're lily padding from task to task and accomplishing very little.	Multi-tasking feels like the thing to do to get it done. However, this can in fact cause anxiety, and we end up juggling and getting nowhere. Make a plan or to do list and prioritise. Work on one task at a time.

You start to second guess everything. You begin tasks, only to be distracted when the mental clock starts ticking in your head.	Through time people will be easily distracted as their inner stopwatch starts a count down. Time boxing and focusing on activities for a set period means we can set an actual stopwatch for our activities. Our inner stopwatch shuts down and the distraction disappears.
You are not using your time well and end up working too hard for too little gain.	It is common for us to believe that the harder we work the more we will be rewarded. This is sadly untrue when it comes to entrepreneurship. Decide on the hours you want to work and stick to it. It is better to work at full capacity for 4 days a week than at 40% for 7 days a week.
You are overworking and overwhelmed and so avoid marketing and promoting your business.	Step back. Plan out your ideal day. Make a list of key tasks that need to happen and prioritise those that bring in income.
You begin to resent your business and your clients because you are not spending enough time with your family and doing things that you enjoy.	It is easy to prioritise our clients over our own needs – they are after all the ones paying the bills. Make yourself your best paying client, without you there's no business. Block out time for yourself, including your own admin and downtime.

You have no idea if you are achieving anything because you have no way to measure productivity.	Our goals are often measured over time and if we fail to set deadlines or check points how can we know if something is working. Include timescales in all your goal setting activities and check in regularly. Adjust where necessary.
You are reluctant to step back from your business to enjoy downtime for fear that things will be missed or that you will be overwhelmed when you return.	If you are holding back from taking time off for fear that things will be missed or pile up in your absence, then this needs attention. We all have peaks and troughs however our business should be able to survive without 24-hour surveillance. Plan ahead and prepare for taking time off to maintain your energy levels.
You believe you are failing when targets and goals aren't reached on time, which starts to chip away at your confidence and leads to a drop in motivation.	Setting realistic timescales for achieving our goals is essential – too much and we procrastinate too little and we panic. Review your goals regularly. If you are putting too much pressure on yourself, rethink your timescales. It's ok to miss the boat every now and then, but constant failure is demotivating.

BOOK RECOMMENDATION

Grow Your Tribe: How to scale and skyrocket your business by loving your audience – by Lauryn Bradley

Getting your head around time and using it well is the number one skill for a successful businessowner. When we are employees, our time is dictated, set boundaries are there to ensure we get what we need to do done. But when we are the boss, general manager, accountant, advertising manager, manufacturing department, and project manager, we must be clear about how we manage ourselves and our time. No one is clocking you in and out, so you must set those boundaries. Growing a business requires business expertise and we cannot always have that expertise in house. Successful businesses and entrepreneurs think nothing of engaging the services of other experts to help them run and grow their business. Lauryn Bradley is a business expert, lifelong entrepreneur, and business mentor. She has walked the walk and she certainly talks the talk. I was lucky enough to have been introduced to Lauryn at a networking meeting in September 2019 and just minutes after meeting her, I was sold. My passion for what I do is undisputed; however, my lack of business basics was evident. When I met Lauryn, I was just starting to find my feet, and thanks to her business mentoring programme and the 80/20 Club, I grew my business more in 6 months than I had in 3 years.

    I highly recommend her book *Grow Your Tribe*. Lauryn's no-nonsense approach is refreshing, and she has the most incredible insight into the behaviours we have around time and how to use it. She has a huge following in the business world, with online platforms and courses all targeted at businessowners just like you and me. Her passion and values to share her skills and give back are heart-warming not to mention a lifesaver.

CHAPTER 8

Big 7 No. 7
Overwhelm to *Resilience*

"Many of us feel stress and get overwhelmed not because we're taking on too much, but because we're taking on too little of what really strengthens us".

MARCUS BUCKINGHAM

Overwhelm

To defeat someone or something by using a lot of force.

Overwhelm is a physical response. It comes as a result of our brain shutting down. Just like a computer, if we have too many tabs open at once, when the Wi-Fi dips we will not perform well. Overwhelm is to an extent a chosen response because we have the power to stop it. Either before or as soon as it starts to consume us.

That said, there are times in life and business when we fall victim to outside pressures, and this will cause us to react rather than respond. Overwhelm looks like fatigue, overthinking, lily padding, procrastination, anxiety, confusion, and fear. Basically, all the struggles rolled into one. So hopefully once you have got to this part of the book, you will already have a good idea about what might be causing your overwhelm and know how to stop it.

Our brains work very well without our interference, much of the time. This can be difficult, as we have discovered, when limiting beliefs and values trigger our fear response. However, we need our brains to work unsupervised, or else we would simply implode. We can't be thinking every time we need to breathe – "Oh I need to breathe" – or consciously remember how to walk every day. Our brains are doing that for us. Overwhelm is a sign that we're putting too much pressure on our unconscious. Breathing and remembering how to walk take up a lot of energy and if we're drawing on that energy to do too much else, the brain sends out a warning. Fear, confusion, and self-doubt all trigger our brains to respond, and this drains our reserved energy and leads quickly to feelings of overwhelm, as our bodies try to cope with the demand for more energy.

Overwhelm, while it can be caused by difficult situations, is not in itself a bad thing, and like all the other struggles, you can notice it and manage it. Significantly, the opposite of overwhelm is not underwhelm. Overwhelm is a warning sign, a barrier in the road that says continue at your own risk. Its opposite is resilience. Resilience is our ability to take another path or to put the brakes on and do a U'ie!

Resilience

The ability to be happy, successful, or calm again after something difficult or bad has happened.

Mental resilience is a conscious process of mindset techniques. Those who are mentally resilient can decide how they wish to experience situations and control their responses. We all experience challenges in life and business, and some are harder than others. The difference is not the level of challenge but our ability to deal with it. Mindset is how we achieve this, and mental resilience is the umbrella under which positive mindset sits. Ever had a frantic phone call from a friend with an issue that to you seems petty? Ever wonder why some people seem to glide through life unaffected by the need to please others or become a slave to stressful situations? Mental resilience is the difference between a person who can navigate challenge and one who becomes a martyr or victim to it. A person who can own the process of experiencing their surroundings without blame or criticism of others is a person who holds power.

Resilience is a result of acceptance. Acceptance that life will challenge us all and in order to survive, we need to choose. Perception and reality are tools used in coaching to offer clients perspective. Resilience is like a superpower, and the more it's tested, the stronger it gets, provided we manage our energy and focus. Resilience needs to be respected and nurtured. If you notice a consistent drain on your resilience, then it might be time to take action to remove the drain or plug the leak.

Just as overwhelm can be a culmination of all the struggles, resilience is the antidote. And how we get there is through our mindset.

My struggle with overwhelm

OVERWHELM IS A WARNING NOT A RESULT

It took me a long time to get my head around what overwhelm was really doing to my thought process and to my energy. I used to think of overwhelm as a sign that I could no longer manage or cope. I've experienced overwhelm more times that I care to recall. Behaviours such as completion compulsion, consistency, perfectionism, and organisation have led me to exhaustion on many occasions. I don't do things by halves, and the story I was told as a child echoes in my head: "If you are going to do something, do it properly or not at all". I grew up surrounded by perfectionists; a family who commit, who show up, who sacrifice, and who tirelessly go all in and rock at what they do. For example, my mum is super skilled at all types of craft and creativity; she can literally turn her hand to anything and make it magnificent. Her eye for detail and imagination is enviable, and it has often been my wish that she would turn her hand to creating things that could be sold. But she has no need or desire to earn money from what she considers her fun activities. Also, my dad (now a retired submariner) is a boss when it comes to DIY, my older sister Rebecca is an outstanding teacher, and

Kate is an absolute genius when it comes to payroll processing and Excel spread sheets. Each of them going over and above whatever is asked of them and performing to the point of excess and perfection. A trait I too portray. However, this engrained need for perfection can cause trouble.

Like so many of the business owners I work with, I've found that dedicating my life to something I feel passionately about comes at a price. I found my old employee mindset wasn't helpful in starting or growing my business; I couldn't just push forward with my head down.

You know I love a new challenge, and when an opportunity arises, I step up willingly to meet it head on. I welcome the chance to learn and enjoy all manner of new experiences. I can manage my fear now and confusion; however, my constant loop of self-reflection means this can be an exhausting experience. New situations, new questions, new ways to judge myself, new ways to question my feelings and responses and new ways to descend into overwhelm will not get it done.

> **When Covid19 hit the UK in March of 2020 like many others, I was in shock and disbelief. Honestly, most people weren't taking it seriously, and until someone close to me came down with it, I too was in denial. The news became a barrage of information and instruction, confusion, and misinformation; social media went nuts, and suddenly I found myself in the middle of not only a pandemic but a debilitating attack on my values and civil liberties. I work hard to keep my attention in the moment, and I resist the urge to think too far into the future. As I discussed in chapter 7, I'm a through time person; however, I work tirelessly to keep my focus on the now. I can see and**

visualise tomorrow, the next day, next week, next year – but I don't put any of my energy there. Suddenly I and the rest of the nation were being forced to consider how we would survive for what could be months without the full use of our freedom. Panic buying in the shops will become the stuff of legends, and we'll be telling stories for generations to come about loo rolls and empty shelves.

So much anxiety in an already mentally fatigued world. Arguments, ignorance, denial, as well as courage, belief, compassion, and kindness exploded on social media, and for me, it was all too much.

My values drive my business at the best of times. I wanted to be helpful and useful, to care about others, and to support and respond to every request that came my way. But omg this was unsustainable, and I had to take control quickly. For several days I, like many flooded the internet with offers of help and support, and then on day 4, I broke. My voice was gone, and I could not stop crying. My energy and focus were being torn between family, myself, friends, and the entire planet. I needed to regain control. So, I stopped and recharged. Deleted stuff I could not control. Streamlined my energy and went to work on helping those who were my priority, starting with family and then my tribe. I had to safeguard those who were paying me, I owed them that, as well as the people who have stood by me and those I care about. Suddenly, I was feeling just as useful and helpful, except I was energised by helping the 100 or so clients and tribe members and supporting the networks where I bring most value. Billions suddenly became around 1000 or so, and that was a number I could manage.

When your phone goes red and says you have 13% battery life, what do you do?
   a. Carry on and think who cares if it dies it dies, I will worry then?
   b. Panic and stare at the screen trying to send all your emails and messages before it's too late?
   c. Reach for your phone charger, plug it in, and go make a cup of tea while it tops up?

Well, I have done all these many, many times, and the one that offers the best result is of course C. Why would you choose A or B? What possible reason could you have to let your phone die, unless there were no viable alternative?

If you are down to the red on your energy levels, then you need to stop and recharge. Plug yourself into whatever recharges your battery. Sleep, exercise, a conversation, or a podcast. Whatever it is, do it. A good work ethic is essential, but powering through when you're exhausted is not a 'good work ethic'; it's stupidity. Hopefully by adopting some of the practices shared here in the book and learning from some of my mistakes you'll avoid overwhelm most of the time, but only if you keep your charger handy and use it regularly.

Overwhelm is a trigger. It's the warning on your phone that says your battery is low, which means you have time to reach for the charger. If your phone (your brain) has been using up the battery with hidden apps and push notifications, when you come to download or watch a video or install a new app, the phone (your brain) is going to struggle and probably refuse.

Overwhelm is not simply a sign of too much to do or bad organisation – although both can contribute heavily to our mental burden. Overwhelm comes because we haven't taken the time to top ourselves up. If you have too much to do in your business, then fantastic. It means you're moving forward; in which case, you need to be minding your energy in accordance with your workload.

In simple terms – find the balance.
Monitor your battery level and charge accordingly.

DON'T FIGHT THE FIRE. GET THE FUCK OUT.

When in May 2018 I took the job at Atlantic Refrigeration, I was expecting it to be varied. I love to do the crap no one else wants to do, because for me I get to do it my way. Tidy the stationery cupboard, empty the fridge, shred a load of paper, laminate documents. I love "mindless tasks", or as I like to call them "mindful tasks", because I get to retreat into my own little world and drift off into a place of quiet sanctuary whilst still being useful. Love them cannot get enough of them and at Atlantic there was lots of opportunity for these kinds of tasks. Once I convinced everyone to stop apologising before they handed me a 'boring task', it was a pleasure.

When I was asked to step up as a fire marshal I was not quite as enthusiastic: urgh that sounds very responsible to me; it sounds important, and I am not sure that's what I want. I like simple stuff that I can hide in. My business is scary enough I don't need to be fighting actual fires.

Still I did it, obviously, and to be honest the risk of fire was minimal as Penny's obsession with health and safety meant that prevention was most definitely a priority. One of the activities we did was learn to use a fire extinguisher properly, and wow I did not know how complicated that was until I did the training. Not complicated as such, but you must do it right or else you're going to fail, and lives could be at risk.

After a day of videos and a practical demonstration, we sat a test. It was all great fun. I, like my colleagues, did well in the test, though I don't remember much of it now. The takeaway that I do remember, after all our training and demonstrations and our contrived bravery to become amateur fire fighters, is this: always sound the alarm before you tackle a fire. Call for help first; and if the fire is bigger than you, get the fuck out and call the fire brigade. If the fire is bigger than you, I thought to myself. Wow there is a metaphor right there.

Know your limits. Ask for help before you start to fight the fire. And if it gets too much, call in the experts. Now business doesn't often come with emergencies, but it does present us with uncertainty, unpredictability, and surprises. With the best preventative measures in the world – we cannot prepare for every eventuality, and when we are the product and our home life is intertwined with our business, then honestly anything can happen.

If you've worked hard on social media and have a load of orders or enquires in, then your kid gets chicken pox and the babysitter lets you down, this can lead to overwhelm. Our values are suddenly in question because our brain is already trying to work out clever and imaginative ways to nurse our child with a combination of large doses of Calpol and screen time without feeling like a total shit bag of a mother and still complete the orders. Too many apps are now in play. Our battery is suddenly being sucked dry because the things we took for granted – like time to get stuff done and a healthy child – are now a major concern. If the problem starts to look bigger than you, ask for help.

My constant need for self-exploration means that instead of just sitting back and taking on information and learning, I begin with questioning myself and looking for ways to define the struggle. A few times the fire got out of control, and in the past, it felt like I was fighting my fire with cups of water. Like the firefighters who tackle bush fires in Australia, I was dampening the edges to stop the spread. I would stay in the room, staring down a fire, watching it grow, feeling the heat, and refusing to leave. Now I call for help; when I need someone who can help me to grow bigger than the fire, I call on my tribe.

Getting all that self-analysing out of my head means that I can process effectively. Hearing others offering perspective helps me to make sense of what is at the root of my overwhelm so I can break it down and tackle it. Instead of one massive inferno, in front of me were candles. I just have to blow them out one by one. My tribe are awesome, and frequently, Dee is my saviour. With a kind heart and kick ass skills as a small business owner, charity fundraiser, marketing expert, and mum, she has tackled many a fire in her life. Dee has a way of hearing the struggles of others and offering kick ass solutions; she's the firefighter I need. Do I take things a bit too seriously sometimes? Yes, and that is all I need to hear.

If the fire is bigger than you, then get the fuck out, find a friend, and go back with a water cannon.

KEEP CALM; IT'S ONLY PANIC.

Mark Manson has an amazing talent for writing, and his perspective on humans is amusing, insightful, and for me very real. We do take ourselves too seriously sometimes, and overdoing the self-analysis is for sure a behaviour I have been guilty of since beginning my journey in 2002. I know when overwhelm is on its way. I can recognise the signs now. For me it feels like turning up to school only to find you have a test that day and you haven't revised. Everyone else seems fine with it and can't understand your panic, but you're dying. Your mind is blank, and you cannot for the life of you remember your name, let alone any of the answers.

I did this once on my Home Economics 'O' Level. I like cooking – I do not love it. I like eating and I like feeding people, but mastering the art of cookery is not something I aspire too. I detest recipes and tend to go off road on even the simplest of concoctions, much to my meat-and-two-veg-loving husband's chagrin; he's politely endured some rather eclectic meals over the years. I chose cookery at school because it sounded less like work than some of the other "Fun" subjects and my sewing skills are atrocious, much to my mum's dismay. God do I wish I had opted for computer studies now. Anyway, cookery it was. In those days bunking off school was a thing; nowadays, if a child went missing in the middle of the day, the police and parents would be called and Facebook would have an alert out in seconds. Back then, communication was a little slower, and honestly, I'm sure some teachers were relieved when certain pupils failed to show up to their lesson. Home Economics was the last lesson on a Wednesday. Prime bunking off time. I want to say I made it to maybe 40% of the practical lessons. Never wrote a single thing down and made only a handful of the required dishes that were necessary for a pass in the exam. So, when I arrived on the morning of the exam, a 3-hour exam I might add, it will not come as a shock to you that when I opened the paper, I was feeling less than confident. Oh, my days what is this? There are questions in here about chemical compounds of food and storage options and ideal cooking temperatures. *I don't remember learning any of this in class. What the hell.* I sat there and flicked through pages and pages of questions that I had no way of answering. *Surely, I didn't miss this much? Maybe I should have revised a bit then. Why did I think this was going to be easy? You have really cocked this one up Ab.* If I could, I would have got up and walked out. But instead I had to sit there for 3 hours, watching everyone else writing and the home economics teacher, who just happened to be invigilating that day, smirking at me with her fat, round face soaking up every second of my obvious discomfort.

Every time overwhelm hits, I go back to that hall. I see myself sat at the desk, frozen and unable to work. Desperately flicking through to find something I can answer, maybe this will be the question that will give me the marks, maybe I'm reading it wrong? With every flick of the page getting more and more anxious and distressed.

I dig when in overwhelm. At least for a long time I did, until I happened upon a blog written by Mark Manson in which he details a story of the wise old sage. I have sampled it here for you. For the full blog on Self-awareness visit https://markmanson.net/self-awareness

> So basically ... There is an old apocryphal story from 16th-century India where a young man climbs a large mountain to speak to the sage at the top. Supposedly this sage knew, like, everything and stuff. And this young man was anxious to understand the secrets of the world.
>
> Upon arriving at the top of the mountain, the sage greeted the young man and invited him to ask him anything (note: this was way before Reddit threads).
>
> The young man then asked him his question, "Great sage, we stand upon the world, but what does the world stand upon?"
>
> The sage immediately replied, "The world rests upon the back of a number of great elephants."
>
> The young man thought for a moment, and then asked,

"Yes, but what do the elephants stand upon?"

The sage replied again, without hesitation, "The elephants rest upon the back of a great turtle."

The young man, still not satisfied, asked, "Yes, but what does the great turtle rest upon?"

The sage replied, "It rests upon an even greater turtle."

The young man, growing frustrated, began to ask, "But what does–"

"No, no," the sage interrupted, "stop there – it's turtles all the way down."

What if I had been realistic when I walked into that exam. What if I had accepted that I bunked off 60% of the year. That I had not done 1 minute of revision and did not even own the textbook for the lesson. What if I had gone in there, looked at the paper and said to myself, "well it's no surprise you can't answer a single question you cockwomble. You only have yourself to blame. Accept it and move on." I would still have got an "Ungraded" and the teacher would still have a fat face and smug grin, but those 3 hours would have felt a lot easier, and I probably wouldn't have remembered that day at all.

The moral of the story – Stop digging. Start building.

How I built resilience

STOP, BREATHE, LISTEN

The first thing I say to a client who's experiencing overwhelm is breathe. In fact, whenever I receive an unexpected or slightly panicked email or FB message from a client, my response will almost always begin with *breathe*. It may sound a little flippant, but it's sound practical advice. Overwhelm triggers a physical response. Our minds become foggy and we can become disorientated. Stumbling from one situation to another achieving very little. Pushing forward, refusing to stop for fear of rolling back down the hill. Overwhelm is not like anxiety or panic. Breathing exercises for anxiety are designed to slow down our breathing so we aren't taking on too much oxygen. When in overwhelm, we actually want to feed our brains and so deep breaths are recommended. Instructing a client to sit and just breathe gives them a mechanism to STOP. Once they have stopped and breathed for a minute or two, then I can begin to help. We do not hear well in overwhelm and our concentration is affected. Have you ever tried to talk sense to someone who is in full overwhelm? They cannot and will not listen. So, for me to coach them or for them to coach themselves – they need to be ready and able to listen.

My core completion driver means I have pushed through on many occasions, and honestly the results weren't always bad. I need to know how the story ends and so when I am mid-flow watching a webinar or listening to a chapter of an audio book or tidying the shelves of my office, I push though. This means a few late nights and dark circles under my eyes; however, I stay present with my decision to do this. I do not allow myself to be driven by a subconscious desire. I am driven by the feeling of getting it done. And it is almost always worth it.

When it comes to writing and coaching, I am far more disciplined. Learning how to stop and recharge is an essential tool I teach; and therefore, I too need to demonstrate it. It's not as easy as some might think; we're conditioned to work hard, so taking a break is loaded with judgement and discomfort. Rest and reward are essential to avoid overwhelm and switching our mindset to see them as part of the process helps reduce the noise of judgement.

A client told me recently that she always felt guilty when she wasn't working. She struggled with procrastination for most of her life and had at this point been in business, 'her lovely hobby' as she calls it, for over 23 years. Since working with me, she had begun to overcome much of her struggle and be more consistent with the tasks around her business. She was, however, now plagued with guilt every time she chose to take a break. Remember the 4 stages of competence? She had become painfully aware of what needed to be done, and this became noise and judgment. "What if you look at the down time as the goal?" I asked. "What if the downtime was the reward? How would that feel?" "Like I am meant to have it," she replied. "Can you do that?" I asked. "Well, yeah, absolutely," was the reply.

I don't have many life coaching clients. In order to grow my business, I had to niche, and niche I did. I feel at my most "useful" when helping fellow female entrepreneurs and small business owners find success and fulfilment in their work. I love working with women in business and occasionally this means women working in business not just business owners.

> When Covid19 hit us hard, many women who were used to packing up and leaving for the office each day suddenly found themselves sat at home in front of a laptop, no makeup on, and screaming kids under their feet. All trying to navigate the struggles that those of us who are used to working from home have been juggling for years; we found ourselves in the same boat. Well, in the same storm, but maybe not the same boat. Suddenly, everyone is on Zoom and tuning into daily FB lives (that used to be something only us home workers could do).

> No routine, no boundaries, no idea of what time it was or how to structure their day. So, my niche became a lot more fluid. I suddenly had working mums wanting to join my FB group searching for a magic mindset solution for home-schooling and home working. And the biggest struggle many of them face, apart from the obvious disconnection from their normality and a massive dose of gratitude for the peace and quiet they used to get on their 2-hour commute. The biggest struggle was overwhelm. Unable to give themselves permission to pivot, they were stuck in a wilderness of nostalgia. Unable to let go of their old ways of working was causing overwhelm. Although some will, of course, have leaned in hard to the flexibility and advantages of "working from home", many struggled to police their time and found themselves on a constant loop of juggling and judgement.

I was overjoyed when my stepdaughter Lauren referred a client to me. As any parent will know when one of your children recommends you to a friend ... you are doing something right! Lauren is the most extroverted of our girls. She has always loved to party and lives for every opportunity she can to have fun, laugh dance and socialise. She has a wide circle of friends and is dedicated to maintaining those friendships. Her love of music is something she shares with her Dad and her huge capacity for empathy and emotional intelligence, mean that she and I get on like a house on fire. She has been a massive supporter of the work I do, and this fills my heart with joy. Much of what I do and why I do it is to pave the way for the next generation. Right now, the millennials are nailing it when it comes to global and social awareness and it is my generation who seem to be failing. My mission is to demonstrate to our girls that life is about choices and to be the best version of yourself, is how you get life to work for you. Lauren has embraced this wholeheartedly. Making the most of each day while planning hard for the amazing and exciting goals I know she will achieve. Lauren has big plans and no one and nothing will stand in her way. Her love of travel will take her far for sure, and I cannot wait to share in the wonderful life I know she will create.

Maria and Lauren work together at a local firm of solicitors and during a lunchtime conversation Lauren was showing Maria my new website. Maria was keen to engage in coaching as she values the process, having been coached and mentored at work; she was keen to get back on track with her personal goals, and so the next day she emailed me and the rest, as they say, is history.

Maria is part of the human resources management team and she was, at the time, single. Her company, like many businesses during Brexit, had gone through some big changes. Brexit, the other arse wart of an issue that we'd had to endure for best part of 4 years was taking its toll. People were fearful and businesses were getting ready for what they thought would be a shit storm of issues once we departed the EU. Who knew that Brexit would be the nation's trial run for how to cope in a crisis? So there had been a lot of upheaval at work and this was taking its toll.

After a few tough years since returning from Dubai, Maria had originally approached me for support with getting back on track with fitness, selfcare, and getting herself back to the fun, healthy person she had been before. She had just bought a flat and decided 2020 was the year to get her shit together. After only a few sessions, Maria was nailing it. It is a joy to coach someone who is already resourceful, positive, and determined. All she needed was a nudge in the right direction. Then there was a huge shake up at work and all hell broke loose. Long hours, huge responsibility shifts, and a massive increase in her workload meant she was working even harder than she was before. Now Maria is one of those "ideal" employees. Someone everyone can rely on to get it done. Without kids and a husband, Maria believed it was her duty to step up and fill in the ever-increasing gaps in the workforce. Her dedication, determination, and a driver to serve and step up, left her exhausted. By the time she arrived for her session just prior to the covid19 outbreak, she was done:

What has happened to me Abbie? I was doing so well and now I feel like I am failing. I'm exhausted from all the upheaval at work, and I cannot even begin to think straight.

Classic employees' mindset and strong values had triggered the overwhelm warning. For Maria, her exhaustion had come from not only taking on multiple new responsibilities at work, but also from failing to maintain her own selfcare. See, overwhelm comes when we stop prioritising the things we love, not from having too much to do. The things that build our resilience and the things that feed our souls and top up our energy. Maria loved to run; she had stopped. Maria likes to eat healthily, as she knows this will help keep her energy up. But during the upheaval, she was now making poor food choices out of guilt and convenience. See its quicker and easier to snack on a packet of crisps at your desk, while continuing to work through your lunch, than it is to step away, take 30 mins, and eat a salad. Maria was working long hours, so was missing her morning or evening run, something she knows is essential for her wellbeing. Her core behaviours to be useful and her value to serve meant she was constantly in work mode. Switching on her phone and emails in the early hours and working late at home so she could be ahead of the game the next day. Guilt and her determination to step up to the challenges at work meant she was putting her own needs way down the list.

"Well done for noticing the warning signs" I said. "Perfect timing; you are in the right place". We chatted for a while, and soon Maria was back on track and we had come up with a plan. The next time I met with Maria – this time on Zoom because by then we were in lockdown – she was much happier and more focused. She had risen to her own challenge of maintaining her wellness by putting herself first. Thus she was able to continue to meet the challenges at work because she was stronger and more focused. By the time we were in lock down, there were, of course, many other unprecedented demands to face. Though neither of us knew what lay ahead, for Maria the decision she'd taken to maintain her mental resilience meant she was about as ready to face the uncertainty as she could be. So, here is the thing, we cannot predict much in life – only that life is unpredictable. No one could have anticipated the global crisis we would face and the inevitable shit storm that will no doubt hang over us for many years to come. The only way we can stay sane is to stay in control of our minds. Mindset tools are for sure what is needed, and like many of my coaching colleagues, I feel that everything I have learnt up to this point has been preparing me for what lies ahead.

We cannot serve others if we refuse to serve ourselves. So, the first thing on the list is breathe. Take the oxygen mask and place it firmly on your face and breathe. Then, and only then, are you ready to serve.

TAKE A BREAK AND DO A DUMP

When a person is experiencing overwhelm, they will often feel as though it's too late to reach out for help. They feel consumed with confusion and low on energy and the thought of adding a coaching session in feels too much. They retreat and avoid. This can be a tricky situation and is often why "selling our services" can be hard – those most in need of support will be actively avoiding it. Coaching is challenging, and when clients realise they are the ones doing the work, it can put them off. We think we want to control our lives, but many of us, particularly those who're struggling, just want answers. We want to be told what to do and then get on with it.

So, when Maria came to me asking for life coaching, I made it very clear that working with me would require commitment from her. My role as a coach is to facilitate not advise, and while my coaching style and approach are compassionate and supportive, rather than challenging and directive, the work will be done by her.

Maria accepted the challenge without hesitation. This inner capacity for determination has stood her in good stead, and throughout our coaching relationship she has never once waivered. She has maintained responsibility for her struggles and her solutions, and I have seen her grow in both confidence and self-awareness. Maria has enormous capacity to serve, and her drive and determination are undeniable. All she had to do was turn those drivers onto herself. To give herself the same kindness, priority, and consideration that she so easily offers to her family and employers.

Overwhelm is, as we know, a warning. Like the beep on your fridge when you leave the door open too long. Something I often do when searching for inspiration for what to cook for tea, or looking furiously for the Mars bar I know I left at the back of the shelf. It is a warning and when it beeps, I get annoyed. "Shut up Karen (our fridge is called Karen). Calm your tits can't you see I'm looking for a Mars bar?" I get annoyed with Karen and overwhelm works in much the same way.

It's inconvenient, it drains our energy, and we focus all our attention on the overwhelm rather than the solution. In business, overwhelm comes in many forms. People letting us down or a sudden influx of orders or issues with IT that send us spinning. It is so easy to put all our energy into screaming and bashing a computer screen rather than stepping back to look at the source of the fury.

When a client attends a session already experiencing overwhelm, they may have been operating on autopilot for quite some time. The priority is to get them to a state where they can release the frustration, put their hands back on the wheel and see the road ahead. Only then can we begin to plan.

The best way to take control again is to stop and get it out of your head. Listen to the warning and act accordingly. Do not sit with a hundred things in your head, get them out and on to paper/computer whatever. I advocate paper for overwhelm. Our brain works in a completely different way when we write than when we type. Handwriting offers a freer flowing process, but go with what works for you.

Having a coach or business buddy will assist you in this process. I like to use post it notes, and I know for sure when the overwhelm beeper is buzzing in my head because I end up surrounded by a sea of multi-coloured squares. This is a sign that I need to begin to make a more structured plan. A brain dump onto 'post its' works wonders to get me ready.

In chapter 7, we talked a lot about using priorities to manage time. Time can be a major cause of overwhelm, so the two really go hand in hand. They both help and hinder each other. Prioritising requires a clear mind. In order to prioritise effectively, our brains need to be operating at a higher level of consciousness, and this requires additional energy. Doing a brain dump allows us to close down a few of the tabs we have open and helps us perform better.

I love to brain dump. Mind maps are cool too, although they can be tricky in the middle of overwhelm, so unstructured dumping is just the ticket. When I helped Maria with overwhelm, once we were both breathing calmly, she took a piece of paper and began to dump.

"What have you stopped doing, Maria, since this all began?"
Running. Eating well. Reducing screen time. Maintaining boundaries. Reading. Prioritising me.

"Let's revisit the goals you set at the start of the year to help you maintain wellness."
Health. Wellbeing. Happiness. Fulfilment.

"What is driving you right now?"
I want to do well and support others at work.
I need to feel that I am being as useful as I can be.

"What values are you meeting?"
Others are struggling and I need to help them.
I feel like if I stop someone will notice and think I'm not pulling my weight or doing my best.
I value commitment, and I'm committed to my team

"What values are you neglecting?"
I value my own wellbeing, and I'm ignoring that right now.

"What is the cost of neglecting your value for wellbeing?"
I will not be able to do any of the other things.

"So, what is the priority right now?"
Me.

Dump, dump, dump. Realisation kicks in when we start to brain dump and the answers start to jump out. This makes prioritising much less of a drain and ensures that we prioritise the right things.

For example, without this process, Maria may have chosen to cut back her hours, or asked for a pay rise, or told her boss she needed help or couldn't cope. None of these options were what she desired, and none would have solved the situation long term. Asking for help is great, getting a pay rise is awesome; however the point is that if Maria had taken those things and continued to work as she was, they would have made no difference to her wellbeing and overwhelm. In fact, she would probably have become more overwhelmed, feeling she needed to justify the help and extra money.

If you are experiencing overwhelm on a regular basis, then getting good at dumping and planning is recommended. Incorporate a regular dump into your process and notice if patterns appear:

- Is there is a person or situation that triggers your overwhelm alarm?
- Where are you leaving the fridge door open too long?
- What are you searching for?

As soon as you begin to feel like your head is in the fridge looking for the Mars bar you know your husband has already eaten, stop. Shut the door, sit down, and do a dump.

Building *your* mental resilience

I saved the best for last. I began this book by sharing with you how my amazing journey began, with Lisa by my side, guiding me through this magical process of building mental resilience. Mindset is the process through which we filter the outside world. Mental resilience is how we respond to what is being allowed in. Overwhelm is, I believe, the physical response to the combination of the other 6 struggles. They rarely appear alone, so we need mindset tools to help decipher what's really going on. Fear feels like confusion; self-doubt feels like guilt; and mindset tools are how we divide and conquer. Struggle is exhausting – mindset gives us energy and mental resilience is where the true power sits. It is my wholehearted belief that those who regularly take steps to build mental resilience will be the happiest and most satisfied among us.

I genuinely believe that in order to navigate life and all its challenges and remain well, both mentally and physically, we need to choose. Life is not easier for those who choose to practice mental resilience. Life doesn't become richer or more satisfying for those with growth mindsets, and business is not made simpler or less challenging because you choose an entrepreneurial mindset. It simply *feels* easier, less challenging more accommodating. If we want to be happy, we need to choose to be happy. If we want to be successful, then we must choose to define our own version of success; and if we want to be surrounded by others who lift us up, support, and inspire us, then we too need to choose to be that for others.

Self-pity is a place I sat for many years. I felt sorry for myself for the hand I was dealt. I resented the way I was treated by others in relationships. I blamed those closest to me for allowing me to make poor choices. I punished myself with pity and remorse for the situations I found myself in. Asking "why me" instead of "what next".

The warning signs were there. I didn't just learn how to notice my overwhelm. Or to wonder why my instincts were screaming "step back you fool! WFT are you doing?" All the signs were there. From the age of 5, I was able to tell a good choice from bad one; what I have learnt to do now is listen. That is true strength.

Since Lisa passed away in 2009, I have continued what she helped me to start. I have become infatuated with the process of self-awareness, and my life has improved massively. I have all I could ever wish for, and I can honestly say without hesitation that despite the struggles I have faced in starting a business, I wouldn't change a thing. My struggles have meant that I can write this book. Without them I would have little to say. This book marks the end of yet another cycle of personal growth and the beginning of another level of fulfilment and excitement.

Since starting my business in 2017 I have been through just about every emotion and struggle possible. I have wanted to give up and walk away many times, and yet something stopped me. My belief that I am here as part of something much bigger than myself has kept me going. And though I have experienced serious dips in my mental resilience, I was able each time to bounce back using this one simple question "what part are you playing in this?" If I had chosen to continue to blame others as I had in the past, my journey would have been over before it even began.

My issue in the past was relationships. It was the place I always seemed to lose my power and fail. When we start a business, this is also a form of relationship. Partners, customers, and of course the obvious online platforms. We are basically in a relationship with the entire online community, so almost the whole planet – in this potentially chaotic situation, boundaries are essential to maintaining mental resilience.

Boundaries are essential, as they form the basis for our mindset processing, which allows us to retain the power to deal with whatever comes our way. If we drop our boundaries and let others get in our heads, then we lose control and struggle to find solutions.

If social media is triggering anxiety in you then, limit the time you spend on there. If other people are causing you to question and doubt your decisions, then only dig so far. Feedback is fine, but we only dig so deep when we begin with the question, "what do I want at the end of this?" Starting here helps you avoid the vortex of "what if ..." Or "I can't because ..." These only lead to overwhelm confusion and indecision. If someone gives you feedback, listen, evaluate, and then choose what you want to do next. Boundaries also help us do this and stay true to who we are. No business is worth compromising on who you are and by building mental resilience, who you are will become your biggest asset.

I let my boundaries drop at the start of my business journey. My low self-confidence when it came to being in business meant I craved collaboration. And for a while I forgot what I had learnt. Those 8 years working with Lisa and then a further 5 years of training and pushing through to find me, meant overcoming unimaginable fears. Business had brought all those fears back, and so I reverted to the co-dependency that had gotten me into so much trouble in the past. Much like I had in my relationships, I believed I was unable to succeed on my own merits. So, I craved collaboration to satisfy my desire to serve others. Whilst I love to buddy up, and I do miss working in a team, I was ignoring the reasons why I felt I had to collaborate.

I was trying to meet everyone else's needs and ignoring my

own. My need to be liked meant that I continuously put myself out there, accepting all offers and requests, even those that weren't good for me or my business. I lost sight of who I was and was clinging to the hope that one of these offers would be the one to save me. I was playing the victim because I didn't believe I could do it for myself.

When I finally stopped, I remembered that I could.

Do not ever let anyone say you cannot do it. Not even YOU. Stop doubting your story and just tell it – whether anyone reads it or not. The magic is in the process. Life and business are just a story to be told, a play to perform. You get to choose your part and you get to choose your lines, and if you have the courage to speak up, you will be the star.

WHERE OVERWHELM SHOWS UP IN BUSINESS

No one ever said it was going to be easy. When I began my business journey, I believed that it would be hard work, but I didn't for even one moment imagine it would challenge me to my very core. I thought I was walking away from stress, anxiety, frustration, and bullshit when I left work. I hadn't anticipated that my own values, behaviours, and beliefs would be at the root of much of my discomfort. I'm much better at noticing where they work and where they don't, and this has certainly helped me to navigate through tough times. Overwhelm can't be avoided, and honestly, we don't want to eliminate it. It's a warning and it has purpose. We can, however, get better at doing things that help replenish our energy as well as avoiding the situations that lead us there.

As I write the final chapters of this book, we are still very much in the grips of the Covid19 pandemic. When we recover,

I hope that we will have a renewed appreciation for ourselves and our own selfcare and that we will understand that with mental resilience, we each have the power to endure. I hope that despite difficult times, the passion projects and creative businesses will rise and become more important and sought after than ever. No longer will we put off that massage or yoga class. We will prioritise days out with our family and support small local businesses. We will prioritise selfcare and we will recognise the important part that mindset and mental resilience has played in our survival.

If you are just starting out, then I applaud you. If you are coming back after the losses of Covid19, then congratulations. If you are choosing to rethink or retrain after this all has passed, then I am here for you. Maintaining mental resilience is essential no matter what stage of business you are at, and right now, passion, joy, and positive prosperity are what the doctor ordered. Make mindset your number one priority, remain curious and be ready to pivot. I hope this book will offer each of its readers the support and insight to help them anticipate and overcome their struggles.

Top tips summary – Overwhelm to resilience

Keep these tips to hand to help you stop overwhelm when it starts:

Where Overwhelm Shows Up	Top Tips to Beat Overwhelm
You experience consistent feelings of anxiety over things that are normally not an issue.	When you notice the signs of anxiety, stop immediately. The quicker you stop and take a breath, the quicker you can recover. Take a short break and regroup. Don't try to outrun it.
You have dips in energy, and it becomes harder and harder to pull yourself up.	Coping with overwhelm takes up a lot of physical and mental energy. Rest and good nutrition are key to maintaining energy levels. Do something physical to boost your happy hormones. Also, step into the role of a friend. What advice would you give someone experiencing overwhelm? What might they need?
You are overthinking activities that require action.	Logic goes out of the window when we are in full overwhelm. And we will overthink rather than take action. Breathing exercises are great for kicking logic back in. Writing stuff down or brainstorming are also great ways to reduce overthinking and put us back in to action mode.

You are firefighting problems that are bigger than you, instead of calling for help.	Trying to tackle things alone will only send you deeper into overwhelm. Don't be a hero, be a warrior. Be ready to walk away if you need to and ask for help when you need it.
You lily pad from problem to problem as soon as it starts to get real.	Take some time to ask if it is the problem that you are jumping away from or the outcome. If the problem is too big, ask for help. If the outcome itself overwhelms you, then you might want to revisit what it is you are trying to achieve.
You ask for help in the wrong places and avoid looking at what might be at the root of a problem.	You need to be sure you are facing the right problems. Be sure to ask for help with what caused the overwhelm as well as help to feel better.
Your brain switches off and refuses to allow any more information in; you go into to shut down.	Grab a piece of paper and write down what you are going to do TODAY (don't worry about yesterday or tomorrow, just focus on today).
You feel like you are failing and unable to come up with positive or practical solutions.	Remember it is your mindset that decides whether you take action or fall into overwhelm. If you are struggling to come up with practical solutions, then reach out to those with business knowledge or expertise specific to your needs. Let them be your voice of reason.

You start to resent clients and customers because they intrude on your time. More clients mean more work. More work means more overwhelm.	Don't let sales or clients predict your productivity. Plan and prepare as much as you can. Plan activities that keep your productivity steady. Make mental wellness a priority every day.

BOOK RECOMMENDATION

The Last Lemon – by Lisa Swerling & Ralph Lazar

During my friendship with Lisa, our relationship pivoted on many occasions. Her impeccable skills and dedication to therapy meant she rarely stepped out of her role, and her language and behaviours were consistent. For 8 years she sat beside me through my own journey of self-discovery, offering solid ground at times when I simply wanted to give up. She is, as I am sure you will have realised by now, still very much a part of my journey. And her passion for life lives on inside me, a daily reminder to show up as myself and live life to the full. Lisa's love of books was inspiring, and I always left her house with something to read. It seemed whatever predicament I found myself in, there was a book she had to hand that could offer comfort and insight. This is a tradition I have continued with my clients and of course here within my own book. Lisa would be overjoyed that I have chosen to write a book of my own, even though she would have been mortified to be in it. As a book designed to offer support and guidance to women in business, I debated whether to include Lisa's influence, for fear it would distract from the core purpose of the book. I'm very glad to have made the decision to include her. In all honesty, without her, it isn't my story. My life makes no sense without her, and I like to think I have her blessing.

Lisa remains to this day the most naturally talented therapist I have ever worked with. I still recall the words of her humble insistence each time I thanked her for everything she had done: "Abbie this is not about me, you have done the work; you have made the changes, not me", she would say, and then she would hug me so tight I could feel the energy flow through my body and deep into my heart.

Of all the books Lisa passed on to me, *The Last Lemon* was the most challenging. "I don't get it", I said one afternoon after reading the book for the third time. "I don't get it". "What is it you want to get?", Lisa asked. "Why did you give me this? Is it because I need to protect my tree? Who is on my tree? What is on my tree? Do I stop helping others is that it? I don't get what you are asking me to do". "Asking you?", she said with a little smile and tilt of her head that always made my stomach twitch.

I sat and looked at the book. "Am I the tree?", I said quietly. Lisa smiled – this time a big happy grin. "You can be anything you choose to be Abbie, anything".

It turns out I was the tree. This little book of enlightenment was a simple, yet profound message of selfcare and mental resilience. Show yourself love first and you can survive anything. A message I remind myself of every day, as I practice gratitude and acceptance for the life I love so much and the amazing people in it.

CHAPTER 9
Inspirational Stories

*"There is power in allowing yourself
to be known and heard,
in owning your unique story
and using your authentic voice."*

MICHELLE OBAMA

The part I enjoy most about my coaching practice is connecting women who can support and encourage each other during their business journeys. Working with me means becoming a part of a vast network of likeminded individuals, each invested in the practice of supporting each other to thrive. I love the energy that comes from facilitating these relationships and the power that can be drawn from accountability, engagement, and congruence. I have many friends in business, and every day I meet more amazing women who blow me away with their passion and courage. I never tire of hearing the stories of how they too have overcome struggle and setbacks to make their dreams a reality. Some of those women have generously offered to share their stories here. It is an honour to have their contributions and I hope you find their stories as uplifting and inspiring as I do. Enjoy.

Emma Hannay – Stamped with Love
www.stampedwithlove.uk

I started my business by accident really. It was 2014, I was on maternity leave with my first child and felt like I needed to be doing something. I'm not one for sitting around day in day out, and although raising a new-born was challenging, I just needed something for me. I've never been creative, but I reckoned I could hit things with a hammer and after some internet research I found some items and thought I'd give it a go. Initially, I made some pieces for friends and family, posted some pics online as you do, and then people started asking me if I was selling them – hey why not, and in 2015 Stamped with Love was born.

    5 years has now passed and I've 'given up' twice. The first time was quite soon after I started the business, I had joined a

Facebook group for other stampers and had casually asked about Pinterest, asking if it was a platform for inspiration and whether we could recreate items we found there. I knew nothing about copyright, nothing about business either really. I was jumped on by the admin who ran the group, my word she was mean! I got a virtual ear bashing, and she scared me; it took me a little while to realise this is exactly what she wanted to do. She ran one of the biggest stamping pages on Facebook, thousands of likers, and she was considered the forefront of knowledge on UK stamping. Her aim was to scare off new competition like me, and initially it worked. But I had more and more people asking me to make things; it was a massive confidence boost, and I found another marketplace to sell on, and she wasn't there.

I did my thing over on Etsy, I still kept a presence on Facebook as you need to these days, but I didn't join any groups and focused my attentions on Etsy. I was getting busier and busier but a break down in my marriage meant that I put the business on hold again. Frustratingly, my business was one of the causes of the breakup. The success was hard for my husband to understand; he just saw it as a glorified hobby and didn't realise that it was topping up our income and paying for all the baby groups my son and I did. I moved back in with my parents and tried to stamp, but my heart wasn't it in; after 8 months we managed to get our own place and I started renting a small studio. My mojo started coming back and my relationship with my husband was being rekindled; we started marriage counselling and eventually got back together. I felt a real change in my mindset. I felt so enthusiastic, and now I had my husband's support. I wanted to really make a go of this business; I wanted to someday turn it into my fulltime job. It's still my side-hustle, but I'm getting there...

My customer base are mums. I love making pieces for

their husbands on Father's Day, gifts for their own mothers on Mother's Day, and presents for their little ones when they start school. In 2018 I had another baby and my eldest was starting school, during my maternity leave I threw myself into my business and had my most successful year to date. I considered leaving my part-time job at the local council, but then Brexit ramped up. The handmade world went quiet, super quiet. The uncertainty of finances with a No Deal exit meant people in the UK weren't buying much, and huge changes with Etsy meant that my international market had all but disappeared. I was so grateful for that hesitation in leaving my 'day job'. It was tough; it took every ounce of energy I had to get the enthusiasm to promote myself, but it also meant I needed to up my game. I needed to look at other avenues to make money.

    I built a brand-new website, learnt about SEO and started investigating Craft Fairs and stockists. I did a 5-Day challenge on Facebook a friend had recommended and learnt so much from the lady who ran it that I joined her paid for group. This was so against what I usually do; I'm one of those people who is fiercely independent. I want to learn it, and I want to do it myself. But this group has helped me take my business to the next level, and when COVID19 hit the UK, I knew I needed to use this to my advantage. As small businesses all over Facebook were announcing they were closing, I decided to stay open and make some new products. Through the group, I learnt that Facebook adverts were becoming cheaper and cheaper, as fewer big businesses were advertising. I decided to take the plunge and give it a go; it was a leap, as I had to basically write off that money in case it didn't work. And that money would have bought me a lot of stock. Well, it was a huge success! After a week, I had to turn off the adverts to catch up with orders! I took 2 weeks off from the 'day job' to focus on completing the orders, and everyone pitched in and helped. The kids enjoyed walking to the post box with me every other day and helping me post the lovely items all over the country.

Many people in crafting groups on Facebook didn't like that businesses were still trading and putting postal workers and delivery drivers at risk, but I reached out to my customers and asked them if they had friends or family working for Royal Mail. I had lots of positive messages: Posties were happy to still be working and I had some lovely messages from customers thanking me for being open and allowing them to send little tokens to their loved ones. The community feel around my business, amongst both my customers and fellow small business owners was wonderful. I didn't feel lonely, as you can do sometimes when working away at a business; I found some lovely support networks locally and we spent time promoting each other's businesses. I was lucky to get 3 months free from my email marketing company and used this to promote other small businesses. Also, with some of my profits I was creating Thank You keyrings for key workers. My business kept me going, both mentally and financially.

My best advice from my first 5 years is to find a tribe. Find a group of likeminded women (and whilst I don't mean to be sexist, men and women do look at business in a very different way). Learn from them, let them inspire and teach you what they know. If you have an opportunity to get a mentor or business coach and you can afford it (even if it's only just), then go for it. One of the hardest things to do is to stay positive, but tomorrow is always a new day. You don't have to be 'on it' every day. Give yourself time off: take a morning off, go for a walk, take time to reassess. Some things you'll try won't work. Chalk it up to experience, scrap it, and move on – you can always try it again at a later date. Having a tribe that you can use as a sounding board will help you so much with this. Run ideas past them and see what they think; commiserate the failures, celebrate the successes, and do it together. Opportunities will arise and it will be scary making that decision to go for it, but you just never know what it might lead to. One day you might even be invited to write a piece for a book!

Jennie Smith – Sole to Soul
Yoga Instructor, Holistic Therapist & Life Coach.
www.beautysalonhavant.co.uk

When I look back to 2009, I suppose I never really intended to seriously run my own business! It was more a case of my children becoming less dependent and me thinking I would fill my time by creating a "cottage industry" that would enable me to buy my husband a Christmas present with money I had earnt myself, and possibly to contribute some spending money to the family holiday. I had been a kept woman for 16 years of marriage.

I had always fancied dabbling in beauty therapy, even though my mother had wrinkled her nose at the idea ("all those feet and unwanted body hair!"). Encouraged by my own beautician, it seemed a good place to start, something I could easily fit around my children – I still wanted to get to sports day and the school concert!

I trained over the course of a year to complete my VTCT levels 2 and 3 in Beauty and Body Massage and set myself up in the granny annex attached to my parents' home. I was lucky to have this option since the overheads were minimal compared to a shop premises, and let's face it, I had yet to source a client!

I felt pretty confident at that point that I could make this work, having come from a family who ran their own small business; anyway, it was really only to enhance the income generated by my husband.

I got busy shopping: couch, towels, varnish, wax pots, tweezers, uniforms, chairs, desk ... on I went, all on a credit card I might add.

I spent a small fortune having a logo designed and price lists printed on premium quality paper. I set about posting them through doors in the hope of drumming up custom. I also paid for small adverts in a local free directly from which I acquired 5 clients over the period of about 18 months! It was SLOW. Feeling less confident now!

Despite my efforts, I'm not sure anyone, including myself, could really have said I was running a business at this point, and I worked as and when a client arose, school hours only. It was a maybe one client today and one or two in three days' time scenario. I needed to advertise.

I got a website; in fact, I got two websites. The first was designed by an acquaintance and when that didn't work, I let it go and moved on to having one professionally designed and managed. That worked!

Further down the line, I was invited to teach at The Southern School of Beauty Therapy where I had trained. I repeatedly turned down the opportunity until the day the owner called and said, "so if I pay for the teaching qualification will you come and teach here?" – I recognised an opportunity when I saw one, and said yes. I started teaching one day a month as a freelance instructor and continue to do so now, every week.

Now I had two jobs and a better income; all should have been well. Except for a couple of "not so small" matters: two major surgeries, one of which was a "near miss" and both of which caused me to be unable to work for a few months each time. Then there was another pressing issue ... I wanted out of my 20-year marriage.

Divorce is never pleasant, never easy, but mine was complicated by the fact that my husband was employed by my father. I won't bore you with the details, but it was BAD.

Anyone could see this was going to be acrimonious, and to make a long story short, by the time we completed the divorce I was in dire need of money. I walked out of the court having lost the family home and with a very poor financial settlement, plus considerable debt, but the most important thing to me was the welfare of my teenagers: I knew I owed it to them to keep going! All the time they were alright I was alright.

In the middle of all this, I took two years to train as a yoga teacher to enhance my income further, another string to my bow. This was the one thing that kept me sane, and whilst the course was challenging in so many ways, it brought mental focus, emotional support, and hope my way.

These days I have four roles: holistic therapist, beauty/holistic educator, essential oils wellness advocate, and yoga instructor. I work pretty much all the time during the week, including some evenings. It is true that I wish I didn't have to work quite so hard at my age (52), but I am proud of succeeding in creating a beautiful space we call home and even more proud that my girls have turned out beyond "just fine", despite so much turbulence faced at important times in their lives.

Most of the time I LOVE my work. There is no greater prize than seeing a client arrive, maybe in a low mood or embarrassed about their feet, and then watch them leave uplifted, rejuvenated, and positive. It is a joy to teach my students to embrace this industry in their own ways. And as for teaching about oils and leading yoga classes, those things are simply gifts. I am lucky to have variety in my day and a range of wonderful clients who pull me into their confidence, which is an utter privilege.

Until three weeks ago, my income had stabilised (in recent

years) and I had turned a corner from the fall out of divorce. I was "doing alright", debt free.

Then came Co-Vid19 ... The tap turned off overnight, and I seem to have fallen into a no man's land in terms of financial help from the government. That is something that I have no power to change, so I consciously choose to accept it and look at what I can do for myself. However, the impact of no money coming in is, of course, not something anyone could ignore.

My technology skills are somewhat limited, to say the least. I have had to reach out to friends and my daughters to really "get with the program" and bring myself up to speed with online platforms to offer yoga classes or essential oils tutorials from my home, which offers no space for such things. That has been a very steep learning curve. I am so uncomfortable in front of a camera, can't stand the sound of my own voice, have had to practice, rerecord, overcome dips in the internet service. I am learning at a rate of knots.

In the end, I have come to the conclusion that in this climate, "done" is better than "perfect", and I have been heartened by positive feedback and encouragement from many clients, so I am determined to keep going with it.

I have had the discomfort of having to ask for donations in return for online classes when I'm aware that so many offer their service for free – sadly I am not financially secure enough to do that. I question whether what I can offer is good enough, but actually I am offering the best I can, so I know I can do no more. I've given up taking it personally if people don't show up – most of the time they have something else on, and it's actually nothing to do with the quality of my class, and then they turn up next week.

Most importantly, this lockdown period has allowed me to embrace precious time with my daughters living back home, a first for five years. I know that since they are now adults with lives of their own, this is unlikely to happen again, so I am drinking in every drop.

Though I am earning very little at present, I'm taking the time to study further in the areas I already cover, whilst planning some yoga day retreats so that when normality resumes, I will have all the tools in place. I am back on board with an online Life Coaching qualification I've been meaning to complete. These are things that are normally put on the back burner in my busy life. I'm posting regularly on social media in order to keep my name in the frame and remind people that I'm still here.

When Co-Vid19 is all over, I anticipate that in terms of teaching at the training school, I will hit the ground running; likewise with my own clients, who I am sure will be in much need of grooming and selfcare.

For any woman starting her own business, I would say: don't expect your business to grow overnight, it takes time, maybe even years, I don't believe "get rich quick" exists.

Do not look at others who are successful and assume they did it easily; it's hard work, but tenacity pays off.

My final bit of advice: Keep going, even on the days you really don't feel like it; Just keep going.

Jess Walton – Fresh Air Learning
www.freshairlearning.co.uk

I was diagnosed with breast cancer aged 37; at the time, I was a teacher and a lone parent to one boy; I knew this was my wake up to my mantra "One life, live it". Following my treatment, I trained to become a Forest School Leader and began to dream about starting my own business and creating a happier place in my life for both myself and Noah. When I returned to my teaching post, I became increasingly frustrated with the classroom-based restrictions to the creativity and learning of children at school and the pressure on me as a teacher to push development at a rate not specific to their needs. Regular testing and constant assessment of skill and academic achievement meant that not all the children I worked with were enjoying learning as I would like them to. I believe that natural learning, following interests when ready and recognising achievements other than scores and green ticks in books are best for children, along with gaining real life experiences of resilience, risk, adventure, and imagination. I was offered redundancy from the school I worked at and decided it was now or never to take the leap of faith and launched Fresh Air Learning in June 2019.

The majority of my clients are local families with young children who have heard through word of mouth or my Facebook page about the services I offer. I began with very small educational sessions with a few friends and their children, and through the power of social media I gained momentum each week and my groups slowly grew. I feel great enjoyment from seeing my educational beliefs coming to life in the young minds I work with. Children from 12 months through to 16 years have benefitted from working with me and spending time connecting with the outdoors and learning from nature.

Self-belief and acceptance that I am talented enough to provide a service that people will pay for has been a major battle for me to overcome. I have always wanted to run my own business but stepping up to the line and going ahead has been blocked on many occasions by a variety of life situations. I have an incessant fear that failure is always on the horizon. I recognise that I go through fits and starts with energy and concentration either full on or full off! It's how I have always been. During my time at university, my assignments were either a week early or literally on the deadline. Those were the days when we had to print the text, write a covering sheet, and personally deliver it to the course letterbox at the faculty offices!

I've had to work really hard to keep a positive mindset with regards to my life and making decisions to continue the business beyond the Covid-19 lockdown. That I am actually providing a quality service that families want to experience and pay for has been a realisation, as I reviewed messages and feedback online. I know families are wanting directed time in the outdoors, and there is a natural-world knowledge deficit which I can plug through my own passion for the outdoors and ability to instil passion in others through my own love of the outdoors.

Back in March 2020, when the government announced that schools would be closing, my business stopped immediately. Running a business 100% reliant on families with children, I knew I would be badly affected by the Covid-19 pandemic. My motivation stayed for a while, as I gave daily live feed ideas via my Facebook page. I then hit a rather hard brick wall of worry, upset, and fear of the unknown as I began wondering when and if people would be allowed to return to social gatherings, even if they were educational.

I wrote a blog post about the impact of the lockdown on me as a person, how I missed the children I work with, and the regular weekly adult contact with the parents who are customers but who have become friends. It made me realise that I am truly committed to sharing my business with as many people as possible.

I will wait and see if the business regenerates itself after lockdown. There are so many unknowns, will families want to socialise, will people have money to pay for extra experiences? Having time to reflect has been a really positive opportunity.

I have a 9-year-old son, and therefore being able to be at home with him during this time has been a wonderful opportunity to connect and explore new things together. We had never been for a night time walk together, but during lockdown, we went out at midnight to search for a lost item. Also, we've slept downstairs in a tent made of blankets and sheets and celebrated time together, which is a gift to all parents.

I wish I'd known from the start that there are so many supportive people out there who want to listen to ideas and are happy to be sounding boards, contributing and commenting positively on my thoughts and ideas. A gentle nudge here or a link to a new idea there has made all the difference to my mindset and ability to believe I can achieve my long-term goals. Having support from the people you value in your life makes all the difference.

Think of a mantra and live with it. Think it, say it, write it every day. Paint it on your wall, make a keyring with it, choose one for yourself and believe it. Afterall, if you don't ever try, you won't know if you will succeed.

Kari Ann Roberts
Emotional Strength Coach
www.facebook.com/kariann2309

I chose this career path, or I should say it chose me, because in 2004 I went from being excited and passionate about my job to total emotional and physical exhaustion. Eight months before I reached this point, I was full of excitement, passion, and expectations. Working in a job I loved and believed in.

I was a parenting expert in a large local authority, managing a team of family workers, delivering training, writing programmes, and ensuring the parenting strategy was delivered. I knew what we were providing was making a difference to families, as we delivered support to and worked with the families in a holistic way, rather than just telling them what they needed to do. There were some challenges; however, these were manageable, and it was a joy to work with my team. I trained as a coach during this time and learnt so much, which in turn enriched me and my work.

Then transformation happened. We had months of consultations and proposals. The idea was to bring all the services under the banner of The Early Help Teams. Fast forward, and all of a sudden everything is happening quickly. Moving offices, changing teams, recording systems, and a new way of working where I found I had become an assistant team manager in a social care frontline team.

No training on the new recording system and no authorisation to access the system, this was a great start. Trying to keep positive and support my team, even though I felt unsafe and like I was part of a conveyor belt of box ticking time frames. This pigeonhole was just too tight for me to be squeezed into, causing me intense emotional pain. Two things I loved doing, delivering training and workshops with partners and local charities, came to an end.

My workdays became longer and longer, and the one thing I held dear, Wednesday night family night, was threatened. I asked for support and spoke to management on many occasions and was told to just keep doing my good job. I was not sleeping, and I was dreading work every day. Even weekends were taken up with thinking about work or working, not through passion but fear. There was no work life balance.

Teams were unhappy, and it was a struggle to keep my mask of false positivity and confidence from slipping. I had cowritten a programme on emotional health with Solent Health and felt I should know what to do. I felt confused, scared, and very unsafe. My confidence and self-belief crumbled, and I felt myself falling into despair.

One Friday, I left work heavy hearted, tears flowing under my sunglasses, and I drove up to Camberley to see a good friend and mentor. I cried the whole 1-hour journey. I told her how I was feeling, and she looked at me and said, "You have to hand your notice in." I went into panic mode; I was the main wage earner, and we had a mortgage and debts. My job had good holiday schemes, good sickness benefits and a great pension scheme that would be threatened if I left at my age. How could I leave after 12 years of building my career? By the time I left her house, I knew the action I needed to take.

I thought telling my husband was going to be tough. As I walked through the door, he greeted me with a smile, asking how my day had gone. This simple question was the perfect one; I burst into tears and told him exactly how I was feeling, all the pent up feelings and fears came pouring out. He agreed I needed to leave. "We will cope", he said.

So Monday morning came, and I spoke to my manager, handing him my letter of resignation. He asked me to reconsider and hold fire. I knew that whatever happened from that moment on that letter needed to be handed over. From the moment I took this action, even though it felt scary and frightening, I leaned into it. I felt like a ten-ton weight had been lifted from my shoulders.

I viewed work with different eyes, realising this was a job I would not have applied for, and it was not aligned with my beliefs, values, and passion. I knew without a shadow of a doubt I could not just do a job that was more about box ticking, deadlines and fear than what it had been when I applied for the role, which was supporting families to connect with their strengths and make sustainable healthy changes.

It was like a veil being lifted and seeing things through new eyes. Financially it was tough; we sold our house and downsized. Again another major decision; and another huge weight lifted from me. Initially, I became an independent parenting specialist, as this felt comfortable and made sense at the time. Delivering training, writing programmes, and working with services that I knew from my previous role.

There was still restlessness inside me and after two years; I hired my coach who helped me to focus on the restlessness, leaning into a whisper that I was ignoring; drawing me more and more towards coaching. One day she asked me why I was not coaching; I didn't have an answer. That is when I started my business as an emotional strength coach.

I predominantly work with women in business who were like me 5 years ago, on the outside everything looks like it's going well. Good job, nice home, nice car, and nice holidays. All while, being pigeonholed into a space that feels uncomfortable, yearning for something different. Feeling caged because society and created beliefs have built a wall of fear around them. Wearing many different masks and living in fear of them slipping and their real selves being seen. But deep inside them they know how freeing that would be. Getting distracted by everything around them, keeping themselves busy, decorating, remodelling, taking courses to better themselves, joining groups, and clubs to fit in, making sure it all looked perfect if anyone was looking through the window of their life. Not because they want to, but because they think that is what they should do.

Although it may seem a totally different field to work in, I also work with companies exploring social pain, which is cited in every piece of research on work-related stress. It's a huge driver for absenteeism, presenteeism, and leavism. Put simply, it affects people personally, mentally, physically, and professionally. Looking after the wellbeing of everyone within teams is fundamental to personal and the company's business success.

When you can be real, there's no pressure to be permanently positive. Therefore, I explore created and conditioned beliefs. If you choose to, you can be optimistic, hopeful and have more opportunities to feel better. Even if it's only by the smallest margin. This is a big part of why I do what I do.

My biggest mindset struggles have been self-belief and the belief that unpleasant emotions should not be felt. I grew up in a country with a large mixture of cultures. I constantly felt I was only seen because of the colour of my skin. I was the only White British person in my school. I would constantly hear statements from teachers and others that I was not worth teaching or being friends with because White people have no morals, and I would only end up getting pregnant at a young age or taking drugs. Some teachers even called me stupid and told me I would not do anything with my life. If I spoke up or answered back, it seemed like I was just confirming the beliefs they had.

I was never encouraged to feel the anger, hurt, disappointment, fear, and frustration that naturally arose. I chose some unhealthy coping strategies, which at the time I truly believed worked for me, and in all honesty, it did short term. The line from *Frozen* comes to mind "be the good girl you always have to be, conceal don't let them know". So it became hidden in me, and at times that's still my default. I would put myself through so much anguish, my inner voice was constantly saying not to bother as I would fail in the end.

There has been something deep inside me that has whispered at every stage of my life, 'keep going, you have a reason for being here; you are more than they say you are'. In 2017, I met Nicola Snoad, the woman who became my coach. I went to a retreat she was running in Wales after a recommendation from a friend. She was known as the Renegade Coach. The whisper within me that had been there since I can remember got louder and louder. Shouting "GO!" After an hour-long call, everything was arranged.

What I learnt was no experience, no thought, no dream, no result, no life, and no emotion is better than another. All of it is created equal and simply here for you to experience. It was the first time I was able to see myself as enough, not broken, and it was simply a misunderstanding, a story I had created that I had believed to be true. I started to embrace all the things I had believed to be 'wrong with me'. To nurture my emotions and feelings and reconnect with my emotional strength, because I believe nothing can be healed if it is not felt first. Journaling and meditation has really helped me create a space to hear myself, and I am part of a global network that holds weekly listening calls.

This fresh outlook on life gave me a sense of freedom to be me and realise that by showing up as me, I was able to work authentically and openly. Full transparency here, this does not mean things are all sunny and rosy: I still have self-doubt, but I know that this is just a default safety mechanism. I know I don't have to run from it, in fact I do the opposite, I lean into it and thank it for trying to protect me, as I know it is from an organic place. Recognising this gives me the strength to be visible, show up, and hold the space for my clients to connect with themselves.

In November 2019, I sat and really thought about my business. It was at the end of my first year as a coach, and I seriously considered what I was offering. There was a fear of offering something that seemed different from what others were offering, and I asked if I should dilute myself. I sat with this, spoke to my coach, and worked through what was really showing up for me. What I learnt was it's showing up as me, not diluting myself, and letting the ripples and the heartbeats come through and not hiding from it. This has given me the clarity and confidence in my business and the coaching I provide.

Just before COVID 19, I had decided to run workshops using a programme I had created called Building Emotional Strength. I had a launch date and venue. Then the safe isolation lockdown rules came into place two weeks before the first workshop. I had spent a lot of my energy, time, and money into creating these workshops, and they all had to be cancelled. Initially there was disappointment, frustration, and fear; I had a few individual clients that I saw over Zoom and ran a few virtual groups, so fortunately that helped keep the business going. I knew that more and more people would be struggling with their emotional health and wellbeing, but there was a part of me that felt guilty for looking at promoting myself during the first few weeks of the pandemic. I felt I had to play small, but I knew this was coming from a fear of being judged.

So I decided to journal and write down everything I was feeling, talk openly in groups and get support from a few coaches I am blessed to know, who helped me to see that what I was offering was needed now more than ever, and I took the step to contact everyone I had worked with in the past. One of the companies responded by paying me a retainer to keep ten hours a week free for their directors and team leaders to have one to one emotional strength coaching and create some training for the company. Taking that one action opened up an opportunity I am extremely grateful for. It also opened up the opportunity to become an online volunteer to help people who were struggling during COVID 19.

Some parents I used to support also reached out to me and

gave me the idea to open up some virtual parents' emotional strength groups to help them with their emotional health.

I have learnt how to use social media more efficiently and the platform Zoom has become a very important part of my day to day life. I am able to hold online groups and coaching calls with confidence, speak to friends, even had a virtual 60th birthday party for one of them and regular family group calls.

What I have noticed is that the importance of emotional health and wellbeing is being talked about more and there is a sense of kindness that I have not seen before. Even having all the understanding that I have, the pandemic has been a tough rollercoaster of emotions. Connecting with people virtually has given me so much more confidence in running online groups and workshops. Things I had not thought I would/could do. I have kept the spark of passion and confidence I have for my business ignited and shown how important it is to be flexible to change. My family have realised how close we are, even though we have had to be apart. It has helped us all reconnect with our own individual emotional strength.

If you truly love what you offer, then everything else will fall into place. Not everything has to be perfect to take action. You can spend a lot of time and money on things that are not the priority to get your business started. I would encourage you to speak to someone about your branding and think about how you are going to market yourself, who your ideal client is and where they are. I wish I had done this at the very beginning. One thing that has been a godsend to me is my coach. Without her I would not have continued in my business. She was able to help me prioritise where I focus my time and energy.

Ask yourself what you would do if there were no rules, no restrictions, who you would be and how you would turn up, the answers may surprise you. Don't dilute yourself, be yourself, as that is who your clients will resonate with. Hire a coach. Invest in yourself and your company.

Tracey Blake – Aloe Energetix Health and Wellness
https://www.facebook.com/aloeenergetix/

My name is Tracey Blake and my working life started in the Armed Forces. I spent many years in the Royal Navy, living the life of Riley. I loved the sport and fitness, and the team spirit and camaraderie were second to none. Unfortunately, I damaged my spine whilst rescuing two Royal Marines off a cliff. This led to me losing my job and my whole way of life. I was lucky enough to walk straight into another job, initially in a call centre and then later with the NHS, but there I found an atmosphere of bullying and a general lack of care for colleagues and staff. I was very unhappy, and this began to affect both my physical and mental health.

A friend introduced me to Multilevel Marketing with a company called Forever Living. Initially, I fell in love with the products and bought the business in order to get my products at a discounted price, but, as time went on, I began to see a whole new way of earning a living. A way that I could fit around my autistic son and family commitments.

Now, the only way to make a big income with any MLM company is by recruiting new team members, and I am an introvert. I always found it really difficult to get to know people, find out how I can help them and then offer them the business opportunity. So, I have decided that my heart lies with providing a service to my clients, and they can decide what is best for them. I attend events all over the country, showing people different products, how they can use those products to improve their health and wellbeing, and the income they could have by signing up to the different companies I work with. Then leave it up to them to decide what they want. Coming to this realisation was not easy. For 3 years I have given myself a really hard time for not building my business "correctly". But, do you know what? I have built my business in a way that makes me happy, and rather than focusing on just one product, I can offer many products and, therefore, a choice that suits the client. This way of working provides me with enough to have a full and contented life, knowing that I am coming from a place of giving, rather than focusing on building an empire. The other benefit to working on this is that when I was taken poorly, last year, I was able to continue to work according to my ability each day. So, my business works for me, and I work for my business.

Finding the right business coach has been the key to me finding my place. Someone who is able to make me see what I have already achieved and how I can move forward. But you have to find the right coach. I haven't been told anything that I didn't know during my coaching sessions. I just had to hear it in a way that I connected with. Corona virus has brought many businesses to a halt, but, with the support of my coach, I have been able to pivot my business and turn it into something that could survive and even thrive during lockdown and beyond.

One of the most important hurdles to overcome, for me anyway, has been a poor mindset. The saying, "Whether you believe you can or believe you can't, you are right" is so true. If you believe you can't do a thing, you will convince yourself it can't be done. So, believe in yourself and aim for the moon. At least if you fail, you will have reached the stars.

Vicki Hudson
Vicki Hudson Reflexology
https://www.facebook.com/VHReflexology/

I have always been a carer; as a child I wanted to be a nurse, but the realisation of the things a nurse does did not enthral me!

When I was in my late 20's and I was not living my best life, I joined a yoga group and the instructor was a massage therapist as well. She became a mentor (although wasn't called that back then). Then in 2001, I found a course running at Southdowns' which was a 2-year complete complementary therapies course. I gave up my job and my family to do what my heart wanted. It was such an amazing opportunity and one I have never regretted.

My clients are mainly women dealing with issues around fertility, pregnancy, or menopause! They usually struggle with anxiety and need relaxation. My business gives me enormous satisfaction. I love that when people leave me, they feel much better than when they came in.

I've always struggled with feelings of not being good enough, and not having confidence in my abilities and money. These affected me in every area of my life, so why would I think I could run a first-class business without those feelings come up there as well? These feelings stopped me getting out there, for fear that someone would call me out for the fraud I was! I struggled to set good prices and felt awful when telling people how much I charged because they might challenge me to prove I was worth it!

I started my journey of self-discovery a long time ago, looking at family dynamics and my feelings of worth. I didn't get the connection between this and my business. Last year I sought out a coach to help give me direction. Well if only I'd known! Looking at all the things that Abbie now talks about in her book and seeing the evidence there in front of me, with someone else telling me this was true and getting some help with the tools to reframe these beliefs. I've found out how I can work with my core behaviours, drivers, and beliefs and stopped fighting against myself.

I now have some tools that enable me to recognise when I'm feeling out of sync with my mind, so I can stop that spiral of downward chatter. Personally, it has enabled me to look at other areas of my life and use the same tools to feel more confident and connected to people. Revealing the natural caring person inside me, without believing I was pretending. Business wise it has given me the confidence to be less rigid and experiment with what I want from my business and give more of my genuine self to my clients to help them make changes.

Being a hands-on therapist, I have had to step away from my comfortable world during lockdown. Currently my business is not earning any money, which is bringing up a whole lot of new mindset issues! However, because I'm coming at this from a new perspective, a new mindset, my confidence and motivation are on the whole higher, and I've have actively looked at ways to maintain contact with my clients and build my following on social media.

I've never been great at marketing myself and certainly the idea of videos horrified me. After much persuasion, I now do just 2 videos a week, on two different areas of my business, and I'm thinking of adding others! The changes have been incredible, I am much more comfortable with myself 'out there', and the process has become much easier. The first one took all day of my recording it, watching it and deleting it, and starting again, trying to read from a script, but not look like I was reading from a script, not waffling, not scratching, picking my nose or whatever. I now pretty much record and schedule them for when I want them to go out. It has also made me start looking after myself a bit more, as I could see from the videos how dry my skin looked and the bags under my eyes. So, I've started a better routine and even use a little make up! I will continue to build the online community when back at work as a way of getting myself out there, and if nothing else, I hope that I may have a few new clients coming to see me.

Generally, as I go through the day, I start a list of things to do; goal setting has been great – I didn't realise I could be quite so competitive even if it is just with myself.

Living alone has been a struggle as I miss my grandchildren so much, but watching my daughter on videos and chatting over the phone has been lovely as she takes to keeping two little ones entertained all day, every day! I also have a daughter who lives abroad, and the distance is hard now. She hasn't been allowed out for about 8 weeks now and is coping incredibly well, there is a new side to her we are all seeing for the first time.

Given my old mindset, I would have ignored my business until this was over and wondered where everyone had gone. I'd then have blamed the virus for me having to get a 'proper job'. But now, by taking responsibility, I'm building a stronger me and a stronger business.

So far, the positives have given me a chance to stop and understand what 'working on' my business means without being involved 'in' my business. I hadn't realised how stressed and busy I was all the time, and, in some ways, it has been a great break.

Keeping in contact with family and friends via the many social platforms has been great – seeing people while chatting is so much nicer. I've recently moved into a new area, so having time and such fabulous weather to explore it has been something I'm really grateful for.

Taking responsibility for your change and development,

rather than leaving it to fate, will empower and motivate you. Being grateful really does work, you will see the good and kindness in everything and everyone.

Be brave and get out there!

One of my favourite quotes has always been: "if you do what you've always done, you will get what you've always got!"

Sami Turner – Sparkle with Sami
Natural skincare and beauty consultant
www.facebook.com/sparklewithsami

Hi, I'm Sami; mother of 4 children, one of whom has extra support needs. I'm also a fully qualified beauty therapist, something I had wanted to be since leaving school.

I went to college after leaving school to train as a beauty therapist, but my fear of feet got the better of me and I left! I bounced through different courses and jobs. After I had my first child at the age of 17, a daughter, everything changed for me – my whole outlook on life and what I wanted.

Fast forward to 4 years ago, when my thoughts turned to starting and growing my own business. I was working in a garage just to get me off of benefits and to have a little extra income, when my boss brought in some products from his partner for me to try. First off, I wasn't interested as I'm not a girlie girl and I worked in a garage, but I gave in and tried the hand cream. Wow – am I glad I did; I was blown away! I got home and researched the company to see Alan Sugar's picture, a man I love. His business strategies and the ethics of the company blew me away, and I was excited to join up and be able to sell the natural skincare products, but I couldn't afford to invest in myself or the business so I couldn't move forward with it.

I spoke to my bosses' partner more about the business and how things worked. I realised I would have to save up some money to be able to join in and grow my own business. However, between them they believed in me and felt I had something beautiful to give, and they both agreed to invest in me and buy the business in a box, agreeing that I could pay them back weekly. I was blown away by their belief in me. I could do this!

Being with the company has lifted my spirits, helped me come off of the antidepressants that I had been on for about 5 years and develop the courage and confidence to make a better life for me and my children. One I didn't have when I was younger.

So, I researched going back to college and worked out if there was a way I could do it with a part-time job and 4 children. I did I find a way, and I made it work! I'm so glad I did. A year of hard work, plenty of tears, and 8 new qualifications later, I passed and now I'm a fully qualified beauty therapist.

Most of my clients and customers are busy mums like me, as I understand them and can help with their skincare needs as well as reminding them of the importance of self-love. I show them techniques and tips that they can use daily to feel as amazing as they can and help them get their sparkle back, too.

I've had quite a few ups and downs along the way, and I've not always been as present in my business as I should be, due to my own personal mindset of not feeling good enough or scared of failing at anything I do. Feeling so terrified that I couldn't make a better life for my children or not making my business as amazing as I know it can be.

This scared me, so I found a coach and invested into improving on my low self-esteem. Working with the coach was hard, very hard, but it has shown me that the negative voice in my head is just that, a voice, and I could change that. I could believe in myself and prove to myself that I am good enough to achieve anything I set my mind to. So, with all this new information and the friends, like Abbie, I have made along the way through network marketing, I am confident I will make this work.

Covid19 has hit as I write this story, so my beauty treatments have come to a halt, but I still have my online skincare business and can continue to help people with their skincare and self-love through this difficult time. Having to change the way I work a little bit has set the anxiety and worry off again, but the tools I have learnt from my coach has helped me through. Helping others has always been something I've loved to do – something I have often done and then forgotten about myself! Not any more! I have learnt that looking after myself is just as important as helping others, so I say this with an open heart to all of you: self-love is very important in everyday life and in running a business. Not only does it lighten your mood, it makes you feel better about yourself too. My biggest tip is learn, learn, and learn some more; find what interests you and research it. Don't be afraid to ask for help, if you don't know the answer someone else will. I wish I had known from the start what I know now: that mindset and focus is everything, along with your goals and dreams. It hasn't been easy, but everything has been worth it, as I've learnt so much and I'm looking forward to learning more. Good luck and enjoy every day with an abundant heart. Much love Sami xx

CONCLUSION

Does it *really* **need** to be this hard?

You've read my story about how I used the mindset tools I learnt through coaching to navigate my journey into business and overcome the 7 Big struggles. There are a million ways to describe struggle. Our behaviours, values, and beliefs make us who we are. They help us and they hurt us, and this book is my way of explaining what this meant for me. Demonstrating the process of transformation that is possible by using mindset tools.

Mindset is all about energy. Internal struggle is exhausting, both physically and mentally, and the Big 7 that I've shared with you in this book are, I believe, the most common for women in business from the start and throughout their journey. The distractions and behaviours they cause, such as procrastination, avoidance, self-sabotage, and addiction, are what truly hold us back. Developing a growth mindset and maintaining mental resilience offers us a constant source of energy, vital for life and for running a business.

No one says, *I think I will start a business because I need more stress in my life*. They do it because they believe it will offer joy and freedom and flexibility. There is no flexibility in struggle; we are by definition restrained and if we allow the struggle to continue, we will eventually become exhausted and broken.

Mindset tools offer us a way to own our process. To place our internal drivers, values, and beliefs onto a platform where we can step back and gain perspective. From that perspective, we can begin to sort what is helpful from what is not. The process of change is not about deleting parts of who we are; it is simply a process of choosing to learn something new. If something isn't working, we find a way to move past it. To overcome it. To reduce its negative effect by applying an antidote. Bad habits develop over time as a coping mechanism for pain. We simply choose to create new habits that offer a more resourceful cure for the pain. We need the pain to feel alive; we don't, however, need to let it consume us. We make choices.

Even those who grew up with a fixed mindset have the ability to learn new skills; we simply need to make the choice to do so. Just by making that choice, we are signifying a commitment towards a growth mindset.

Struggle, to a point, is necessary and inevitable, but it does not need to be constant or consuming. All that separates those who succeed in business from those who struggle is mindset. Yes, you need a good idea. You must have a good idea and something to sell for sure, and the ability to take action and execute the plans necessary to promote and sell that idea. But those who succeed in delivering on their idea, their dreams, and their goals are those who work purposefully to adopt an entrepreneurial growth mindset: the ability to believe and trust in your dreams even when the going gets tough.

You must believe success is possible to be a success; those who struggle have yet to embrace this simple, yet life changing, concept: self-belief. The struggles are part of the journey, but once we decide that what we want is at least possible, that the script from our past no longer defines or dictates our future, that is the difference.

We are all born with self-belief, although many of us will inevitably lose some of it over time. It's reduced by experiences, situations, setbacks, and other people's agendas. Messages absorbed subconsciously are all stored away in our minds just waiting for someone or something to trigger them. Thankfully, our past does not define our future.

We all have a choice to do better and to feel better. If you have chosen to work for yourself, if you have chosen a path of entrepreneurship, a path of risk and reward, of unpredictability and fulfilment, then choosing to invest time and money in yourself too, should not be difficult. Your business will not save you. Your business, however amazing it is, will not give you the joy and satisfaction you seek, nor will it offer the life altering changes you hoped it would. That is on you. You are the business; therefore, you will need to become the source of joy and fulfilment. Your business is simply the vehicle for the journey.

If you are the business you had better learn to understand, love, appreciate, and prioritise every part of who you are. Do this and you have the recipe for success.

Postscript

SUPPORT FOR THE ONWARD JOURNEY

Navigating the elusive work life balance. What does that even mean? For me balancing my work, my family, and myself is a process that requires behavioural flexibility and acceptance. No two days are the same. Life demands our attention in ways that we cannot predict, and for someone like me, who thrives on organisation and consistency, this in itself is challenging.

Mental resilience is how I find balance. Focusing my attention inwardly to build confidence in my process, shaping behaviours that enable me to show up every day without always knowing what that day will bring. If you have chosen to use your skills your talents and your passion to earn income, then you are the business. You must, therefore, look after YOU.

We are who we are, and our struggles will forever be a part of our journey; they do not need to define us. Switching our mindset to be able to use time effectively to become our own boss so we call the shots, so time no longer enslaves or drains us. Controlling our fear of success and making money – a simple tool that leads to the things we desire like more time with our family, enjoyment, fulfilment, and peace. Finding connections in our business world that energise and inspire us. Giving ourselves permission to let go of the guilt and cease self-sabotage. Noticing when our minds and bodies are crying out for rest and introducing daily routines that navigate us away from overwhelm. Making peace with our past, forgiving others for the part they played, and taking responsibility for our own journey. Overcoming self-doubt and confusion by committing to a journey of curiosity and growth.

I named my business Now Watch Me Fly to remind me of

the last time Lisa and I met in this world. I knew on that day it was to be the last time she and I would be together and that our journey in this life was coming to an end. I felt the anger and sadness well up inside of my chest as my heart struggled to keep a beat. And yet I felt strong. Lisa made sure of that. It was as though everything we had worked on together up to this point, had been preparing me for this moment. She placed her hands gently onto my face and whispered, "It's your time now Abbie; it's your time to fly". A few days later she was gone.

I sincerely hope that my story has inspired you, either to begin your own journey or to continue one that you have started. This is my story and I am honoured to have been able to share it with you. Discovering I had choices was the start of an incredible journey for me, one that I hope, never ends. I thrive on the energy of self-actualisation and I am incredibly grateful that I now have the pleasure of supporting and coaching other women in business to discover who they are too. To embrace their uniqueness and thrive beyond the struggle.

I did not walk this path alone. Although at times I felt disconnected, isolated, and alone, I did not spend a single day alone. I had me. There were times when I ignored this amazing person. Took for granted her wisdom and friendship. Treated her with contempt and ignored her cries for help. But she never left my side. I believed for a long time that Lisa was the voice inside of me spurring me on, offering me guidance, and supporting me to grow. Through the later years of my journey, I have come to realise what Lisa always knew. What she had been trying to tell me all along. That person is me. I have the answers I have the strength. I can be anything I choose to be. I just needed to listen. "You have to love who you are, once you do that everything else is easy", Lisa once said. "Is that it? Just love me?", I whispered. "Yes, it's that simple, know and love yourself", she replied. "Does it have to be this hard though?", I replied with a sigh. "No, my friend it doesn't, just lean in and enjoy the ride", was the reply.

WORK WITH ME

I would be honoured to have you as a member of the Mindset Coaching Tribe, a free Facebook group I facilitate, offering connection and support to women in business. If you would like to work with me directly, then you can join the Mindset Coaching VIP Members Club. Details of which can be found on my website. Here are the links to my website and social media platforms.

The resources that accompany the book can be found in the Free Facebook group Abbie Broad Mindset Tribe, and I would encourage you to join the group, access the workbook downloads, and use it to support your learning.

- https://nowwatchmefly.co.uk/
- www.facebook.com/groups/AbbieBroadMindsetTribe/
- www.instagram.com/nowwatchmeflyltd
- www.linkedin.com/in/abbiebroad/
- https://twitter.com/AbbieBroadCoach

The 80/20 Club
YOU'VE GOT A PASSION FOR BUSINESS!

The 80/20 Club is for small business owners at any stage in business. Or, you might have the passion, but need the practical know-how and access to the experts who can show you how to be brilliant in your business.

Maybe you've not yet taken the leap to go full-time but hey, you have buckets of passion to turn your creative ideas into your full-time business baby.

Perhaps you're on the cusp of your passion becoming a REAL, serious business, or maybe you're already running a business and experiencing 'wins', but a small part of you still feels like an imposter. Let's change that right now!

The 80/20 Club is best suited for businesses with an online presence. You already have a website and some social media stuff going on, but you want to shake things up!

As a founding member of the 80/20 Club I can tell you first-hand just how amazing this mentorship programme is. It has everything a small or micro business owner could need to support them to scale and grow their business. After working through the struggles, I was experiencing in my business, I was ready to begin building a solid brand. What I didn't know was 'how to do it'. What I needed was a plan to follow, a structure to work to, and advice I could trust.

The 80/20 ticked every box for me and after joining the program my business and income grew a staggering 500% in just a few short months.

I am still a member of the 80/20 Club and can offer you a link to join the awesome community today. It is my belief that Mindset Coaching and Professional Business Mentorship work perfectly together, offering the highest quality support and the best possible chances of success.

For more information visit my website at Now Watch Me Fly https://nowwatchmefly.co.uk/

Acknowledgements and thanks

MY FAMILY

To my gorgeous and devoted husband Dave and our beautiful girls, Ellie, Lauren, Taylor, and Maya. For being so patient and supportive throughout this journey. For believing in me even when I was doubting myself. For putting up with so many compromises and for giving me a life worth fighting for.

MY COLLABORATORS

Dr Jennifer Jones – Author & writing coach https://ewc.coach/
Writing a book has been a dream of mine ever since I can remember. One I confess I never truly believed would happen, until I met Jennifer. Thank you for giving me that final push to believe in myself, for sitting beside me throughout this journey and for helping me to see myself so completely within this process and become confident enough to pull it off.

Rico Patzer https://uspmaker.com/
Thank you for your tireless commitment to dragging me kicking and screaming into the 21st century. For seeing my USP even when I couldn't and for guiding me so beautifully towards a business that I now love. Your expertise together with such patience and kindness has enabled me to overcome my biggest fears about business. Thanks to you, I can now embrace the process of sales and marketing with renewed confidence and determination.

Christine Hammacott https://book-design.co.uk
Writing a book is the easy part, taking that idea and turning it into a product that can be seen and sold, requires a professional. Thank you Christine for your advice guidance and support

throughout this last and most important stage of the process. Thank you for caring as much about my book as I do and for helping me to create something I am truly proud of.

MY CLIENTS

To each and every person who has invited me to walk beside them. You are my biggest source of learning and motivation. I am and will forever be grateful for all that you have given me. I am what I am because of you. Thank you for seeing me.

MY TRIBE

Devida Bushrod, Vicki Hudson, Pauline MacNamara, and Penny Moore. You were the start of this amazing journey. Your faith and belief in me was the inspiration for the business I have today. Discovering that it was not only ok to be me, but that it was in fact the only viable option. You helped me to regain the belief that for a while had been forgotten. Through friendship, kindness, and laughter, you sat beside me, you picked me up, and you have walked bedside me ever since. Many more have joined our wonderful community since, and those values still remain as we work to pay it forward.

Printed in Poland
by Amazon Fulfillment
Poland Sp. z o.o., Wrocław